FREE CHOICE PETRI

Cambridge Tracts in Theoretical Computer Science

Managing Editor Professor C.J. van Rijsbergen,
Department of Computing Science, University of Glasgow

Editorial Board

S. Abramsky, *Department of Computing Science, Imperial College of Science and Technology*
P.H. Aczel, *Department of Computer Science, University of Manchester*
J.W. de Bakker, *Centrum voor Wiskunde en Informatica, Amsterdam*
J.A. Goguen, *Programming Research Group, University of Oxford*
Y. Gurevich, *Department of Electrical Engineering and Computer Science, University of Michigan*
J.V. Tucker, *Department of Mathematics and Computer Science, University College of Swansea*

Titles in the series

FREE CHOICE PETRI NETS

Jörg Desel
Technical University of Munich

Javier Esparza
University of Edinburgh

CAMBRIDGE
UNIVERSITY PRESS

CAMBRIDGE UNIVERSITY PRESS
Cambridge, New York, Melbourne, Madrid, Cape Town, Singapore, São Paulo

Cambridge University Press
The Edinburgh Building, Cambridge CB2 2RU, UK

Published in the United States of America by Cambridge University Press, New York

www.cambridge.org
Information on this title: www.cambridge.org/9780521465199

© Cambridge University Press 1995

First published 1995
This digitally printed first paperback version 2005

A catalogue record for this publication is available from the British Library

ISBN-13 978-0-521-46519-9 hardback
ISBN-10 0-521-46519-2 hardback

ISBN-13 978-0-521-01945-3 paperback
ISBN-10 0-521-01945-1 paperback

Contents

Preface

Free-choice Petri nets have been around for more than twenty years, and are a successful branch of net theory. Nearly all the introductory texts on Petri nets devote some pages to them. This book is intended for those who wish to go further. It brings together the classical theorems of free-choice theory obtained by Commoner and Hack in the seventies, and a selection of new results, like the Rank Theorem, which were so far scattered among papers, reports and theses, some of them difficult to access.

Much of the recent research which found its way into the book was funded by the ESPRIT II BRA Action DEMON, and the ESPRIT III Working Group CALIBAN.

The book is self-contained, in the sense that no previous knowledge of Petri nets is required. We assume that the reader is familiar with naïve set theory and with some elementary notions of graph theory (e.g. path, circuit, strong connectedness) and linear algebra (e.g. linear independence, rank of a matrix). One result of Chapter 4 requires some knowledge of the theory of NP-completeness.

The book can be the subject of an undergraduate course of one semester if the proofs of the most difficult theorems are omitted. If they are included, we suggest the course be restricted to Chapters 1 through 5, which contain most of the classical results on S- and T-systems and free-choice Petri nets. A postgraduate course could cover the whole book.

All chapters are accompanied by a list of exercises. Difficult exercises are marked with asterisks.

We would like to express our warmest thanks to the many people who have helped us to write the book. Eike Best encouraged us, offered advice and criticism, and was a good friend. Raymond Devillers flooded us with helpful comments, and corrected many mistakes. Glenn Bruns, Ekkart Kindler, Maciej Koutny, Agathe Merceron, Alan Paxton, Anette Renner, P.S. Thiagarajan and Walter Vogler made useful suggestions.

This book was written while the first-mentioned author was at the Technical University of Munich and the Humboldt University of Berlin, and the second author was at the University of Hildesheim and the University of Edinburgh. We thank our colleagues Eike Best, Julian Bradfield, Glenn Bruns, Hans-Günther Linde-Göers, Wolfgang Reisig, Colin Stirling and Rolf Walter for creating a very enjoyable working atmosphere.

Finally, many thanks to Jaco de Bakker for suggesting that we publish the book
as a Cambridge Tract in Theoretical Computer Science, and to David Tranah and
Roger Astley, from Cambridge University Press, for their help in the production.

Chapter 1 ———————————

Introduction

Petri nets are one of the most popular formal models of concurrent systems, used by both theoreticians and practitioners. The latest compilation of the scientific literature related to Petri nets, dating from 1991, contains 4099 entries, which belong to such different areas of research as databases, computer architecture, semantics of programming languages, artificial intelligence, software engineering and complexity theory. There are also several introductory texts to the theory and applications of Petri nets (see the bibliographic notes).

The problem of how to analyze Petri nets – i.e., given a Petri net and a property, how to decide if the Petri net satisfies it or not – has been intensely studied since the early seventies. The results of this research point out a very clear trade-off between expressive power and analyzability. Even though most interesting properties are decidable for arbitrary Petri nets, the decision algorithms are extremely inefficient. In this situation it is important to explore the analyzability border, i.e., to identify a class of Petri nets, as large as possible, for which strong theoretical results and efficient analysis algorithms exist.

It is now accepted that this border can be drawn very close to the class of free-choice Petri nets. Eike Best coined the term 'free-choice hiatus' in 1986 to express that, whereas there exists a rich and elegant theory for free-choice Petri nets, few of its results can be extended to larger classes. Since 1986, further developments have deepened this hiatus, and reinforced its relevance in Petri net theory.

The purpose of this book is to offer a comprehensive view of the theory of free-choice Petri nets. Moreover, almost as important as the results of the theory are the techniques used to prove them. The techniques given in the book make very extensive and deep use of nearly all the analysis methods indigenous to Petri nets, such as place and transition invariants, the marking equation, or siphons and traps. In fact, the book can also be considered as an advanced course on the application of these methods in Petri net theory.

1.1   Petri nets

The Petri net is a mathematical model of a parallel system, in the same way that the finite automaton is a mathematical model of a sequential system. Petri nets have a faithful and convenient graphical representation, which we shall use in this informal introduction.

A Petri net has two components: a *net* and an *initial marking*. A net is a directed graph with two sorts of nodes such that there is no edge between two nodes of the same sort. The two sorts of nodes are called *places* and *transitions*. Places are graphically represented by circles, and transitions by boxes.

Places can store *tokens*, represented by black dots. A distribution of tokens on the places of a net is called a *marking*, and corresponds to the 'state' of the Petri net. A transition of a net is *enabled* at a marking if all its input places (the places from which some edge leads to it) contain at least one token. An enabled transition can *occur*, and its occurrence changes the marking of the net: it removes one token from each of the input places of the transition, and adds one token to each of its output places. Figure 1.1 shows on the left a Petri net containing an enabled transition, whose occurrence changes the marking to the one shown on the right.[1]

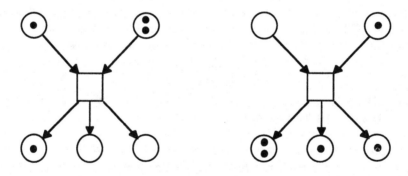

Fig. 1.1   A Petri net before and after the occurrence of a transition

With this simple occurrence rule, Petri nets can be used to model dynamic systems. Consider as an example the Petri net of Figure 1.2, which models a vending machine. At the marking shown in the Figure – called the *initial marking* – the machine is waiting for a coin to be inserted. This is modelled by the token on the place `ready for insertion`, which enables the transition `insert coin`. When this transition occurs, the machine can choose to reject or to accept the coin. In the first case, the machine returns to the initial marking; in the second it gets ready to dispense

---

[1]Petri nets with this occurrence rule are sometimes called marked nets, place/transition systems, or just systems.

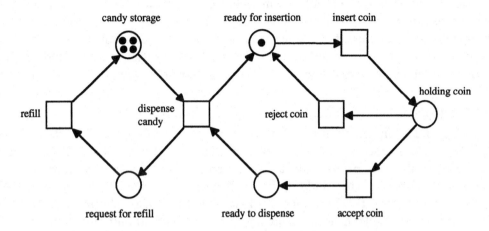

Fig. 1.2 A Petri net model of a vending machine

a candy. However, candies can only be dispensed if there are some available. The available candies are modelled by the tokens in the place candy storage. The storage contains initially four candies. When a candy is dispensed, the marking shown in Figure 1.3 is reached. At this point, transitions refill and insert coin

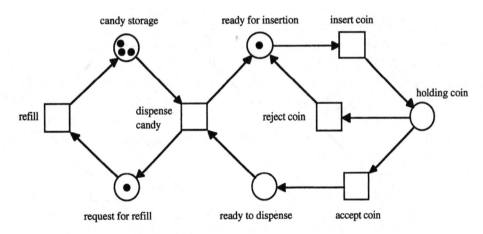

Fig. 1.3 Marking reached after the first candy is dispensed

are enabled. With the given initial marking, the machine can deliver up to four candies without having to refill the storage.

This example can be used to show how Petri nets model a variety of dependency relations between the events of a dynamic system. At the initial marking, the transition `accept coin` can only occur after `insert coin` has occurred: these two transitions are in *causal* relation. After `insert coin` occurs, both `reject coin` and `accept coin` are enabled, but the occurrence of one of them disables the other: they are in *conflict*. At the marking shown in Figure 1.3, transitions `refill` and `insert coin` can occur independently of each other: they are *concurrent*.

Our vending machine can be seen as composed of a storage unit, which takes care of removing and adding candies to the storage, and a control unit, which takes care of the coins. The storage unit can only deliver a candy if, simultaneously, the control unit changes its state from `ready to dispense` to `ready for insertion`; in other words, the delivery of the candy and this change of state have to be *synchronized*. Figure 1.4 shows the Petri net models of these units. The synchronization is modelled by merging the transitions `dispense candy` of the two units into a single new transition, which has as input (output) places all the input (output) places of the two old transitions. Since – according to the occurrence rule – a transition is enabled if all its input places are marked, the new transition is enabled if the two old transitions are enabled. Moreover, its occurrence has the same effect as the simultaneous occurrences of the old transitions.

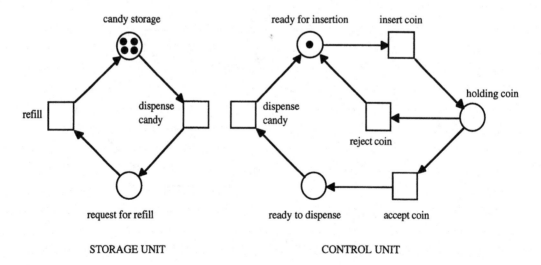

Fig. 1.4 Units of the vending machine

1.2   Free-choice Petri nets

Petri nets have a large expressive power, which makes them suitable to model a rich variety of dynamic systems. As a consequence, the analysis algorithms for arbitrary Petri nets are bound to have a high complexity (when they exist), and it is not possible to develop a comprehensive theory that relates the structure of a Petri net to its behaviour.[2] These obstacles can be removed if we restrict our attention to classes of Petri nets in which – by means of constraints on the graphical structure of the net – certain behaviour is ruled out. In Chapter 3 two of these classes are studied, called S-systems and T-systems. In S-systems, every transition has one input place and one output place, and therefore synchronizations are ruled out. Both the storage unit and the control unit of the vending machine are examples of S-systems[3]. In T-systems, every place has one input transition and one output transition: conflicts are ruled out.[4] The Petri net obtained from the vending machine by removing the transition **reject coin** and its adjacent arcs is a T-system.

The theory of S-systems is very simple. T-systems have been studied since the early seventies, and are today very well understood. These two classes are well within the analyzability border. To get closer to the border, we allow both synchronization and conflict, but in such a way that they do not 'interfere'. A typical situation of interference between synchronization and conflict is shown in the Petri net of Figure 1.5.

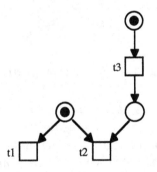

Fig. 1.5   A Petri net in which conflicts and synchronizations interfere

Transitions t_1 and t_2 are not in conflict, because t_2 cannot occur, but will be in conflict if t_3 occurs before t_1. Roughly speaking, due to the synchronization at t_2,

---

[2]There exist high lower complexity bounds and even undecidability results concerning analysis algorithms for arbitrary Petri nets.

[3]The reason of the name 'S-systems' is that places play in them a more important role than transitions, and places are called *Stellen* in German – the language in which Petri nets were originally defined.

[4]The converse does not hold, see Exercise 1.4.

the transition t_3 influences which one of the transitions t_1 and t_2 can occur. The
class of free-choice Petri nets is defined to rule these situations out: in them, the
result of the choice between two transitions can never be influenced by the rest of
the system – in other words, choices are *free*. The easiest way to enforce this is to
keep places with more than one output transition apart from transitions with more
than one input place. More precisely, if there is an arc from a place s to a transition
t, then either t is the only output transition of s (which implies that t cannot be in
conflict with any other transition) or s is the only input place of t (which implies
that there is no synchronization at t). In this way, whenever an output transition
of s is enabled, *all* output transitions of s are enabled, and therefore the choices
in which t takes place are free. The vending machine is an example of a Petri net
satisfying this condition.

There is a slightly more general way to achieve the same effect: if there is an arc
from a place s to a transition t, then there must be an arc from any input place
of t to any output transition of s. We call the Petri nets satisfying this weaker
condition *free-choice Petri nets*[5]. The net of Figure 1.6 is free-choice; for every
token distribution, either the two transitions t_1 and t_2 are enabled, or none of them
is enabled.

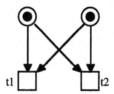

Fig. 1.6   A free-choice Petri net

We show how free-choice Petri nets can be used to model the flow of control in
networks of processors, which provides some insight into their expressive power. We
model a processor as a computing entity having input and output ports. Processors
are connected through unidirectional channels. A channel connects an output port
to an input port. Figure 1.7 shows a graphical representation of a processor.

When a processor receives a value through each of its input ports, it computes a
result. The processor then selects nondeterministically one of its output ports, and
sends the result through all the channels connected to it.

Figure 1.9 shows how to translate a network of processors into a free-choice Petri
net. It is easy to see that the behaviour of a network of processors corresponds to

---

[5]Historically, the Petri nets satisfying the stronger condition have been called *free-choice*, and
those satisfying the weaker *extended free-choice*. Since we only consider the weaker condition in
this book, the distinction between free-choice and extended free-choice is not necessary.

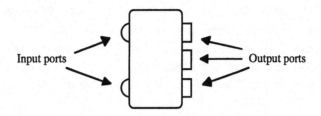

Fig. 1.7 Graphical representation of a processor

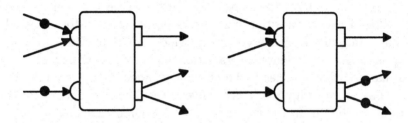

Fig. 1.8 Behaviour of processors

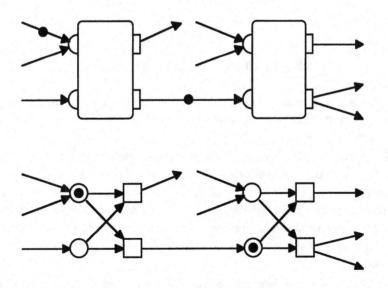

Fig. 1.9 A free-choice Petri net model of networks of processors

the behaviour of the respective free-choice Petri net (notice, however, that we do not model the data manipulated by the processors: for us they are only black dots).

Conversely, every free-choice Petri net can be seen as the Petri net model of a network of processors. The readers are invited to convince themselves of this; it suffices to show that the places and transitions of an arbitrary free-choice Petri net can be grouped into clusters, each of which corresponds to a processor.

1.3   Properties

We describe in this section, in an informal way, some of the properties of Petri nets that are studied throughout the book. The first one we consider is *liveness*. A Petri net is *live* if every transition can always occur again. More precisely, if for every reachable marking (i.e., every marking which can be obtained from the initial marking by successive occurrences of transitions) and every transition t it is possible to reach a marking that enables t. The Petri net model of the vending machine is live, but the Petri net of Figure 1.10 is not live: after the occurrence of the transition t a marking is reached from which t cannot become enabled again.

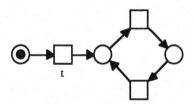

Fig. 1.10   The transition t is not live

Deadlock-freedom is a weaker property than liveness. A Petri net is deadlock-free if every reachable marking enables some transition. The non-live Petri net of Figure 1.10 is deadlock-free.

A Petri net is *bounded* if there exists a number b such that no reachable marking puts more than b tokens in any place. Places in a Petri net are often used to model buffers and registers for the storage of data – this is the case, for instance, of the place **candy storage** of the vending machine. If a Petri net is unbounded, then overflows can occur in these buffers or registers. The vending machine is bounded (no place can ever contain more than four tokens), while the Petri net of Figure 1.11 is unbounded.

A marking is a *home marking* if it is reachable from every reachable marking. A Petri net is *cyclic* if its initial marking is a home marking. The vending machine is an example of a cyclic Petri net. In general, systems which remain in their initial

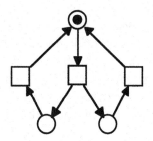

Fig. 1.11   A Petri net in which no place is bounded

state until some user interacts with them, and after the interaction can return to this same state, are modelled by cyclic Petri nets. The Petri nets of Figures 1.10 and 1.11 are not cyclic.

Liveness, boundedness and cyclicity are independent of each other. For instance, there exist Petri nets that are live and bounded but not cyclic. Exercise 1.3 proposes to find Petri nets showing this independence.

Liveness, boundedness, cyclicity, or the reachability of a marking are *behavioural* or *dynamic* properties, i.e., properties of the behaviour of a Petri net, as defined by the rule which governs the occurrence of transitions. In this book, we study the connection between behavioural and *structural* properties for the classes of S-systems, T-systems and free-choice Petri nets. By structural properties we mean those which do not refer to the dynamic aspects of a Petri net, but only to its syntactic description as a graph. For instance, the property 'every circuit of the net contains a place which is marked at the initial marking' is structural. One of the results of Chapter 3 is that a T-system is live if and only if this structural property holds. This is an example of what we call a *structural characterization* of a behavioural property (liveness) for a class of Petri nets (T-systems).

1.4   Structure of the book

Chapter 2 introduces formal definitions and some basic results about arbitrary Petri nets. In particular, it contains five lemmata, namely the Monotonicity, Marking Equation, Exchange, Boundedness, and Reproduction Lemma, and the Strong Connectedness Theorem, all of which are very often used in the next chapters. The chapter also introduces analysis methods for Petri nets based on linear algebra: S- and T-invariants, and the Incidence Matrix.

Chapter 3 studies S- and T-systems. For each of these two classes four theorems are obtained. The first three are structural characterizations of behavioural properties: the Liveness Theorem characterizes the live systems; the Boundedness Theorem characterizes the live systems which are moreover bounded; the Reachability Theorem characterizes the set of reachable markings. The fourth theorem, called the Shortest Sequence Theorem, gives an upper bound on the length of the shortest sequences of transitions that lead to a given marking.

The rest of the chapters develop the theory of free-choice Petri nets. In particular, they generalize the theorems of Chapter 3.

Chapter 4 introduces siphons and traps. They are used to prove Commoner's Theorem, which generalizes the Liveness Theorem for both S- and T-systems. It is shown that deciding non-liveness of free-choice systems is an NP-complete problem.

Chapter 5 contains the S-coverability and T-coverability Theorems, which show that every live and bounded free-choice Petri net can be decomposed into special S-systems and also into special T-systems.

Using these results, Chapter 6 proves the Rank Theorem, which characterizes the free-choice nets which admit a live and bounded marking. It follows from this characterization that live and bounded free-choice Petri nets can be recognized in polynomial time. Another consequence of the Rank Theorem is the Duality Theorem, a classical result of free-choice theory.

Chapter 7 gives reduction rules which reduce all and only free-choice nets which admit a live and bounded marking to very simple nets with just one place and one transition. This provides another algorithm to recognize live and bounded free-choice Petri nets, which is not as efficient as the one of Chapter 6, but gives more information about why a given free-choice Petri net is not live and bounded. The reduction rules can be reversed to yield synthesis rules which generate all and only the live and bounded free-choice Petri nets starting from simple Petri nets.

Chapter 8 studies and characterizes the home markings of live and bounded free-choice Petri nets. It is proved that the problem of deciding if a reachable marking of a live and bounded Petri net is a home marking can be solved in polynomial time.

In Chapter 9, the reachable markings of live, bounded and cyclic Petri nets are characterized. This result generalizes the Reachability Theorem for S- and T-systems. A generalization of the Shortest Sequence Theorems is presented as well.

Finally, Chapter 10 shows how weakened versions of Commoner's Theorem and the Rank Theorem also hold for Petri nets which are not free-choice.

Exercises

Exercise 1.1
Convince yourself that every free-choice Petri net models a network of processors.

Exercise 1.2
Try to prove that the vending machine is live, bounded and cyclic.

Exercise 1.3   *
Show that the properties liveness, boundedness and cyclicity are independent of each other by exhibiting eight Petri nets, one for each possible combination of the three properties and their negations.

Exercise 1.4   *
Construct a live and bounded Petri net which is not a T-system, but where no two distinct transitions are ever in conflict.

Bibliographic notes

The bibliography of Petri nets is periodically compiled by the Special Interest Group FG 0.0.1 'Petri nets and related system models' of the Gesellschaft für Informatik. The last published update is [69].

The most popular introductory books to the applications and theory of Petri nets are possibly those by Peterson [68] and Reisig [70]. There also exists a more recent survey by Murata [67], which contains a solution to Exercise 1.3.

Free-choice Petri nets were first defined in Hack's Master Thesis [42], which is also one of the classical papers on free-choice net theory. Best's paper on the 'free-choice hiatus' is [6]. The networks of processors described in the text were introduced by Desel in his Ph. D. Thesis [21].

Chapter 2 ——————————

Analysis techniques for Petri nets

This chapter introduces elementary definitions, concepts and results concerning arbitrary Petri nets. We start with a short section on mathematical notation. Section 2.2 is devoted to the definition and properties of nets, markings, the occurrence rule and incidence matrices. Section 2.3 defines net systems as nets with a distinguished initial marking. We give formal definitions of some behavioural properties of systems: liveness, deadlock-freedom, place-liveness, boundedness. Section 2.4 introduces S- and T-invariants, an analysis technique used throughout the book. The relationship between these invariants and the behavioural properties of Section 2.3 is discussed.

The chapter includes six simple but important results, which are very often used in later chapters. They are the Monotonicity, Marking Equation, Exchange, Boundedness, and Reproduction Lemma, and the Strong Connectedness Theorem. We encourage the reader to become familiar with them before moving to the next chapters.

2.1 Mathematical preliminaries

We use the standard definitions on sets, numbers, relations, sequences, vectors and matrices. The purpose of this section is to fix some additional notations.

Notation 2.1 *Sets, numbers, relations*

Let X and Y be sets. We write $X \subseteq Y$ if X is a subset of Y, including the case $X = Y$. $X \subset Y$ denotes that X is a proper subset of Y, i.e., $X \subseteq Y$ and $X \neq Y$. $X \setminus Y$ denotes the set of elements of X that do not belong to Y. $|X|$ denotes the cardinality of X.

If X is a subset of some set Y then the mapping $\chi[X]: Y \to \{0, 1\}$, given by $\chi[X](y) = 1$ iff $y \in X$ is called the characteristic function of X with respect to Y. The set Y will always be either the set of places or the set of transitions of a net given by the context. Which one of the two can be inferred from the nature of the elements of X.

$I\!N$ denotes the set of natural numbers including 0. Q denotes the set of rational numbers.

A relation R on a set A is a subset of the cartesian product $A \times A$. Since relations are sets of pairs, the set operations can be applied to them. We use the following notations:

$\text{id}_A = \{(a,a) \mid a \in A\}$ is the identity relation.

$R^{-1} = \{(b,a) \mid (a,b) \in R\}$ is the inverse of R.

For $k \in \{1,2,3,\ldots\}$, R^k is inductively defined by $R^1 = R$ and, for $k > 1$.

$$R^k = \{(a,c) \mid (a,b) \in R^{k-1} \text{ and } (b,c) \in R \text{ for some } b \in A\}.$$

$R^+ = R^1 \cup R^2 \cup R^3 \cup \cdots$ is the transitive closure of R.

$R^* = \text{id}_A \cup R^+$ is the reflexive and transitive closure of R.

$(R \cup R^{-1})^*$ is the symmetric, reflexive and transitive closure of R. This relation is the least equivalence relation which includes R.

Sequences play a particularly important role in this book. We mostly consider finite sequences, which are isomorphic to strings over an alphabet, but also infinite ones. We define the concatenation of two sequences only if the first sequence is finite.

Notation 2.2   *Sequences*

Let A be a set. A finite sequence on A is a mapping $\{1,\ldots,n\} \to A$, including the mapping $\epsilon\colon \emptyset \to A$, called the empty sequence. We represent a finite sequence $\sigma\colon \{1,\ldots,n\} \to A$ by the string $a_1 a_2 \ldots a_n$ of elements of A, where $a_i = \sigma(i)$ for $1 \leq i \leq n$. The length of σ is n, and the length of ϵ is 0.

An infinite sequence is a mapping $\sigma\colon \{1,2,3,\ldots\} \to A$. We write $\sigma = a_1 a_2 a_3 \ldots$ where $a_i = \sigma(i)$ for $i \geq 1$.

If $\sigma = a_1 a_2 \ldots a_n$ and $\tau = b_1 b_2 \ldots b_m$ are finite sequences then the concatenation of σ and τ, denoted by $\sigma\tau$, is the sequence $a_1 a_2 \ldots a_n b_1 b_2 \ldots b_m$ of length $n+m$.

If $\sigma = a_1 a_2 \ldots a_n$ is a finite sequence and $\tau = b_1 b_2 b_3 \ldots$ is an infinite sequence then the concatenation of σ and τ is the infinite sequence $a_1 a_2 \ldots a_n b_1 b_2 b_3 \ldots$

If σ is a finite sequence then σ^ω denotes the infinite concatenation $\sigma\sigma\sigma\ldots$

A sequence σ is a prefix of a sequence τ if either $\sigma = \tau$ or $\sigma\sigma' = \tau$ for some sequence σ'.

The alphabet of a sequence σ is the set $\mathcal{A}(\sigma) = \{a \in A \mid a = \sigma(i) \text{ for some } i\}$, i.e., the set of elements that appear in the string representation of σ.

The restriction of a sequence σ to a set $B \subseteq A$ is inductively defined by $\epsilon|_B = \epsilon$ and

$$(a\,\sigma)|_B = \begin{cases} a\,(\sigma|_B) & \text{if } a \in B \\ \sigma|_B & \text{if } a \notin B \end{cases}$$

Notation 2.3   *Vectors, matrices*

Given a finite set $A = \{a_1, \ldots, a_k\}$, every mapping X from A to $\mathcal{Q}$ can be represented by the vector $(X(a_1) \ldots X(a_k))$. We do not distinguish the mapping X and the vector $(X(a_1) \ldots X(a_k))$.

$X \cdot Y$ denotes the scalar product of two vectors. Similarly, if C is a matrix and X is a vector, $X \cdot C$ and $C \cdot X$ denote the left and right products of X and C. We do not use different symbols for row and column vectors. In the expression $C \cdot X$, the vector X is a column vector, even though we write $X = (X(a_1) \ldots X(a_k))$.

We write $X \geq Y$ ($X > Y$) if $X(a) \geq Y(a)$ ($X(a) > Y(a)$) for every element a of A. The mapping which maps every element to 0 is called the null vector and is denoted by **0**.

A matrix containing only zero entries is also denoted by **0**.

2.2   Nets and their properties

The scientific literature contains many variants of the basic definitions of net theory; different papers tailor them in different ways, depending on the problems studied[1]. The differences in the definitions are not very significant from a conceptual point of view, in the sense that the results of the theory hold for all the variants, possibly after some minor modifications. However, a good choice of definitions helps to simplify both the statement of the results and their proofs. Our choice is based on the principle *as simple as possible and as general as necessary*. For example, we do not define nets with an infinite number of elements since we only study finite nets.

---

[1]This variety also exists in other subjects. For instance, Turing machines may have one or more tapes, overwrite the input or not, have infinite tapes in one direction or in two, etc.

Basic definitions for nets

Definition 2.4   *Nets, pre-sets, post-sets, subnets*

A net N is a triple (S, T, F), where S and T are two finite, disjoint sets, and F is a relation on $S \cup T$ such that $F \cap (S \times S) = F \cap (T \times T) = \emptyset$.

The elements of S are called places, and are graphically represented by circles. The elements of T are called transitions, represented by boxes. F is called the flow relation of the net, represented by arrows from places to transitions or from transitions to places. Often, the elements of $S \cup T$ are generically called nodes of N or elements of N.

Given a node x of N, the set ${}^\bullet x = \{y \mid (y, x) \in F\}$ is the pre-set of x and the set $x^\bullet = \{y \mid (x, y) \in F\}$ is the post-set of x. The elements in the pre-set (post-set) of a place are its input (output) transitions. Similarly, the elements in the pre-set (post-set) of a transition are its input (output) places.

Given a set X of nodes of N, we define ${}^\bullet X = \bigcup_{x \in X} {}^\bullet x$ and $X^\bullet = \bigcup_{x \in X} x^\bullet$.

A triple (S', T', F') is a subnet of N if $S' \subseteq S$, $T' \subseteq T$ and

$$F' = F \cap ((S' \times T') \cup (T' \times S'))$$

If X is a set of elements of N, then the triple $(S \cap X, T \cap X, F \cap (X \times X))$ is a subnet of N, called the subnet of N generated by X.

We use the following convention: if N' is a subnet of a net N and x is a node of N', then ${}^\bullet x$ and $x^\bullet$ denote the pre-set and post-set of x *in the net N*.

Figure 2.1 shows again the Petri net model of the vending machine used in Chapter 1. For convenience we have shortened the names of transitions and places. If we ignore for the moment the black dots in the places, the figure shows the graphical representation of the net (S, T, F), where

$S = \{s_1, s_2, s_3, s_4, s_5\}$ is the set of places,

$T = \{t_1, t_2, t_3, t_4, t_5\}$ is the set of transitions, and

$F = \{(s_1, t_2), (s_2, t_1), (s_3, t_3), (s_4, t_4), (s_4, t_5), (s_5, t_2),$
$\quad (t_1, s_1), (t_2, s_2), (t_2, s_3), (t_3, s_4), (t_4, s_5), (t_5, s_3)\}$ is the flow relation.

Examples for pre- and post-sets are $t_2^\bullet = \{s_2, s_3\}$ and ${}^\bullet\{s_2, s_3\} = \{t_2, t_5\}$. The two units of the vending machine shown in Figure 1.4 of Chapter 1 are the subnets generated by the sets $\{s_1, s_2, t_1, t_2\}$ and $\{s_3, s_4, s_5, t_2, t_3, t_4, t_5\}$.

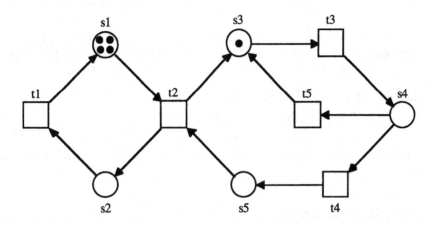

Fig. 2.1   The example of Figure 1.2 again

Since nets can be viewed as special graphs, graph terminology also applies to nets:

Definition 2.5   *Paths, circuits*

A path of a net (S, T, F) is a nonempty sequence $x_1 \dots x_k$ of nodes which satisfies $(x_1, x_2), \dots, (x_{k-1}, x_k) \in F$. A path $x_1 \dots x_k$ is said to lead from x_1 to x_k.

A path leading from a node x to a node y is a circuit if no element occurs more than once in it and $(y, x) \in F$. Observe that a sequence containing one element is a path but not a circuit, because for every node x we have $(x, x) \notin F$.

A net (S, T, F) is called weakly connected (or just connected) if every two nodes x, y satisfy $(x, y) \in (F \cup F^{-1})^*$.

(S, T, F) is strongly connected if $(x, y) \in F^*$, i.e., for every two nodes x, y there is a path leading from x to y.

By this definition, every net with less than two elements is strongly connected. Every strongly connected net is weakly connected because $F^* \subseteq (F \cup F^{-1})^*$.

In the example of Figure 2.1, $t_2\, s_2\, t_1\, s_1\, t_2\, s_3$ is a path and $s_3\, t_3\, s_4\, t_5$ is a circuit. The net is strongly connected. The subnet generated by all elements except t_1 is connected but not strongly connected. The subnet generated by all elements except t_2 is not connected.

The following proposition gives alternative characterizations of connectedness and strong connectedness. Its proof is left for an exercise.

Proposition 2.6   *Characterization of connectedness and strong connectedness*

    (1) A net (S, T, F) is connected iff it does not fall into unconnected parts, i.e.,
iff no two subnets (S_1, T_1, F_1) and (S_2, T_2, F_2) with disjoint and nonempty
sets of elements satisfy $S_1 \cup S_2 = S$, $T_1 \cup T_2 = T$ and $F_1 \cup F_2 = F$.

    (2) A connected net is strongly connected iff for every arc (x, y) there is a path
leading from y to x (this path is a circuit by definition).   □

The next definition introduces markings and the occurrence rule, which transform
a net into a dynamic system.

Definition 2.7   *Markings, occurrence rule*

A marking of a net (S, T, F) is a mapping $M: S \to I\!N$. A marking is often
represented by the vector $(M(s_1) \dots M(s_n))$, where $s_1, s_2, \dots, s_n$ is an arbitrary
fixed enumeration of S.

A place s is marked at a marking M if $M(s) > 0$. A set of places R is marked if
some place of R is marked.

The total number of tokens on a set of places R is denoted by $M(R)$, i.e., $M(R)$
is the sum of all $M(s)$ for $s \in R$.

The restriction of a marking M to a set of places R is denoted by $M|_R$.

The null marking is the marking which maps every place to 0.

A marking M enables a transition t if it marks every place in ${}^\bullet t$. If t is enabled
at M, then it can occur, and its occurrence leads to the successor marking M'
(written $M \xrightarrow{\ t\ } M'$) which is defined for every place s by

$$
M'(s) = \begin{cases}
M(s)   & \text{if } s \notin {}^\bullet t \text{ and } s \notin t^\bullet, \ \text{ or } \ s \in {}^\bullet t \text{ and } s \in t^\bullet \\
M(s) - 1 & \text{if } s \in {}^\bullet t \text{ and } s \notin t^\bullet \\
M(s) + 1 & \text{if } s \notin {}^\bullet t \text{ and } s \in t^\bullet
\end{cases}
$$

(a token is removed from each place in the pre-set of t and a token is added to
each place in the post-set of t).

A marking M is called dead if it enables no transition of the net.

Graphically, a marking M is represented by $M(s)$ tokens (black dots) on the place
s. The marking of the net of Figure 2.1 maps s_1 to 4, s_3 to 1 and all other places
to 0. Its vector representation is $(4\,0\,1\,0\,0)$. The transition t_3 is enabled, and the
marking reached after its occurrence is $(4\,0\,0\,1\,0)$.

Definition 2.8   *Occurrence sequences, reachable markings*

Let M be a marking of N. If $M \xrightarrow{t_1} M_1 \xrightarrow{t_2} \cdots \xrightarrow{t_n} M_n$ are transition occurrences then $\sigma = t_1 t_2 \ldots t_n$ is an occurrence sequence leading from M to M_n and we write $M \xrightarrow{\sigma} M_n$. This notion includes the empty sequence ϵ; we have $M \xrightarrow{\epsilon} M$ for every marking M.

We write $M \xrightarrow{*} M'$, and call M' reachable from M, if $M \xrightarrow{\sigma} M'$ for some occurrence sequence σ. The set of all markings reachable from M is denoted by $[M\rangle$.

If $M \xrightarrow{t_1} M_1 \xrightarrow{t_2} M_2 \xrightarrow{t_3} \cdots$ for an infinite sequence of transitions $\sigma = t_1 t_2 t_3 \ldots$ then σ is an infinite occurrence sequence and we write $M \xrightarrow{\sigma}$.

A sequence of transitions σ is enabled at a marking M if $M \xrightarrow{\sigma} M'$ for some marking M' (if σ is finite) or $M \xrightarrow{\sigma}$ (if σ is infinite).

Proposition 2.9   *Enabledness of occurrence sequences*

A (finite or infinite) sequence σ of transitions is enabled at a marking M iff every finite prefix of σ is enabled at M.

Proof:

($\Rightarrow$): Immediate from the definition.

($\Leftarrow$): If σ is finite then it is a finite prefix of itself and the result holds trivially. So we only have to consider the case that σ is infinite. Assume that $\sigma = t_1 t_2 t_3 \ldots$

Let $i \geq 1$ be an index. We have to prove that t_i is enabled at the marking reached after the occurrence of $t_1 t_2 \ldots t_{i-1}$.

Define $\tau = t_1 t_2 \ldots t_i$. Since τ is a finite prefix of σ, it is enabled at M by the hypothesis. Therefore, there exist markings $M_1, M_2, \ldots, M_i$ such that

$$M \xrightarrow{t_1} M_1 \xrightarrow{t_2} \cdots \xrightarrow{t_{i-1}} M_{i-1} \xrightarrow{t_i} M_i$$

The result follows because M_{i-1} enables t_i. $\square$

Note that for every *finite* sequence of transitions σ of a net there exists a marking that enables σ. For instance, if σ has length k, then we can take the marking that puts k tokens on every place.

The incidence matrix of a net

Consider an arbitrary place s and an arbitrary transition t of some net. With respect to the flow relation F, s and t are related in one of the following four ways:

- $(s, t) \notin F$ and $(t, s) \notin F$.

  Then s and t are completely unrelated: s has no influence on when is t enabled, and the occurrence of t does not change the number of tokens on s.

- $(s, t) \in F$ and $(t, s) \notin F$.

  In this case the occurrence of t is only possible when s carries at least one token, and the occurrence of t reduces the number of tokens on s by one.

- $(s, t) \notin F$ and $(t, s) \in F$.

  Here the occurrence of t increases the number of tokens on s by one.

- $(s, t) \in F$ and $(t, s) \in F$.

  As in the second case, t can only occur when s is marked. However, the occurrence of t does not change the number of tokens on s.

It is important to observe that the change of the number of tokens on s caused by the occurrence of t does not depend on the current marking. Instead, it is completely determined by the net. Therefore, in order to keep track of the distribution of tokens while transitions occur it suffices to consider the relative changes for every place and each transition. This is most conveniently done in form of a matrix, the so-called incidence matrix of the net.

Definition 2.10   *Incidence matrix*

Let N be the net (S, T, F). The incidence matrix $\mathbf{N} \colon (S \times T) \to \{-1, 0, 1\}$ of N is defined by

$$\mathbf{N}(s, t) = \begin{cases} 0 & \text{if } (s, t) \notin F \text{ and } (t, s) \notin F, \quad \text{or} \quad (s, t) \in F \text{ and } (t, s) \in F \\ -1 & \text{if } (s, t) \in F \text{ and } (t, s) \notin F \\ 1 & \text{if } (s, t) \notin F \text{ and } (t, s) \in F \end{cases}$$

Similarly to the vector representations of simple mappings, the matrix representation of the incidence matrix depends on enumerations $\{s_1, \ldots, s_n\}$ of places and $\{t_1, \ldots, t_m\}$ of transitions. The entry in the i-th row and j-th column of the matrix is then $\mathbf{N}(s_i, t_j)$.

The column vector $S \to \{-1, 0, 1\}$ of $\mathbf{N}$ associated to a transition t is denoted by $\mathbf{t}$. Similarly, the row vector $T \to \{-1, 0, 1\}$ associated to a place s is denoted by $\mathbf{s}$.

The incidence matrix of the net N of Figure 2.1 is

	t_1	t_2	t_3	t_4	t_5
s_1	1	−1	0	0	0
s_2	−1	1	0	0	0
s_3	0	1	−1	0	1
s_4	0	0	1	−1	−1
s_5	0	−1	0	1	0

The entry $\mathbf{N}(s,t)$ corresponds to the change of the marking of the place s caused by the occurrence of the transition t. Hence, if t is enabled at a marking M and $M \xrightarrow{t} M'$ then $M' = M + \mathbf{t}$. For a generalization of this equation to sequences of transitions, we need the following definition:

Definition 2.11   *Parikh vectors of transition sequences*

Let (S,T,F) be a net and let σ be a finite sequence of transitions. The Parikh vector $\overrightarrow{\sigma}: T \to I\!N$ of σ maps every transition t of T to the number of occurrences of t in σ.

The Parikh vector of the sequence $t_3\, t_5\, t_3\, t_4\, t_2$ is $(\,0\,1\,2\,1\,1\,)$, while the Parikh vector of the sequence t_1 is $(\,1\,0\,0\,0\,0\,)$.

Now, observe that for every transition t, we have $\mathbf{t} = \mathbf{N} \cdot \overrightarrow{t}$. Therefore, if $M \xrightarrow{t} M'$, then $M' = M + \mathbf{N} \cdot \overrightarrow{t}$ (where M and M' are taken as column vectors). For an arbitrary finite occurrence sequence $M \xrightarrow{\sigma} M'$, we get $M' = M + \mathbf{N} \cdot \overrightarrow{\sigma}$, as shown in the following Marking Equation Lemma:

Lemma 2.12   *Marking Equation Lemma*

For every finite occurrence sequence $M \xrightarrow{\sigma} M'$ of a net N the following Marking Equation holds:

$$M' = M + \mathbf{N} \cdot \overrightarrow{\sigma}$$

Proof:

By induction on the length of σ.

Base: $\sigma = \epsilon$. Then $M = M'$. We have $\overrightarrow{\sigma} = \mathbf{0}$, which proves the result.

Step: Assume that σ is not the empty sequence. Then $\sigma = \tau t$ for a sequence τ and a transition t.

Let $M \xrightarrow{\tau} L \xrightarrow{t} M'$. We have

$$
\begin{aligned}
M' &= L + \mathbf{t} & \text{(definition of } \mathbf{t}) \\
&= L + \mathbf{N} \cdot \overrightarrow{t} & \text{(definition of } \overrightarrow{t}) \\
&= M + \mathbf{N} \cdot \overrightarrow{\tau} + \mathbf{N} \cdot \overrightarrow{t} & \text{(induction hypothesis)} \\
&= M + \mathbf{N} \cdot (\overrightarrow{\tau} + \overrightarrow{t}) & \\
&= M + \mathbf{N} \cdot \overrightarrow{\tau t} & \text{(definition of the Parikh vector)} \\
&= M + \mathbf{N} \cdot \overrightarrow{\sigma} & (\sigma = \tau\, t)
\end{aligned}
$$

$\square$

For the sequence $\sigma = t_3\, t_5\, t_3\, t_4\, t_2$ we have

$$
\begin{pmatrix} 3 \\ 1 \\ 1 \\ 0 \\ 0 \end{pmatrix} = \begin{pmatrix} 4 \\ 0 \\ 1 \\ 0 \\ 0 \end{pmatrix} + \begin{pmatrix} 1 & -1 & 0 & 0 & 0 \\ -1 & 1 & 0 & 0 & 0 \\ 0 & 1 & -1 & 0 & 1 \\ 0 & 0 & 1 & -1 & -1 \\ 0 & -1 & 0 & 1 & 0 \end{pmatrix} \cdot \begin{pmatrix} 0 \\ 1 \\ 2 \\ 1 \\ 1 \end{pmatrix}
$$

As a consequence of the Marking Equation Lemma, the marking reached by an occurrence sequence only depends on the number of occurrences of each transition, and not on the order in which they occur. Every permutation leads to the same marking, provided it is also an occurrence sequence.

We now show that if a marking M enables a transition sequence σ, then any marking greater than M also enables it.

Lemma 2.13   *Monotonicity Lemma*

Let M and L be markings of a net.

(1) If $M \xrightarrow{\sigma} M'$ for a finite sequence σ then $(M + L) \xrightarrow{\sigma} (M' + L)$.

(2) If $M \xrightarrow{\sigma}$ for an infinite sequence σ then $(M + L) \xrightarrow{\sigma}$.

Proof:

(1) We proceed by induction on the length of σ.

Base. If σ is the empty sequence then it is enabled at every marking.

Step. Assume $\sigma = \tau t$ where t is a transition and suppose $M \xrightarrow{\tau} M'' \xrightarrow{t} M'$. By the induction hypothesis, $(M + L) \xrightarrow{\tau} (M'' + L)$. By the occurrence rule, and since M'' enables t, $M'' + L$ enables t. By the Marking Equation Lemma,

$(M'' + L) \xrightarrow{t} (M'' + L + \overrightarrow{t})$. Since, again by the Marking Equation Lemma, $M' = M'' + \overrightarrow{t}$, we get $(M'' + L) \xrightarrow{t} (M' + L)$. The result $(M + L) \xrightarrow{\sigma} (M' + L)$ follows from $\sigma = \tau t$.

(2) Using Proposition 2.9, it suffices to show that every finite prefix of σ is enabled at $M + L$. Also by Proposition 2.9, every finite prefix of σ is enabled at M. The result follows from (1). $\qquad \square$

The Exchange Lemma

Occurrence sequences do not provide full information about the causal relationship between transition occurrences. If a marking M enables a sequence $t_1 t_2$, it is not necessarily the case that t_2 can only occur after t_1. It is not difficult to see that if the sets ${}^\bullet t_1 \cup t_1^\bullet$ and ${}^\bullet t_2 \cup t_2^\bullet$ are disjoint, then the transitions occur concurrently and $t_2 t_1$ is also enabled at M. The Exchange Lemma provides a more general condition under which transitions of an occurrence sequence can be exchanged.

Lemma 2.14   *Exchange Lemma*

Let U and V be disjoint subsets of transitions of a net satisfying ${}^\bullet U \cap V^\bullet = \emptyset$. Let σ be a (finite or infinite) sequence of transitions such that $\mathcal{A}(\sigma) \subseteq U \cup V$.

(1) If $M \xrightarrow{\sigma} M'$ is a finite occurrence sequence, then $M \xrightarrow{\sigma|_U \, \sigma|_V} M'$.

(2) If $M \xrightarrow{\sigma}$ is an infinite occurrence sequence and $\sigma|_U$ is finite, then $M \xrightarrow{\sigma|_U \, \sigma|_V}$.

(3) If $M \xrightarrow{\sigma}$ is an infinite occurrence sequence and $\sigma|_U$ is infinite, then $M \xrightarrow{\sigma|_U}$.

Proof:

(1) We start by proving the following claim: if $L \xrightarrow{v} K \xrightarrow{u} L'$ for arbitrary markings L, K, L' and transitions $u \in U$ and $v \in V$, then $L \xrightarrow{u} K' \xrightarrow{v} L'$ for some marking K'.

We get ${}^\bullet u \cap v^\bullet = \emptyset$ from ${}^\bullet u \subseteq {}^\bullet U$, $v^\bullet \subseteq V^\bullet$ and the assumption ${}^\bullet U \cap V^\bullet = \emptyset$. We show

$L(s) \geq 1$ for every place $s \in {}^\bullet v$,

$L(s) \geq 1$ for every place $s \in {}^\bullet u$, and

$L(s) \geq 2$ for every place $s \in {}^\bullet v \cap {}^\bullet u$.

Assume $s \in {}^\bullet v$. Then $L(s) \geq 1$ because L enables v.

Assume $s \in {}^\bullet u$. Then $K(s) \geq 1$ because K enables u. Since ${}^\bullet u \cap v^\bullet = \emptyset$ we have $s \notin v^\bullet$. So the number of tokens on s does not increase by the occurrence of v, i.e., $L(s) \geq K(s)$. Therefore $L(s) \geq 1$.

Assume $s \in {}^\bullet v \cap {}^\bullet u$. Again, $K(s) \geq 1$ because K enables u and $s \in {}^\bullet u$. Since $s \in {}^\bullet v$ and $s \notin v^\bullet$ we get $K(s) = L(s) - 1$. So $L(s) \geq 2$.

We have that L enables u because $L(s) \geq 1$ for every place $s \in {}^\bullet u$. Let $L \xrightarrow{u} K'$; we show that K' enables v. Let s be a place of ${}^\bullet v$. If $s \notin {}^\bullet u$ then $K'(s) \geq L(s) \geq 1$. If $s \in {}^\bullet u$ then $K'(s) \geq L(s) - 1$ and $L(s) \geq 2$ whence $K'(s) \geq 1$. So K' marks every place in ${}^\bullet v$, and therefore K' enables v.

The sequences $u\,v$ and $v\,u$ have identical Parikh vectors. By the Marking Equation, both lead from L to the same marking, namely to L'. This completes the proof of the claim.

Now we consider the finite occurrence sequence $M \xrightarrow{\sigma} M'$. By the claim, the exhaustive exchange of adjacent elements $v\,u$ in σ, where $v \in V$ and $u \in U$, yields another occurrence sequence τ, also leading from M to M'. Since U and V are disjoint and every transition occurring in σ is an element of $U \cup V$, τ is the sequence $\sigma|_U\,\sigma|_V$, which proves the result.

(2) Let σ', σ'' be two sequences such that $\sigma = \sigma'\,\sigma''$ and only transitions of V occur in σ''. Such sequences exist because $\sigma|_U$ is finite by assumption.

Let $M \xrightarrow{\sigma'} M' \xrightarrow{\sigma''}$. We can apply (1) to σ' and obtain $M \xrightarrow{\sigma'|_U\,\sigma'|_V} M'$. Now $\sigma|_U = \sigma'|_U$ because no transition occurring in σ'' belongs to U. Moreover, $\sigma|_V = \sigma'|_V\,\sigma''$ because every transition occurring in σ'' belongs to V. Since M' enables σ'', M enables $\sigma|_U\,\sigma|_V$.

(3) By Proposition 2.9, it suffices to show that every finite prefix of $\sigma|_U$ is enabled at M. Consider a finite prefix τ' of $\sigma|_U$ and a corresponding finite prefix τ of σ satisfying $\tau' = \tau|_U$. By (1), M enables the sequence $\tau|_U\,\tau|_V$, and in particular its prefix $\tau|_U = \tau'$.   □

2.3 Systems and their properties

The name 'Petri net' is precise enough for an informal discussion – like that of the Introduction – but can lead to confusion when used in a technical sense. The names 'net' and 'Petri net' are rather similar, but they denote very different objects. A net is static – a special kind of graph – while a Petri net is dynamic and has a behaviour. To emphasize this difference between the static and dynamic levels, we shall use the name *net system* or just *system* instead of 'Petri net'.

Definition 2.15   *Net systems, initial and reachable markings*

A net system (or just a system) is a pair (N, M_0) where

- N is a connected net having at least one place and one transition, and
- M_0 is a marking of N called the initial marking.

A marking is called reachable in a system if it is reachable from the initial marking.

The two conditions on N are required only for technical convenience. Consider a net system composed by several smaller subsystems without connections between them. We can decide if the system satisfies any of the properties we are interested in by examining if the subsystems satisfy it. For instance, the system is live if and only if all its subsystems are live, and it is deadlock-free if and only if at least one of its subsystems is deadlock-free. So no generality is lost by restricting our attention to connected nets, whereas some proofs can be simplified. Nets without places or without transitions have little interest, but their inclusion in Definition 2.15 would lead to ugly special cases in some theorems.

We transfer properties from nets to systems (but not vice versa!), e.g., we sometimes say that a system is connected, meaning that its underlying net is connected. We now give formal definitions of some of the properties of systems that were mentioned in the Introduction.

Definition 2.16   *Liveness and related properties*

A system is live if, for every reachable marking M and every transition t, there exists a marking $M' \in [M\rangle$ which enables t. If (N, M_0) is a live system, then we also say that M_0 is a live marking of N.

A system is place-live if, for every reachable marking M and every place s, there exists a marking $M' \in [M\rangle$ which marks s.

A system is deadlock-free if every reachable marking enables at least one transition; in other words, if no dead marking can be reached from the initial marking.

Loosely speaking, a system is live if every transition can always occur again. A live system remains live under the occurrence of transitions, i.e., if (N, M_0) is live and $M_0 \xrightarrow{*} M$, then (N, M) is also live. The same holds respectively for place-liveness and for deadlock-freedom.

Observe that liveness is stronger than the property 'every transition can occur at least once from the initial marking'. In a live system every transition can occur at least once from *any* reachable marking. The next two propositions show that liveness is also stronger than both place-liveness and deadlock-freedom.

Proposition 2.17   *Liveness implies place-liveness*

Live systems are place-live.

Proof:

Let (N, M_0) be a live system, $M \in [M_0\rangle$ and s a place of N. Since the underlying net of a system is connected and has at least one transition by definition, there is a transition t in ${}^\bullet s \cup s^\bullet$. By liveness, t is enabled at some marking $L \in [M\rangle$; let $L \xrightarrow{t} L'$. If $t \in {}^\bullet s$ then $L'(s) \geq 1$. Choose then $M' = L'$. If $t \in s^\bullet$ then $L(s) \geq 1$ and $M' = L$ can be chosen.   □

Proposition 2.18   *Liveness implies deadlock-freedom*

Live systems are deadlock-free.

Proof:

By definition, a system has at least one transition t. Assume that a system has a reachable dead marking M. Then the set of markings reachable from M is $\{M\}$. So t is not enabled at any marking reachable from M and the system is therefore not live.   □

Observe that the previous propositions would not hold if marked nets without transitions were admitted as systems.

The liveness of a system depends very much on the initial marking. Changing the initial marking may easily render the system non-live. It is not hard to exhibit nets which have no live markings at all. We give a name to the nets which do have live markings:

Definition 2.19   *Structural liveness*

A net N is structurally live if there exists a marking M_0 of N such that (N, M_0) is a live system.

Next we define and study boundedness of systems.

Definition 2.20   *Bounded systems, bound of a place*

A system is bounded if for every place s there is a natural number b such that $M(s) \leq b$ for every reachable marking M. If (N, M_0) is a bounded system, we also say that M_0 is a bounded marking of N.

The bound of a place s in a bounded system (N, M_0) is defined as

$$\max\{M(s) \mid M \in [M_0\rangle\}$$

A system is called b-bounded if no place has a bound greater than b.

Proposition 2.21   *Elementary properties of bounded systems*

  (1) Every bounded system is b-bounded for some $b \in I\!N$.

  (2) Every bounded system has a finite set of reachable markings.

Proof:
Both claims depend on the finiteness of the set of places.

  (1) b can be chosen as the maximal bound of all places.

  (2) If a system is b-bounded, then it has at most $(b+1)^{|S|}$ reachable markings, where S is the set of places.   □

The next lemma shows that the markings of bounded systems cannot properly increase by the occurrence of transitions.

Lemma 2.22   *Boundedness Lemma*

  Let (N, M_0) be a bounded system and M_1 a reachable marking. If $M_1 \geq M_0$, then $M_1 = M_0$.

Proof:
Let $M_0 \xrightarrow{\sigma} M_1$ be an occurrence sequence and assume that $M_1 \geq M_0$. By the Monotonicity Lemma we have

$$M_0 \xrightarrow{\sigma} M_1 \xrightarrow{\sigma} M_2 \xrightarrow{\sigma} \cdots$$

where $M_i = M_0 + i \cdot (M_1 - M_0)$ for every $i \in I\!N$. By the boundedness of the system, this implies $M_1 - M_0 = 0$.   □

Systems which are both live and bounded enjoy many interesting properties. One example is the Strong Connectedness Theorem, which states that the nets underlying live and bounded systems are strongly connected. Before proving the Theorem, we give these nets a name.

Definition 2.23   *Well-formed nets*

  A net N is well-formed if there exists a marking M_0 of N such that (N, M_0) is a live and bounded system.

Observe that every well-formed net is structurally live. By the definition of system, well-formed nets are connected and have at least one transition and one place (the same holds for structurally live nets).

We need the following lemma:

Lemma 2.24

Every live and bounded system (N, M_0) has a reachable marking M and an occurrence sequence $M \xrightarrow{\sigma} M$ such that all transitions of N occur in σ^2.

Proof:

Let T be the set of transitions of N and let k be the number of reachable markings of (N, M_0). Observe that the set of reachable markings of (N, M_0) is finite because the system is bounded.

Since (N, M_0) is a live system, there is an occurrence sequence $M_0 \xrightarrow{\sigma_1} M_1$ satisfying $\mathcal{A}(\sigma_1) = T$ (this follows immediately from the definition of liveness). Since the system (N, M_1) is also live, there is again an occurrence sequence $M_1 \xrightarrow{\sigma_2} M_2$ satisfying $\mathcal{A}(\sigma_2) = T$. We obtain in this way a sequence of occurrence sequences

$$M_0 \xrightarrow{\sigma_1} M_1 \xrightarrow{\sigma_2} M_2 \xrightarrow{\sigma_3} \cdots \xrightarrow{\sigma_k} M_k$$

By the choice of k, the $k+1$ markings $M_0, M_1, \ldots, M_k$ cannot be pairwise different. Suppose that $M_i = M_j$ for $0 \leq i < j \leq k$. Define $M = M_i = M_j$, and $\sigma = \sigma_{i+1} \cdots \sigma_j$. Then $M \xrightarrow{\sigma} M$. Since $\mathcal{A}(\sigma_{i+1}) = T$ and σ_{i+1} is a prefix of σ, we have $\mathcal{A}(\sigma) = T$.

$\square$

Theorem 2.25   *Strong Connectedness Theorem*

Well-formed nets are strongly connected.

Proof:

Let $N = (S, T, F)$ be a well-formed net and let M_0 be a marking of N such that (N, M_0) is live and bounded.

Since N is well-formed, it is weakly connected. By Proposition 2.6(2), it suffices to prove that for every arc (x, y), there exists a path leading from y to x.

By Lemma 2.24 there exists a reachable marking M and an occurrence sequence $M \xrightarrow{\sigma} M$ such that every transition of N occurs in σ at least once. Since the marking M is reproduced by σ, it enables the infinite sequence $\sigma \sigma \sigma \ldots$.

---

[2]note that the occurrence of σ reproduces the marking M.

We consider two cases:

Case 1. $(x, y) = (s, t)$ for some place s and some transition t.

We construct a path from t to s. Define

$$V = \{v \in T \mid \text{there is a path from } t \text{ to } v\},$$

$$U = T \setminus V.$$

We claim that $M \xrightarrow{\sigma|_V} M$ is also an occurrence sequence leading from M to M. This claim clearly holds if σ contains no transitions of U. So it remains to consider the case that $\sigma|_U$ is not the empty sequence.

By the definition of V, $(V^\bullet)^\bullet \subseteq V$. Hence U and V are disjoint sets satisfying $^\bullet U \cap V^\bullet = \emptyset$. So we can apply the Exchange Lemma to $M \xrightarrow{\sigma\,\sigma\,\sigma\dots}$ and get that M enables the infinite sequence $(\sigma\,\sigma\,\sigma\dots)|_U = \sigma|_U\,\sigma|_U\,\sigma|_U\dots$

Let $M \xrightarrow{\sigma|_U} M'$. Since $\sigma|_U$ can occur infinitely often from M, the number of tokens on a place cannot decrease by the occurrence of $\sigma|_U$. Therefore we have $M' \geq M$. By the Boundedness Lemma, $M' = M$. The application of the Exchange Lemma to $M \xrightarrow{\sigma} M$ yields $M \xrightarrow{\sigma|_U\,\sigma|_V} M$. Hence $M \xrightarrow{\sigma|_U} M \xrightarrow{\sigma|_V} M$, which completes the proof of the claim.

By the definition of V, $t \in V$. Hence t occurs in $\sigma|_V$. Since $t \in s^\bullet$ and $\sigma|_V$ reproduces the marking, there is a transition $v \in {}^\bullet s$ that also occurs in $\sigma|_V$. The transition v belongs to V, whence there is a path π leading from t to v. Since $v \in {}^\bullet s$, the path $\pi\,s$ leads from t to s.

Case 2. $(x, y) = (t, s)$ for some place s and some transition t.

We construct a path from s to t. Define

$$U = \{u \in T \mid \text{there is a path from } u \text{ to } t\},$$

$$V = T \setminus U.$$

An analogous argument to the one used in Case 1 shows that $M \xrightarrow{\sigma|_U} M$ is an occurrence sequence. Since the transition t occurs in $\sigma|_U$ and $t \in {}^\bullet s$ there exists a transition $u \in s^\bullet$ that also occurs in $\sigma|_U$. u is in U, whence there is a path π leading from u to t. Since $u \in s^\bullet$, the path $s\,\pi$ leads from s to t. $\square$

2.4   S-invariants and T-invariants

An invariant of a dynamic system is an assertion that holds at every reachable state. In net systems it is possible to compute certain vectors of rational numbers – directly from the structure of the net – which induce invariants. They are called (with a certain abuse of language) S-invariants.

In the first part of the section we introduce S-invariants and study their connection with different behavioural properties. We then observe that the definition of S-invariant suggests to study other vectors, called T-invariants. They are introduced and discussed in the second part of the section. Finally, a third part deals with results that apply to both S- and T-invariants.

S-invariants

Consider the system of Figure 2.2. It is easy to see that for every reachable marking M the equation $M(s_1) + M(s_3) = 1$ holds, i.e., it is an invariant of the system. We can rewrite this equation as:

$$(1\,0\,1) \cdot \begin{pmatrix} M(s_1) \\ M(s_2) \\ M(s_3) \end{pmatrix} = 1 \text{ or just } (1\,0\,1) \cdot M = 1$$

Given an arbitrary net system, it is difficult to characterize all the vectors I such that $I \cdot M$ remains constant for every reachable marking M. However, it is easy to derive a sufficient condition from the Marking Equation.

Definition 2.26   *S-invariants*

An S-invariant of a net N is a rational-valued solution of the equation $X \cdot \mathbf{N} = \mathbf{0}$.[3]

Proposition 2.27   *Fundamental property of S-invariants*

Let (N, M_0) be a system, and let I be an S-invariant of N. If $M_0 \xrightarrow{*} M$, then $I \cdot M = I \cdot M_0$.

Proof:

Since $M_0 \xrightarrow{*} M$, we have $M_0 \xrightarrow{\sigma} M$ for some occurrence sequence σ. By the Marking Equation, $M = M_0 + \mathbf{N} \cdot \vec{\sigma}$. Therefore

$$I \cdot M = I \cdot M_0 + I \cdot \mathbf{N} \cdot \vec{\sigma} = I \cdot M_0$$

because $I \cdot \mathbf{N} = 0$. □

---

[3]We could also consider real-valued solutions; however, since incidence matrices only have integer entries, every real-valued solution is the product of a real scalar and a rational-valued solution.

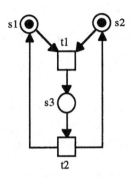

Fig. 2.2 (1 0 1) is an S-invariant

By definition, the set of S-invariants of a net constitutes a vector space over the field of rational numbers. The vector (1 0 1) is an S-invariant of the net of Figure 2.2. In fact, it is easy to see that the set $\{(\,1\,0\,1\,),(\,0\,1\,1\,)\}$ is a basis of the space of S-invariants.

The following proposition can be seen as an alternative definition of S-invariant. The proof of the proposition follows easily from the definition of incidence matrix, and is left for an exercise.

Proposition 2.28   *An alternative definition of S-invariant*

Let (S, T, F) be a net. A mapping $I: S \rightarrow \mathbb{Q}$ is an S-invariant iff for every transition t holds

$$\sum_{s \in {}^{\bullet}t} I(s) = \sum_{s \in t^{\bullet}} I(s) \qquad\qquad \square$$

This alternative definition is very useful in some proofs. For instance, it allows to show that the two vectors given above are S-invariants of the net of Figure 2.2, without having to construct the incidence matrix.

The next results show relations between S-invariants and system properties. First, we define positive and semi-positive S-invariants.

Definition 2.29   *Some definitions about S-invariants*

An S-invariant I of a net is called semi-positive if $I \geq 0$ and $I \neq 0$. The support of a semi-positive S-invariant I, denoted by $\langle I \rangle$, is the set of places s satisfying $I(s) > 0$ ($\langle I \rangle \neq \emptyset$ because $I \neq 0$).

An S-invariant I is called positive if $I > 0$, i.e., $I(s) > 0$ for every place s.

Theorem 2.30   *A necessary condition for liveness*

If (N, M_0) is a live system, then every semi-positive S-invariant I of N satisfies $I \cdot M_0 > 0$.

Proof:

Let I be a semi-positive S-invariant and let s be a place of $\langle I \rangle$. Since liveness implies place-liveness (Proposition 2.17), some reachable marking M marks s, i.e. $M(s) > 0$. Since I is semi-positive and markings have no negative entries we obtain

$$I \cdot M \geq I(s) \cdot M(s) > 0$$

Since I is an S-invariant we have $I \cdot M_0 = I \cdot M$, and the result follows.   □

Theorem 2.31   *A sufficient condition for boundedness*

Let (N, M_0) be a system. If N has a positive S-invariant I, then (N, M_0) is bounded.

Proof:

Let M be a reachable marking. Since I is an S-invariant we have $I \cdot M = I \cdot M_0$. Let s be a place of N. Then $I(s) \cdot M(s) \leq I \cdot M = I \cdot M_0$. Since I is positive we can divide by $I(s)$ and obtain $M(s) \leq I \cdot M_0 / I(s)$.   □

In the example of Figure 2.2, (1 2 1) is a positive S-invariant, which proves the boundedness of the system.

S-invariants also give information about the reachability of a marking. We introduce a relation between markings.

Definition 2.32   *Markings that agree on all S-invariants*

Two markings M and L of a net are said to agree on all S-invariants if $I \cdot M = I \cdot L$ for every S-invariant I of the net.

Theorem 2.33   *A necessary condition for reachability*

Let (N, M_0) be a system, and let $M \in [M_0\rangle$. Then M and M_0 agree on all S-invariants.

Proof:

Let I be an arbitrary S-invariant of N. By the fundamental property of S-invariants, $I \cdot M_0 = I \cdot M$. So M_0 and M agree on I and, since I is arbitrary, M and M_0 agree on all S-invariants.   □

This condition for the reachability of a marking is not sufficient; even if M and M_0 agree on all S-invariants, M is not necessarily reachable from M_0. However, it is very efficiently computable: the following theorem shows that, given two markings, we can decide if they agree on all invariants by solving an ordinary system of linear equations.

Theorem 2.34   *Characterization of markings that agree on all S-invariants*

Two markings M and L of a net N agree on all S-invariants iff the equation $M + \mathbf{N} \cdot X = L$ has some rational-valued solution for X.

Proof:

($\Rightarrow$): Since M and L agree on all S-invariants, they also agree on a basis $\{I_1, \ldots, I_k\}$. For every vector I_j of this basis we have $I_j \cdot (L - M) = \mathbf{0}$. A well-known theorem of linear algebra states that the columns of $\mathbf{N}$ include a basis of the space of solutions of the homogeneous system

$$I_j \cdot X = \mathbf{0} \qquad (1 \le j \le k)$$

Therefore, $(L-M)$ is a linear combination in $\mathbb{Q}$ of these columns, i.e., $\mathbf{N} \cdot X = (L-M)$ has some rational-valued solution for X.

($\Leftarrow$): Let I be an S-invariant of N. Since $I \cdot \mathbf{N} = \mathbf{0}$, we have

$$I \cdot L = I \cdot M + I \cdot \mathbf{N} \cdot X = I \cdot M.$$

$\square$

T-invariants

The S-invariants of a net N are the vectors I satisfying $I \cdot \mathbf{N} = \mathbf{0}$. It seems natural to ask if the vectors J satisfying $\mathbf{N} \cdot J = \mathbf{0}$ also have properties of interest. We shall see that they are related to the occurrence sequences which reproduce a marking, i.e., those that lead from a marking to itself.

Definition 2.35   *T-invariants*

A T-invariant of a net N is a rational-valued solution of the equation $\mathbf{N} \cdot X = \mathbf{0}$.

As in the case of S-invariants, there exists an alternative definition.

Proposition 2.36   *An alternative definition of T-invariant*

Let (S, T, F) be a net. A mapping $J: T \to Q$ is a T-invariant iff for every place s holds

$$\sum_{t \in {}^\bullet s} J(t) = \sum_{t \in s^\bullet} J(t)$$

$\square$

The notions of semi-positive, positive, and support of T-invariants are defined as for S-invariants. The set of T-invariants of a net constitutes again a vector space over the field of rational numbers. For the net of Figure 2.2, this space has dimension 1: the vector $(1\,1)$ constitutes a basis of the space.

Proposition 2.37   *Fundamental property of T-invariants*

Let σ be a finite sequence of transitions of a net N which is enabled at a marking M. Then the Parikh vector $\overrightarrow{\sigma}$ is a T-invariant iff $M \xrightarrow{\sigma} M$ (i.e, iff the occurrence of σ reproduces the marking M).

Proof:

($\Rightarrow$): Since σ is enabled at M, we have $M \xrightarrow{\sigma} M'$ for some marking M'. By the Marking Equation we have $M' = M + \mathbf{N} \cdot \overrightarrow{\sigma}$. Since $\overrightarrow{\sigma}$ is a T-invariant we have $\mathbf{N} \cdot \overrightarrow{\sigma} = \mathbf{0}$. So $M' = M$.

($\Leftarrow$): If $M \xrightarrow{\sigma} M$ then, by the Marking Equation, $\mathbf{N} \cdot \overrightarrow{\sigma} = \mathbf{0}$. So $\overrightarrow{\sigma}$ is a T-invariant. $\square$

An immediate consequence of Lemma 2.24 is:

Theorem 2.38

Every well-formed net has a positive T-invariant.

Proof:

The Parikh vector of the occurrence sequence $M \xrightarrow{\sigma} M$ mentioned in Lemma 2.24 is a positive T-invariant. $\square$

By this theorem, if a bounded system is live then it has a positive T-invariant. The next lemma states a similar result: if a bounded system has an infinite occurrence sequence then it has a semi-positive T-invariant.

Lemma 2.39   *Reproduction Lemma*

Let (N, M_0) be a bounded system and let $M_0 \xrightarrow{\sigma}$ be an infinite occurrence sequence.

(1) There exists sequences σ_1, σ_2, σ_3 such that $\sigma = \sigma_1 \sigma_2 \sigma_3$, σ_2 is not the empty sequence and

$$M_0 \xrightarrow{\sigma_1} M \xrightarrow{\sigma_2} M \xrightarrow{\sigma_3}$$

for some marking M.

(2) There exists a semi-positive T-invariant J such that $\langle J \rangle \subseteq \mathcal{A}(\sigma)$.

Proof:

(1) Assume $\sigma = t_1 t_2 t_3 \dots$ Define $M_0 \xrightarrow{t_1} M_1 \xrightarrow{t_2} M_2 \xrightarrow{t_3} \cdots$.

By boundedness, the markings $M_0, M_1, M_2, \dots$ cannot be pairwise different. Suppose $M = M_i = M_j$ for two indices i, j, $0 \leq i < j$. Define $\sigma_1 = t_0 \dots t_i$, $\sigma_2 = t_{i+1} \dots t_j$ and $\sigma_3 = t_{j+1} t_{j+2} \dots$ The sequence σ_2 is not empty because $i < j$.

(2) Take, with the notions of (1), $J = \vec{\sigma_2}$. The result then follows from the fundamental property of T-invariants because $M \xrightarrow{\sigma_2} M$.   □

The Strong Connectedness Theorem states that well-formed nets are strongly connected. Well-formed nets are defined in a behavioural way: they are those for which a live and bounded marking exists. The following theorem is a structural counterpart of this result. It shows that the nets which have a positive S-invariant and a positive T-invariant – a purely structural property – are strongly connected as well.

Theorem 2.40   *Positive S- and T-invariants imply strong connectedness*

Every connected net with a positive S-invariant and a positive T-invariant is strongly connected.

Proof:

Let N be a connected net (S, T, F) with a positive S-invariant I and a positive T-invariant J.

By Proposition 2.6(2), it suffices to prove that for every arc (x, y) in F there exists a path leading from y to x. We consider two cases:

Case 1. $(x, y) = (s, t)$ for a place s and a transition t.

Define the mapping $J': T \to I\!N$ by

$$J'(u) = \begin{cases} J(u) & \text{if there exists a path } t \dots u \\ 0 & \text{otherwise} \end{cases}$$

Let r be a place of S. Assume that $J'(u) = 0$ for every $u \in {}^\bullet r$. Since J' has no negative entries by definition, we get

$$0 = \sum_{u \in {}^\bullet r} J'(u) \le \sum_{u \in r^\bullet} J'(u)$$

Now assume that $J'(u) = J(u) > 0$ for some transition $u \in {}^\bullet r$. Then, by the definition of J', there exists a path from t to r. So for every transition u in $r^\bullet$ there is also a path $t \dots u$ and we get $J'(u) = J(u) > 0$ for all transitions u in $r^\bullet$. So

$$0 < \sum_{u \in {}^\bullet r} J'(u) \le \sum_{u \in {}^\bullet r} J(u) = \sum_{u \in r^\bullet} J(u) = \sum_{u \in r^\bullet} J'(u)$$

Hence in both cases we have $\sum_{u \in {}^\bullet r} J'(u) \le \sum_{u \in r^\bullet} J'(u)$.

Since $(\mathbf{N} \cdot J')(r) = \sum_{u \in {}^\bullet r} J'(u) - \sum_{u \in r^\bullet} J'(u) \le 0$ and r was chosen arbitrarily, $\mathbf{N} \cdot J'$ has no properly positive entries. Since I is an S-invariant, $I \cdot \mathbf{N} \cdot J' = 0$. Since I has only positive entries, $\mathbf{N} \cdot J'$ has no negative entries and is hence the null vector $\mathbf{0}$. So J' is a T-invariant. We then have:

$$\begin{aligned} \sum_{u \in {}^\bullet s} J'(u) &= \sum_{u \in s^\bullet} J'(u) && (J' \text{ is a T-invariant}) \\ &\ge J'(t) && (t \in s^\bullet) \\ &= J(t) && (\text{definition of } J') \\ &> 0 && (J \text{ is positive}) \end{aligned}$$

So there exists a transition $u \in {}^\bullet s$ satisfying $J'(u) > 0$. By the definition of J', there is a path $\pi = t \dots u$. Then, the path πs leads from t to s.

Case 2. $(x, y) = (t, s)$ for a transition t and a place s.

Consider the net $N' = (T, S, F)$ in which the places of N' are the transitions of N and vice versa. The incidence matrix of N' is equal to the transposed of the incidence matrix of N multiplied by -1. So I is a positive T-invariant of N' and J is a positive S-invariant of N'.

The arc (t, s) leads from a place of N' to a transition of N'. As shown in Case 1, N' contains a path from the transition s to the place t. So N contains a path from the place s to the transition t. $\square$

Observe that in the proof of this result Case 2 follows easily from Case 1 via a duality argument. This technique will be used later on in different chapters.

Semi-positive and minimal invariants

The semi-positive S- and T-invariants of a net are particularly interesting, because most results of the last two sections state relationships between them and dynamic properties. We give two results on semi-positive invariants which will be useful in later chapters (by a semi-positive invariant we mean a vector which is either a semi-positive S-invariant or a semi-positive T-invariant).

Proposition 2.41 *Pre-sets of supports equal post-sets of supports*

Every semi-positive invariant I satisfies $^\bullet\langle I\rangle = \langle I\rangle^\bullet$.

Proof:

Follows immediately from the alternative definitions of S- and T-invariants (Propositions 2.28 and 2.36). □

We now define minimal invariants and show that they generate all semi-positive invariants. Moreover, if a net has a positive invariant, then its minimal invariants generate all invariants.

Definition 2.42 *Minimal invariants*

A semi-positive invariant I is minimal if no semi-positive invariant J satisfies $\langle J\rangle \subset \langle I\rangle$.

Note that by this definition each nonzero multiple of a minimal invariant is again minimal, because the minimality of an invariant depends solely on its support.

Theorem 2.43 *Fundamental property of minimal invariants*

(1) Every semi-positive invariant is the sum of minimal invariants.

(2) If a net has a positive invariant, then every invariant is a linear combination of minimal invariants.

Proof:

(1) Let $I: X \to \mathbb{Q}$ be a semi-positive invariant. We proceed by induction on $|\langle I\rangle|$.

   Base. $|\langle I\rangle| = 1$. Then I is minimal because every semi-positive invariant has at least one non-zero entry.

Step. $|\langle I \rangle| > 1$. If I is minimal, we are done. So assume that I is not minimal. Then, there exists a minimal invariant J such that $\langle J \rangle \subset \langle I \rangle$.

Let x be an element of $\langle J \rangle$ such that $I(x)/J(x)$ is minimal. Define

$$I' = I - \frac{I(x)}{J(x)} \cdot J$$

Since the set of all invariants is a vector space, I' is an invariant. By the choice of x, $I'(x) = 0$ and $I' \geq 0$. Moreover, $\langle I' \rangle \subset \langle I \rangle$. Since $\langle J \rangle$ is a proper subset of $\langle I \rangle$, $\langle I' \rangle \neq \emptyset$. So we can apply the induction hypothesis and conclude that I' is the sum of minimal invariants.

The result follows because $I = I' + \dfrac{I(x)}{J(x)} \cdot J$ and $\dfrac{I(x)}{J(x)} \cdot J$ is also a minimal invariant.

(2) Let N be a net having a positive invariant I, and let J be an arbitrary invariant of N. There exists an integer λ such that $\lambda I + J$ is a semi-positive invariant. By (1), both I and $\lambda I + J$ are sums of minimal invariants. Since $J = (\lambda I + J) - \lambda I$, the invariant J is a linear combination of minimal invariants. □

Exercises

Exercise 2.1

1) Show that (S, T, F) is a net iff (T, S, F) is a net iff (S, T, F^{-1}) is a net. The first equivalence is in fact implicitly used in the proof of Theorem 2.40.

2) Show that if one of these nets is (strongly) connected then all of them are.

3) Show that a net (S, T, F) is connected iff $(S, T, F \cup F^{-1})$ is strongly connected.

Exercise 2.2
Prove Proposition 2.6.

Exercise 2.3
Exhibit counterexamples that disprove the following conjectures:

1) If (N, M_0) is bounded and $M \geq M_0$, then (N, M) is bounded.

2) * If (N, M_0) is live and $M \geq M_0$, then (N, M) is live.

3) * If (N, M_0) is live and bounded and $M \geq M_0$, then (N, M) is bounded.

Exercise 2.4

Give a basis of the space of S-invariants and a basis of the space of T-invariants of the net shown in Figure 2.1.

Exercise 2.5

Prove the characterizations of S- and T-invariants given in Proposition 2.28 and Proposition 2.36.

Exercise 2.6

A semi-positive T-invariant J of a net N is *realizable* in a system (N, M_0) if there exist an occurrence sequence $\sigma\tau$ such that $\overrightarrow{\tau} = J$ (then we get $M_0 \xrightarrow{\sigma} M \xrightarrow{\tau} M$ for some marking M, which implies that $\sigma\,\tau\,\tau\,\tau\ldots$ is an occurrence sequence).

1) Exhibit a system (N, M_0) and a semi-positive T-invariant J of N such that J is not realizable in (N, M_0).

2) * As (1), but (N, M_0) is required to be live and bounded.

Exercise 2.7 *

Prove that every bounded system with a positive T-invariant is strongly connected. Show that this implies the Strong Connectedness Theorem as well as Theorem 2.40.

Bibliographic Notes

The material of this chapter consists mainly of well-known results of Petri net theory. Most of them can be found in the introductory books of Peterson [68] and Reisig [70]. The Exchange Lemma is due to Desel [21]. The Strong Connectedness Theorem is taken from [6]. The concepts of S- and T-invariant are due to Lautenbach [59]. There exist several surveys on the applications of linear algebra to Petri nets: by Memmi and Roucairol [64], by Lautenbach [61], and by Murata (Section VIII of [67]). Solutions to Exercise 2.3 can be found in [50] by Jantzen and Valk. A solution to the second part of Exercise 2.6 is given in Reisig's book [70].

Chapter 3 ——————————————

S-systems and T-systems

This chapter presents the main results of the theory of S-systems and T-systems. It is divided into two sections of similar structure, one for each of these two classes. The main results of each section are a Liveness Theorem, which characterizes liveness, a Boundedness Theorem, which characterizes b-boundedness of live systems, and a Reachability Theorem, which characterizes the set of reachable markings of live systems. Additionally, both sections contain a Shortest Sequence Theorem, which states that every reachable marking can be reached by an occurrence sequence whose length is bounded by a small polynomial in the number of transitions of the net (linear in the case of S-systems and quadratic for T-systems).

3.1 S-systems

Recall from the Introduction that S-systems are systems whose transitions have exactly one input place and one output place.

Definition 3.1 *S-nets, S-systems*

A net is an S-net if $|^\bullet t| = 1 = |t^\bullet|$ for every transition t.

A system (N, M_0) is an S-system if N is an S-net.

The fundamental property of S-systems is that all reachable markings contain exactly the same number of tokens. In other words, the total number of tokens of the system remains invariant under the occurrence of transitions.

Proposition 3.2 *Fundamental property of S-systems*

Let (N, M_0) be an S-system. If M is a reachable marking, then $M_0(S) = M(S)$, where S is the set of places of N.

Proof:

Since N is an S-net, the occurrence of a transition removes a token from one place and adds a token to one place (these two places may be the same). So the total number of tokens remains unchanged. $\qquad\square$

The next theorem characterizes liveness of S-systems.

Theorem 3.3   *Liveness Theorem*

An S-system (N, M_0) is live iff N is strongly connected and M_0 marks at least one place.

Proof:

($\Rightarrow$): (N, M_0) is live by assumption, and bounded by the fundamental property of S-systems. By the Strong Connectedness Theorem (Theorem 2.25), N is strongly connected. Since (N, M_0) is live, at least one transition t is enabled at M_0. So M_0 marks the unique input place of t.

($\Leftarrow$): Let M be an arbitrary reachable marking and let t be an arbitrary transition. We show that some marking reachable from M enables t.

Since M_0 marks at least one place and the total number of tokens of N remains invariant under transition occurrences, M marks some place s. By the strong connectedness of N, there exists a minimal path leading from s to t. As N is an S-net, every transition of this path has exactly one input place, which is its predecessor in the path, and exactly one output place, which is its successor in the path. Let σ be the sequence of transitions of the path, excluding t. Then, $M \xrightarrow{\sigma} M'$ is an occurrence sequence leading to some marking M' which puts at least one token on the last place of the path. Since N is an S-net, this place is the only input place of its successor in the path, which is t. Therefore, M' enables t.   □

We now state and prove the Boundedness Theorem which characterizes b-boundedness of live S-systems, and the Reachability Theorem, which characterizes the reachable markings of live S-systems. Both are consequences of the following lemma.

Lemma 3.4

Let (S, T, F) be a strongly connected S-net, and let M and M' be two markings such that $M(S) = M'(S)$. Then $M \xrightarrow{*} M'$.

Proof:

We proceed by induction on $M(S)$.

Base. $M(S) = M'(S) = 0$. Then both markings are the null marking and henceforth equal.

Step. $M(S) = M'(S) \geq 1$. Define markings K, K', L, L' such that $L(S) = 1$, $L'(S) = 1$ and

$$M = K + L \qquad M' = K' + L'$$

Then $K(S) < M(S)$ and $K(S) = K'(S)$. We can apply the induction hypothesis to K and obtain an occurrence sequence $K \xrightarrow{\sigma} K'$.

Next we show that there is an occurrence sequence $L \xrightarrow{\tau} L'$. Let s be the place marked by L and let s' be the place marked by L'. Since N is strongly connected, there exists a path $s\, t_1 \ldots t_n\, s'$. As in the proof of the Liveness Theorem, we can choose $\tau = t_1 \ldots t_n$, i.e., τ moves the token from s to s'.

Altogether we have, by two applications of the Monotonicity Lemma (Lemma 2.13),

$$M = (K + L) \xrightarrow{\sigma} (K' + L) \xrightarrow{\tau} (K' + L') = M'$$

and hence $M \xrightarrow{*} M'$. $\square$

Theorem 3.5   *Boundedness Theorem*

A live S-system (N, M_0) is b-bounded iff $M_0(S) \leq b$, where S is the set of places of N.

Proof:

($\Rightarrow$): Let s be a place of S, and let M be the unique marking of N satisfying $M(s) = M(S) = M_0(S)$. By the Liveness Theorem, N is strongly connected. By Lemma 3.4, $M_0 \xrightarrow{*} M$. Since (N, M_0) is b-bounded, we have $M(s) \leq b$, and therefore $M_0(S) \leq b$.

($\Leftarrow$): By the fundamental property of S-systems, $M(S) = M_0(S)$ for every reachable marking M. Since $M(s) \leq M(S)$ for every place s and $M_0(S) \leq b$ by assumption, (N, M_0) is b-bounded. $\square$

Theorem 3.6   *Reachability Theorem*

Let (N, M_0) be a live S-system and let M be a marking of N. M is reachable iff $M_0(S) = M(S)$, where S is the set of places of N.

Proof:

($\Rightarrow$): Follows from the fundamental property of S-systems.

($\Leftarrow$): By the Liveness Theorem, N is strongly connected. Apply then Lemma 3.4.
                                                                $\square$

The reachable markings of live S-systems can also be characterized in terms of S-invariants. So we first study the S-invariants of S-nets.

Proposition 3.7   *S-invariants of S-nets*

Let $N = (S, T, F)$ be a connected S-net. A vector $I: S \to \mathbb{Q}$ is an S-invariant of N iff $I = (x \ldots x)$ for some x.

Proof:

Since N is an S-net, every transition t of N has exactly one input place s_t and one output place s'_t. Therefore

$$\sum_{s \in {}^\bullet t} I(s) = I(s_t) \quad \text{and} \quad \sum_{s \in t^\bullet} I(s) = I(s'_t)$$

It follows that I is an S-invariant iff $I(s_t) = I(s'_t)$ for every transition t. Since N is a connected S-net, this is the case iff $I(s) = I(s')$ holds for every two places s and s'; in other words, if there exists a number x such that $I(s) = x$ for every place s of N. $\square$

Observe that the fundamental property of S-systems can also be derived from Proposition 3.7. Since $I = (1 \ldots 1)$ is an S-invariant, we have $I \cdot M_0 = I \cdot M$ for every reachable marking M. Since $I \cdot M_0 = M_0(S)$ and $I \cdot M = M(S)$, it follows $M_0(S) = M(S)$.

Theorem 3.8   *Second Reachability Theorem*

Let (N, M_0) be a live S-system. A marking M is reachable iff it agrees with M_0 on all S-invariants.

Proof:

($\Rightarrow$): Holds for arbitrary systems by Theorem 2.33.

($\Leftarrow$): By the Liveness Theorem, N is strongly connected. Since the place vector $I = (1 \ldots 1)$ is an S-invariant (Proposition 3.7) and M agrees with M_0 on all S-invariants, we have $I \cdot M_0 = I \cdot M$. Since $I \cdot M_0 = M_0(S)$ and $I \cdot M = M(S)$, we get $M_0(S) = M(S)$. By the Reachability Theorem (Theorem 3.6), $M_0 \xrightarrow{*} M$. $\square$

To complete our study of S-systems, we raise the following question: given an S-system (N, M_0) and a reachable marking M, which is the length of a shortest occurrence sequence leading from M_0 to M? We show that it is at most $b \cdot n$, where n is the number of transitions of the system and b is the bound of the system. This bound exists because, by the fundamental property, no place can ever contain more than $M_0(S)$ tokens.

We need two lemmata.

Lemma 3.9

Let $N = (S, T, F)$ be an S-net, γ a circuit of N, and U the set of transitions appearing in γ. Then the characteristic vector of U with respect to T is a T-invariant of N.

Proof:

Let J be the characteristic vector of U. By Proposition 2.36, it suffices to prove that for every place s the equation $\sum_{t \in {}^\bullet s} J(t) = \sum_{t \in s^\bullet} J(t)$ holds.

If s belongs to γ, then it has exactly one input transition in γ and one output transition in γ. So both sides of the equation are equal to 1. If s does not belong to γ, then it has no transition of γ in its pre- or post-set, because N is an S-net; so both sides of the equation are equal to 0. $\square$

Lemma 3.10

Let $N = (S, T, F)$ be an S-net, M a marking of N, and $X: T \to \mathbb{N}$ a vector such that $M + \mathbf{N} \cdot X \geq \mathbf{0}$. If every circuit of N contains a transition t such that $X(t) = 0$, then there is an occurrence sequence $M \xrightarrow{\sigma} M'$ such that $\vec{\sigma} = X$.

Proof:

We proceed by induction on $|X|$, the sum of entries in X.

Base. If $|X| = 0$ then $X = \mathbf{0}$. Take $\sigma = \epsilon$.

Step. $|X| \geq 1$.

We denote the set of transitions t satisfying $X(t) > 0$ by $\langle X \rangle$. We claim that a transition of $\langle X \rangle$ is enabled at M.

Since T is finite and every circuit contains a transition which does not belong to $\langle X \rangle$, there is a place s such that some transition $t \in s^\bullet$ belongs to $\langle X \rangle$ but no transition in ${}^\bullet s$ belongs to $\langle X \rangle$. Since $M + \mathbf{N} \cdot X \geq \mathbf{0}$ by assumption, we have

$$
\begin{aligned}
0 \;\leq\; & M(s) + \sum_{u \in {}^\bullet s} X(u) - \sum_{u \in s^\bullet} X(u) \\
=\; & M(s) - \sum_{u \in s^\bullet} X(u) & ({}^\bullet s \cap \langle X \rangle = \emptyset\,) \\
\leq\; & M(s) - X(t) & (t \in s^\bullet\,)
\end{aligned}
$$

Since $X(t) > 0$, we have $M(s) > 0$, and therefore t is enabled at M, which proves the claim.

Let $M \xrightarrow{t} M''$. Then $M'' + \mathbf{N} \cdot (X - \vec{t}) = M + \mathbf{N} \cdot X \geq \mathbf{0}$. We can apply the induction hypothesis to $(X - \vec{t})$, which yields a sequence $M'' \xrightarrow{\tau} M'$ satisfying $\vec{\tau} = X - \vec{t}$. Taking $\sigma = t\tau$, the result follows. $\square$

Theorem 3.11   *Shortest Sequence Theorem*

Let (N, M_0) be a b-bounded S-system with n transitions. If M is a reachable marking then there exists an occurrence sequence $M_0 \xrightarrow{\sigma} M$ such that the length of σ is at most $b \cdot n$.

Proof:

Let $X \geq 0$ be an integer-valued solution of the Marking Equation $M_0 + \mathbf{N} \cdot X = M$. Such a solution exists because M is reachable from M_0. Assume moreover that X is minimal with respect to the order $\leq$.

We claim that $\langle X \rangle$ does not contain the set of transitions of any circuit of N. Suppose that $X(t) \geq 1$ for all the transitions t of some circuit γ. By Lemma 3.9, the characteristic vector of the set of transitions of γ is a T-invariant, say J. Therefore, $X - J$ is another solution of the Marking Equation, and $X - J \geq 0$. Moreover, $X - J \leq X$ and $X - J \neq X$, contradicting the minimality of X. This proves the claim.

By Lemma 3.10, there is an occurrence sequence $M_0 \xrightarrow{\sigma} M$ such that $\vec{\sigma} = X$. We show that no transition occurs more than b times in σ, which immediately implies the result.

Let t be an arbitrary transition of the alphabet $\mathcal{A}(\sigma)$ of σ. Define

$$U = \{u \in \mathcal{A}(\sigma) \mid \text{ there is a path } u \ldots t \text{ containing only transitions of } \mathcal{A}(\sigma)\}$$

$$V = \mathcal{A}(\sigma) \setminus U$$

We have ${}^\bullet U \cap V^\bullet = \emptyset$. Moreover, U and V are disjoint and $\mathcal{A}(\sigma) \subseteq U \cup V$. So we can apply the Exchange Lemma, and conclude that the sequence $\sigma|_U$ is also enabled at M_0.

By definition, $t \in U$. Let s be the unique place in $t^\bullet$. Since no circuit contains only transitions of $\mathcal{A}(\sigma)$, no transition in $s^\bullet$ belongs to U. So no transition of $s^\bullet$ occurs in $\sigma|_U$. Since (N, M_0) is b-bounded and $t \in {}^\bullet s$, we have that t occurs at most b times in $\sigma|_U$. Therefore, t occurs at most b times in σ, which finishes the proof. $\square$

3.2   T-systems

In T-systems places have exactly one input and one output transition.

Definition 3.12   *T-nets, T-systems*

A net is a T-net if $|{}^\bullet s| = 1 = |s^\bullet|$ for every place s.

A system (N, M_0) is a T-system if N is a T-net.

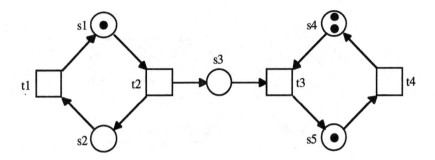

Fig. 3.1 A T-system

Circuits play a very important role in the theory of T-systems.

Definition 3.13   *Token counts of circuits*

Let γ be a circuit of a net and let M be a marking. Let R be the set of places of γ. The token count $M(\gamma)$ of γ at M is defined as $M(R)$.

A circuit γ is marked at M if $M(\gamma) > 0$.

A circuit of a system is initially marked if it is marked at the initial marking.

$s_1\, t_2\, s_2\, t_1$ and $s_4\, t_3\, s_5\, t_4$ are two circuits of the T-system of Figure 3.1. Their token counts at the initial marking are 1 and 3, respectively.

With the help of this definition we can now state the fundamental property of T-systems: the token counts of circuits remain invariant under the occurrence of transitions.

Proposition 3.14   *Fundamental property of T-systems*

Let γ be a circuit of a T-system (N, M_0). For every reachable marking M, $M(\gamma) = M_0(\gamma)$.

Proof:

Let t be a transition. If t does not belong to γ, then the occurrence of t does not change the number of tokens of any place of γ, because N is a T-net. If t belongs to γ, then exactly one of its input places and one of its output places belong to γ. So the occurrence of t removes a token from one place of γ, and adds a token to one place of γ (these two places may be the same). In both cases the token count of γ does not change.   □

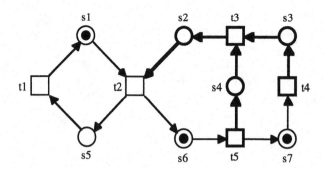

Fig. 3.2   Illustration of the proof of the Liveness Theorem

Liveness of T-systems is characterized by the following theorem:

Theorem 3.15   *Liveness Theorem*

A T-system is live iff every circuit is initially marked.

Proof:

($\Rightarrow$): Assume that some circuit is not initially marked. By the fundamental property of T-systems, this circuit remains unmarked at every reachable marking. Therefore, its transitions can never occur. So the T-system is not live.

($\Leftarrow$): Let t be an arbitrary transition, and let M be an arbitrary reachable marking. We show that some marking reachable from M enables t.

Define the set S_M of places as follows: $s \in S_M$ if there is a path from s to t which contains no place marked at M. In the example of Figure 3.2, if we take $t = t_2$, then we have $S_M = \{s_2, s_3, s_4\}$ (the paths leading to t_2 are shown in boldface). Notice that every place of S_M must become marked at some intermediate marking before t can occur from M.

We proceed by induction on $|S_M|$.

Base. $|S_M| = 0$. Then every place in $\bullet t$ is marked at M and t is already enabled at the marking M.

Step. $|S_M| > 0$. Then t is not enabled at M. By the assumption, every circuit is initially marked. By the fundamental property of T-systems, every circuit is marked at M. Therefore, there exists a path π of maximal length, containing no places marked at M and leading to t (π is not necessarily unique). Let u be the first element of π (in the example, we can take $\pi = t_4\, s_3\, t_3\, s_2\, t_2$, and so $u = t_4$). By the maximality of π, u is a transition and all places in $\bullet u$ are marked at M. So u is enabled at M. Observe that $u \neq t$ because t is not enabled at M.

Let $M \xrightarrow{u} M'$. In order to apply the induction hypothesis we prove that $S_{M'}$ is a proper subset of S_M.

(i) $S_{M'} \subseteq S_M$.

Let $s \in S_{M'}$. Then there exists a path $\pi' = s \dots t$ containing no places marked at M'. We show indirectly that π' has no places marked at M, which implies $s \in S_M$.

Assume that some place r of π' is marked at M. Since r is not marked at M' and $M \xrightarrow{u} M'$, u is an output transition of r. Since N is a T-net, u is the only output transition of r, and hence its successor in π'. Since $u \neq t$, some place of $u^{\bullet}$ is contained in π'; but this place is marked at M', which contradicts the definition of π'.

(ii) $S_{M'} \neq S_M$. Let s be the successor of u in the path π. Since all places of π belong to S_M, we have $s \in S_M$. Since the occurrence of u puts a token on s, $M'(s) > 0$, and so $s \notin S_{M'}$.

By the induction hypothesis, there exists an occurrence sequence $M' \xrightarrow{\sigma} M''$ such that M'' enables t. Since $M \xrightarrow{u} M'$, the marking M'' is reachable from M, and we are done. $\square$

Since all circuits of the example shown in Figure 3.1 are marked, the T-system is live. The same holds for the example shown in Figure 3.2.

Strongly connected T-systems play an important role in the next chapters. We now prove that a strongly connected T-system is live if and only if it has an infinite occurrence sequence. This is not true for all T-systems. Consider the example of Figure 3.1, but with a different initial marking, namely the marking obtained by removing the tokens from s_4 and s_5. This system is not live because the transitions t_3 and t_4 can never become enabled. However, $(t_2\, t_1)^{\omega}$ is an infinite occurrence sequence.

We first state a proposition that characterizes the T-invariants of a T-system. The proof is left for the reader (it can be easily obtained from the proof of Proposition 3.7 by interchanging the role of places and transitions).

Proposition 3.16   *T-invariants of T-nets*

Let $N = (S, T, F)$ be a connected T-net. A vector $J : T \to \mathbb{Q}$ is a T-invariant iff $J = (\, x \dots x \,)$ for some x. $\square$

Theorem 3.17   *Liveness in strongly connected T-systems*

Let (N, M_0) be a strongly connected T-system. The following statements are equivalent:

(a) (N, M_0) is live.

(b) (N, M_0) is deadlock-free.

(c) (N, M_0) has an infinite occurrence sequence.

Proof:

As was seen in Chapter 2, (a) implies (b). It follows easily from the definition of deadlock-freeness that (b) implies (c). We prove that (c) implies (a).

Assume that (N, M_0) has an infinite occurrence sequence $M_0 \xrightarrow{\sigma}$. We claim that the alphabet of σ contains all the transitions of the net.

Since N is strongly connected, every place s is contained in some circuit γ. By the fundamental property of T-systems, the token count of γ remains invariant. Therefore, no reachable marking puts more than $M_0(\gamma)$ tokens on s, which implies that (N, M_0) is bounded. We can then apply the Reproduction Lemma (Lemma 2.39), and conclude that there is a semi-positive T-invariant J satisfying $\langle J \rangle \subseteq \mathcal{A}(\sigma)$. By Proposition 3.16, all semi-positive T-invariants have the same support, namely all the transitions of the net. So, in particular, $\langle J \rangle$ contains every transition of N. The claim then follows from $\langle J \rangle \subseteq \mathcal{A}(\sigma)$.

By the claim, every transition can occur from M_0. Therefore, every place can become marked, which implies that every circuit can become marked. By the fundamental property of T-systems, every circuit must then be initially marked. By the Liveness Theorem, (N, M_0) is live. $\square$

We now characterize the live T-systems which are b-bounded.

Theorem 3.18   *Boundedness Theorem*

A live T-system (N, M_0) is b-bounded iff for every place s there exists a circuit γ which contains s and satisfies $M_0(\gamma) \le b$.

Proof:

($\Rightarrow$): Let s be a place. Since (N, M_0) is b-bounded, the bound of s exists and is at most b. Let M be a reachable marking such that $M(s)$ is equal to the bound of s. Define the marking L of N as follows:

$$L(r) = \begin{cases} M(r) & \text{if } r \neq s \\ 0 & \text{if } r = s \end{cases}$$

We claim that (N, L) is not live. Assume this is not the case. Then, since liveness implies place-liveness, there exists an occurrence sequence $L \xrightarrow{\sigma} L'$ such that $L'(s) > 0$. Since $M \geq L$, σ is also enabled at M (Monotonicity Lemma). Let $M \xrightarrow{\sigma} M'$. Since $L(s) = 0$ we have $M'(s) = L'(s) + M(s) > M(s)$, which contradicts the assumption that $M(s)$ is equal to the bound of s. This finishes the proof of the claim.

Since (N, L) is not live, some circuit γ is unmarked at L (Liveness Theorem). Since (N, M) is live, γ is marked at M. As L and M only differ in the place s, the circuit γ contains s. Moreover, s is the only place of γ marked at M, and therefore $M(\gamma) = M(s)$. So $M(\gamma) \leq b$ because $M(s) \leq b$.

($\Leftarrow$): Let M be an arbitrary reachable marking, and let s be an arbitrary place of N. By the assumption, s belongs to some circuit γ such that $M_0(\gamma) \leq b$. By the fundamental property of T-systems, we have $M(\gamma) \leq b$, and therefore $M(s) \leq b$.

□

We can apply this theorem to the T-systems of Figures 3.1 and 3.2, because both are live. Place s_3 in Figure 3.1 is not contained in any circuit; therefore, the T-system is unbounded. On the contrary, every place in Figure 3.2 is contained in a circuit with at most 2 tokens; therefore, this T-system is 2-bounded.

The proof of the Boundedness Theorem implies the following stronger result:

Corollary 3.19   *Place bounds in live T-systems*

Let (N, M_0) be a live T-system.

(1) A place s of (N, M_0) is bounded iff it belongs to some circuit of N.

(2) If a place s of (N, M_0) is bounded, then its bound is equal to

$$\min\{M_0(\gamma) \mid \gamma \text{ is a circuit of } N \text{ containing } s\}$$

(3) (N, M_0) is bounded iff N is strongly connected.

Proof:

($1 \Rightarrow$) Assume that s is bounded. Then, the proof of the Boundedness Theorem shows that s belongs to some circuit γ such that $M_0(\gamma)$ is the bound of s.

($1 \Leftarrow$) Assume that s belongs to some circuit γ of N. By the fundamental property of T-systems, s can never contain more than $M_0(\gamma)$ tokens.

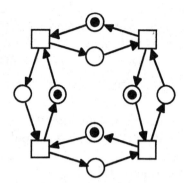

Fig. 3.3 A 1-bounded T-system with a circuit containing three tokens

(2) Let γ be the circuit of (1 $\Rightarrow$). Since $M_0(\gamma)$ is the bound of s, it suffices to prove that for every circuit δ containing s, $M_0(\delta) \geq M_0(\gamma)$.

Let M be a reachable marking such that $M(s)$ is equal to the bound of s. Then $M_0(\gamma) = M(s)$ and, since δ contains s, $M(s) \leq M(\delta)$. So $M_0(\gamma) \leq M(\delta)$ and, by the fundamental property of T-systems, $M_0(\delta) \geq M_0(\gamma)$.

(3 $\Rightarrow$): Follows from the Strong Connectedness Theorem (Theorem 2.25). It also follows from the first part of the Boundedness Theorem: since (N, M_0) is bounded, every place is contained in a circuit of N; since every place has exactly one input transition and one output transition, for every arc (x, y) of N, some circuit has a prefix $x\,y$. Together with the connectedness of N, this implies that N is strongly connected.

(3 $\Leftarrow$): Since N is strongly connected every place is contained in some circuit. Apply then (1). $\square$

The third part of this corollary implies that a T-net has a live and bounded marking if and only if it is strongly connected (and has at least one place and at least one transition). The corollary proves the 'if' direction, while the 'only if' direction follows from the Strong Connectedness Theorem.

In the example shown in Figure 3.1, the bound of the places s_4 and s_5 is 3, because that is the token count on the only circuit they are contained in. In the system of Figure 3.2, the place s_4 has bound 1, but the place s_7 has bound 2.

Observe that a live and b-bounded T-system may have circuits containing more than b tokens. A good example is the T-system of Figure 3.3. The system is 1-bounded, but the inner circuit contains 3 tokens.

Live and 1-bounded systems are of particular interest in many applications. The Liveness Theorem and the Boundedness Theorem imply that strongly connected

T-nets can always be transformed into live and bounded T-systems: it suffices to put one token in each place. The question is if they can also be transformed into live and 1-bounded T-systems. Genrich's Theorem gives a positive answer.

Theorem 3.20   *Genrich's Theorem*

Let N be a strongly connected T-net having at least one place and one transition. There exists a marking M_0 of N such that (N, M_0) is a live and 1-bounded system.

Proof:

By the Liveness Theorem, N has a live marking; it suffices to put a token on every place.

Let (N, M) be an arbitrary live T-system which is not 1-bounded. We construct another marking L such that (N, L) is also live and satisfies the following two conditions:

- for every circuit γ, $L(\gamma) \leq M(\gamma)$, and

- for some circuit γ, $L(\gamma) < M(\gamma)$.

Starting with an arbitrary live marking, an exhaustive application of this construction yields a live marking M_0 such that every place is 1-bounded at (N, M_0).

To construct L, let s be a place which is not 1-bounded in (N, M). Then, there exists a marking M' reachable from M satisfying $M'(s) \geq 2$. Let L be the marking that coincides with M' everywhere except in s, where it puts only one token.

Since (N, M) is live, (N, M') is live. So every circuit of N is marked at M', and, by the construction of L, every circuit of N is marked at L. So (N, L) is live.

By the fundamental property of T-systems, $M(\gamma) = M'(\gamma)$ for every circuit γ of N. By the construction of L, we also have $L(\gamma) \leq M'(\gamma)$. Moreover, if a circuit γ contains s (some circuit does, because N is strongly connected), then $L(\gamma) < M'(\gamma)$.
$\square$

The proof of this theorem is in fact an algorithm for the construction of a live and 1-bounded marking from a live and bounded one. The algorithm lets transitions occur, until a marking is reached which puts more than one token in some place; then, it removes all but one of those tokens. These two steps are iterated until a live and 1-bounded marking is obtained.

We can apply the algorithm to the T-system of Figure 3.2. One iteration suffices: we let t_5 occur, and then remove one of the tokens of s_7. The marking so obtained is live and 1-bounded.

We now show that the reachable markings of live T-systems admit the same characterization as those of live S-systems; i.e., they are the markings that agree with the initial marking on all S-invariants.

Theorem 3.21   *Reachability Theorem*

Let (N, M_0) be a live T-system. A marking M is reachable iff it agrees with M_0 on all S-invariants.

Proof:

($\Rightarrow$): Holds for arbitrary systems by Theorem 2.33.

($\Leftarrow$): Theorem 2.34 implies that there exists a rational-valued vector X satsifying $M = M_0 + \mathbf{N} \cdot X$. Since $J = (1 \ldots 1)$ is a T-invariant of N (Proposition 3.16), we have $\mathbf{N} \cdot (X + \lambda J) = \mathbf{N} \cdot X$ for every λ. Therefore, we can further assume that $X \geq \mathbf{0}$.

Let T denote the set of transitions of N. The proof is divided into two steps:

(i) There exists a vector $Y : T \to I\!N$ such that $M = M_0 + \mathbf{N} \cdot Y$.

Define Y by $Y(t) = \lceil X(t) \rceil$ for every transition t, where, given a rational number x, $\lceil x \rceil$ denotes the smallest integer greater than or equal to x. Since $M = M_0 + \mathbf{N} \cdot X$, we have for every place s:

$$M(s) = M_0(s) + X(t_1) - X(t_2)$$

where t_1 is the unique transition in ${}^\bullet s$ and t_2 is the unique transition in $s^\bullet$.

Since both $M(s)$ and $M_0(s)$ are integer-valued, $X(t_1) - X(t_2)$ is an integer. By the definition of Y, we have $X(t_1) - X(t_2) = Y(t_1) - Y(t_2)$. So

$$M(s) = M_0(s) + Y(t_1) - Y(t_2)$$

and hence $M = M_0 + \mathbf{N} \cdot Y$.

(ii) $M_0 \xrightarrow{\;*\;} M$.

By induction on $|Y|$, the sum of the entries of the vector Y defined in (i).

Base. $|Y| = 0$. Then $Y = \mathbf{0}$ and $M = M_0$.

Step. $|Y| > 0$. We first show that some transition of the support $\langle Y \rangle$ of Y is enabled at M_0. Let S_Y be the set of places in ${}^\bullet \langle Y \rangle$ which are unmarked at M_0.

If a place $s \in S_Y$ has an input transition which belongs to $\langle Y \rangle$, then, since s is unmarked at M_0 and $M_0 + \mathbf{N} \cdot Y = M \geq \mathbf{0}$, some transition in ${}^\bullet s$ belongs to $\langle Y \rangle$ as well.

Every circuit of N is marked at M_0 because the system (N, M_0) is live. Therefore, there exists a path of maximal length containing only places of S_Y and transitions of $\langle Y \rangle$. Since, as shown above, every place of S_Y has an input transition that belongs to $\langle Y \rangle$, the path begins with a transition $t \in \langle Y \rangle$. Moreover, no input place of t belongs to S_Y because the path has maximal length. Therefore, every input place of t is marked at M_0, and hence t is enabled.

Let $M_0 \xrightarrow{t} M_1$. Then $M_1 + \mathbf{N} \cdot (Y - \overrightarrow{t}) = M$. Since $|Y - \overrightarrow{t}| < |Y|$, we can apply the induction hypothesis to M_1. So $M_1 \xrightarrow{*} M$. It follows $M_0 \xrightarrow{t} M_1 \xrightarrow{*} M$, which implies $M_0 \xrightarrow{*} M$. $\qquad\square$

Finally, we obtain a Shortest Sequence Theorem for T-systems. Given a b-bounded T-system (N, M_0) with n transitions and a reachable marking M, we show that the length of a shortest occurrence sequence leading from M_0 to M is at most

$$b \cdot \frac{(n-1) \cdot n}{2}$$

The proof is based on the notion of biased sequence, and requires several lemmata. We prove these lemmata in a more general way than necessary for T-systems. This will make it possible to reuse them later for more general classes.

Definition 3.22   *Permutations, biased sequences*

Two sequences σ and τ of transitions of a net are permutations of each other if $\overrightarrow{\tau} = \overrightarrow{\sigma}$; in other words, if each transition occurs in σ and τ the same number of times.

A sequence σ of transitions of a net is called biased if $^\bullet t \cap {}^\bullet u = \emptyset$ for every two distinct transitions t and u that occur in σ, i.e., if for every place s, at most one transition of $s^\bullet$ occurs in σ.

Assume that τ is a permutation of σ. By the Marking Equation, if $M_0 \xrightarrow{\sigma} M$ and $M_0 \xrightarrow{\tau} M'$, then $M' = M$, i.e., both σ and τ lead to the same marking.

Lemma 3.23

Let $\sigma_1 \sigma_2 t$ be a biased sequence of transitions of a net (where σ_1 and σ_2 are sequences of transitions and t is a transition) such that t does not occur in σ_1 and every transition occurring in σ_2 also occurs in σ_1. If $M_0 \xrightarrow{\sigma_1 \sigma_2 t} M$ is an occurrence sequence, then $M_0 \xrightarrow{\sigma_1 t \sigma_2} M$ is also an occurrence sequence.

Proof:

By induction on the length of σ_2.

Base: If σ_2 is the empty sequence then $\sigma_1 \sigma_2 t = \sigma_1 t \sigma_2$.

Step: Assume that σ_2 is nonempty and define $\sigma_2 = \sigma_2' u$, where u is a transition.

Let $M_0 \xrightarrow{\sigma_1} M_1 \xrightarrow{\sigma_2'} M_2 \xrightarrow{u} M_3 \xrightarrow{t} M$. We prove $M_2 \xrightarrow{t} M_4 \xrightarrow{u} M$ for some marking M_4. If $t = u$, we are done. So assume $t \neq u$.

Let s be an arbitrary input place of t. We claim $M_2(s) > 0$. Since $\sigma_1 \sigma_2 t$ is biased, we have $s \notin {}^\bullet u$. Consider two cases:

Case 1. $s \notin u^\bullet$. Then $M_2(s) = M_3(s)$. Since t is enabled at M_3, we have $M_3(s) > 0$. So $M_2(s) > 0$.

Case 2. $s \in u^\bullet$. Since every transition that occurs in σ_2 occurs in σ_1 and u occurs in σ_2, u occurs at least twice in $\sigma_1 \sigma_2$. Since t does not occur in σ_1, it does not occur in $\sigma_1 \sigma_2$. Since t is the only output transition of s occurring in $\sigma_1 \sigma_2 t$, we have

$$M_3(s) \geq M_0(s) + \overrightarrow{\sigma_1 \sigma_2}(u) - \overrightarrow{\sigma_1 \sigma_2}(t)$$

Therefore, $M_3(s) \geq 2$. Since $M_2 \xrightarrow{u} M_3$, we have $M_2(s) \geq 1$, and the claim is proved.

The transition t is enabled at M_2, because the claim holds for an arbitrary input place of t. Let $M_2 \xrightarrow{t} M_4$. Since $\sigma_1 \sigma_2 t$ is biased, the occurrence of t does not disable u, and so u is enabled at M_4. Since $u\,t$ and $t\,u$ are permutations of each other, we get $M_2 \xrightarrow{t} M_4 \xrightarrow{u} M$. The application of the induction hypothesis to $\sigma_1 \sigma_2' t$ (taking σ_2' for σ_2) yields an occurrence sequence $M_0 \xrightarrow{\sigma_1 t \sigma_2'} M_4$. The result follows since $M_4 \xrightarrow{u} M$ and $\sigma_2' u = \sigma_2$. $\square$

Lemma 3.24

Let (N, M_0) be a system and let $M_0 \xrightarrow{\sigma} M$ be a biased occurrence sequence. There exists a permutation $\sigma_1 \sigma_2$ of σ such that $M_0 \xrightarrow{\sigma_1 \sigma_2} M$, no transition occurs more than once in σ_1, and $\mathcal{A}(\sigma_2) \subseteq \mathcal{A}(\sigma_1)$.

Proof:

By induction on the length of σ.

Base: If $\sigma = \epsilon$, then take $\sigma_1 = \sigma_2 = \epsilon$.

Step: $\sigma \neq \epsilon$. Assume $\sigma = \tau t$, where t is a transition.

By the induction hypothesis, there exists a permutation $\tau_1 \tau_2$ of τ such that no transition occurs more than once in τ_1 and $\mathcal{A}(\tau_2) \subseteq \mathcal{A}(\tau_1)$.

If t occurs in τ_1 then $\sigma_1 = \tau_1$ and $\sigma_2 = \tau_2 t$ satisfy the requirements.

If t does not occur in τ_1 then $\tau_1 \tau_2 t$ satisfies the conditions of Lemma 3.23, and so $M_0 \xrightarrow{\tau_1 t \tau_2} M$ is an occurrence sequence. Take then $\sigma_1 = \tau_1 t$ and $\sigma_2 = \tau_2$. $\square$

Lemma 3.25

Let (N, M_0) be a b-bounded system and let $M_0 \overset{\sigma}{\longrightarrow} M$ be an occurrence sequence such that σ is biased and nonempty. Then there exist sequences σ_1, σ_2 such that $M_0 \overset{\sigma_1 \sigma_2}{\longrightarrow} M$, no transition occurs more than b times in σ_1, and $\mathcal{A}(\sigma_2) \subset \mathcal{A}(\sigma_1)$.[1]

Proof:

By repeated application of Lemma 3.24, there exists a permutation $\tau_1 \ldots \tau_n$ of σ such that

- $M_0 \overset{\tau_1 \ldots \tau_n}{\longrightarrow} M$,

- for every i, $1 \le i \le n$, $\tau_i \ne \epsilon$,

- for every i, $1 \le i \le n$, no transition occurs more than once in τ_i, and

- for every i, $1 \le i \le n-1$, $\mathcal{A}(\tau_{i+1}) \subseteq \mathcal{A}(\tau_i)$.

If $n \le b$ then, taking $\sigma_1 = \tau_1 \ldots \tau_n$ and $\sigma_2 = \epsilon$, we are done because every transition occurs at most once in every τ_i. So we assume that $n \ge b+1$.

If $\mathcal{A}(\tau_{b+1}) \subset \mathcal{A}(\tau_1)$, then $\mathcal{A}(\tau_i) \subset \mathcal{A}(\tau_1)$ for every $i \ge b+1$. So in this case, taking $\sigma_1 = \tau_1 \ldots \tau_b$ and $\sigma_2 = \tau_{b+1} \ldots \tau_n$, we are done. Therefore we also assume $\mathcal{A}(\tau_{b+1}) = \mathcal{A}(\tau_1)$.

Let m be the greatest number such that $\mathcal{A}(\tau_m) = \mathcal{A}(\tau_1)$. We have $b+1 \le m \le n$. Let $M_0 \overset{\tau_1 \ldots \tau_m}{\longrightarrow} M'$. We then have for every place s

$$M'(s) = M_0(s) + \sum_{i=1}^{m} \left(\sum_{t \in {}^\bullet s} \overrightarrow{\tau_i}(t) - \sum_{t \in s^\bullet} \overrightarrow{\tau_i}(t) \right)$$

Since $\mathcal{A}(\tau_m) = \mathcal{A}(\tau_1)$, the sequences $\tau_1, \ldots, \tau_m$ have the same alphabet. Since no transition occurs more than once in them, they are moreover permutations of each other. It follows:

$$M'(s) = M_0(s) + m \cdot \left(\sum_{t \in {}^\bullet s} \overrightarrow{\tau_1}(t) - \sum_{t \in s^\bullet} \overrightarrow{\tau_1}(t) \right)$$

Since (N, M_0) is b-bounded, $|M'(s) - M_0(s)| \le b$. Therefore, since $m > b$

$$\sum_{t \in {}^\bullet s} \overrightarrow{\tau_1}(t) - \sum_{t \in s^\bullet} \overrightarrow{\tau_1}(t) = 0$$

Since s was chosen arbitrarily, we get that $\overrightarrow{\tau_1}$ is a T-invariant, and so are $\overrightarrow{\tau_2}, \ldots, \overrightarrow{\tau_m}$. So $M' = M_0$, and we can take $\sigma_1 = \tau_1$ and $\sigma_2 = \tau_{m+1} \ldots \tau_n$ (or $\sigma_2 = \epsilon$ if $n = m$). $\square$

---

[1]Notice that, in contrast to Lemma 3.24, here $\mathcal{A}(\sigma_2)$ is a proper subset of $\mathcal{A}(\sigma_1)$.

Lemma 3.26   *Biased Sequence Lemma*

Let (N, M_0) be a b-bounded system and let $M_0 \xrightarrow{\sigma} M$ be an occurrence sequence such that σ is biased. Let k be the number of distinct transitions that occur in σ, i.e., $k = |\mathcal{A}(\sigma)|$. There exists an occurrence sequence $M_0 \xrightarrow{\tau} M$ such that the length of τ is at most

$$b \cdot \frac{k \cdot (k+1)}{2}$$

Proof:

By induction on k.

Base: $k = 0$. Then $\sigma = \epsilon$, and we may take $\tau = \epsilon$.

Step: $k > 0$. By Lemma 3.25, there exist sequences σ_1 and σ_2 such that $M_0 \xrightarrow{\sigma_1 \sigma_2} M$, no transition occurs more than b times in σ_1, and $\mathcal{A}(\sigma_2) \subset \mathcal{A}(\sigma_1)$. In particular, this implies that the length of σ_1 is at most $b \cdot k$.

Let $M_0 \xrightarrow{\sigma_1} M_1 \xrightarrow{\sigma_2} M$. The number of distinct transitions occurring in σ_2 is at most $k - 1$. Since (N, M_0) is b-bounded, so is (N, M_1). By the induction hypothesis, there exists a sequence τ_2, of length at most

$$b \cdot \frac{(k-1) \cdot k}{2}$$

such that $M_1 \xrightarrow{\tau_2} M$.

Take $\tau = \sigma_1 \tau_2$. We have $M_0 \xrightarrow{\tau} M$, and the length of τ is at most

$$b \cdot k + b \cdot \frac{(k-1) \cdot k}{2} = b \cdot \frac{k \cdot (k+1)}{2}$$

$\square$

Theorem 3.27   *Shortest Sequence Theorem*

Let (N, M_0) be a b-bounded T-system with n transitions, and let M be a reachable marking. There exists an occurrence sequence $M_0 \xrightarrow{\sigma} M$ such that the length of σ is at most

$$b \cdot \frac{(n-1) \cdot n}{2}$$

Proof:

Since M is reachable, we have $M_0 \xrightarrow{\tau} M$ for a sequence τ. We can moreover assume that τ has minimal length. Since N is a T-net, every sequence of transitions of N is biased, in particular τ.

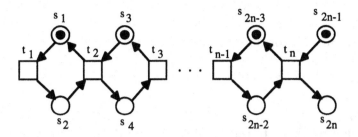

Fig. 3.4 A family of T-systems for which the bound of Theorem 3.27 is tight

We claim that not every transition of N occurs in τ. Assume the contrary. By Lemma 3.24, there exists a permutation $\tau_1 \tau_2$ of τ such that $M_0 \xrightarrow{\tau_1 \tau_2} M$, no transition occurs more than once in τ_1, and every transition that occurs in τ_2 also occurs in τ_1. Since τ contains every transition of N, τ_1 contains exactly one occurrence of every transition of N. Therefore, $\vec{\tau_1} = (\,1 \ldots 1\,)$. By Proposition 3.16, $\vec{\tau_1}$ is a T-invariant, which implies $M_0 \xrightarrow{\tau_1} M_0$. Then we have $M_0 \xrightarrow{\tau_2} M$, which contradicts the minimality of τ.

By this claim, at most $n - 1$ transitions of N occur in τ. Apply now Lemma 3.26.

$\square$

The bound of Theorem 3.27 is tight, i.e., for every number n there exists a T-system (N, M_0) and a reachable marking M for which the bound above is the exact value of the length of a shortest occurrence sequence leading from M_0 to M. Figure 3.4 shows a family of T-systems, one for each value of n. The initial marking M_0 that puts one token in all upper places (shown in the figure) is 1-bounded. It is not difficult to see that the marking M that puts one token in all lower places is reachable from M_0. Moreover, the shortest path leading from M_0 to M has length $\frac{(n-1) \cdot n}{2}$. Therefore, if the only available information is the number of transitions of the net, the bound of Theorem 3.27 cannot be improved.

Exercises

In the exercises, a 'structural characterization' is a characterization that does not involve dynamic concepts like enabledness of a transition or occurrence sequence.

Exercise 3.1

Use Lemma 3.10 to give a structural characterization of the reachable markings of S-systems which are not necessarily live.

Exercise 3.2

Give a polynomial algorithm to decide if a T-system is live.

Exercise 3.3

Give a structural characterization of the bounded T-systems which are not necessarily live.

Exercise 3.4

Let (N, M_0) be a T-system, not necessarily live, and let M be a marking of N. Prove that M is reachable iff the Marking Equation $M = M_0 + \mathbf{N} \cdot X$ has a solution satisfying $X(t) = 0$ for every transition t contained in any circuit of N unmarked at M_0.

Exercise 3.5   *

Let (N, M_0) be a live T-system and let M be a marking of N. Prove: there exists a marking $M' \in [M_0\rangle$ such that $M' \geq M$ iff for every circuit γ of N the token count of γ at M_0 is greater than or equal to the token count of γ at M.

Exercise 3.6   *

Let (N, M_0) be a live T-system, where $N = (S, T, F)$. Prove: a vector $X : T \to \mathbb{N}$ is the Parikh vector of an occurrence sequence of (N, M_0) iff $M_0 + \mathbf{N} \cdot X \geq 0$ (compare with Lemma 3.10).

Exercise 3.7   *

1) Give a structural characterization of boundedness for systems satisfying $|{}^\bullet s| \leq 1$ and $|s^\bullet| \leq 1$ for every place s.

2) Give a structural characterization of the set of reachable markings for the same class of systems.

Exercise 3.8

Prove that the following algorithm yields the set of transitions of a T-system which cannot occur in any occurrence sequence.

> **Input:** A T-system (N, M_0), where $N = (S, T, F)$.
> **Output:** $U \subseteq T$.
> **Initialization:** $U = T$, $M = M_0$.
>
> **begin**
>   **while** M enables some transition t of U **do**
> $U := U \setminus \{t\}$; $M := M + \mathbf{t}$
>   **endwhile**
> **end**

Exercise 3.9

Generalize the Shortest Sequence Theorem for T-systems (Theorem 3.27) to the bounded systems in which every place has one output transition, but maybe more than one input transition.

Bibliographic Notes

T-systems were studied by Commoner, Holt, Even and Pnueli [19] and Genrich and Lautenbach [39] in the early seventies. These two papers contain most of the results of the chapter. Genrich's Theorem was published in [38]. The Shortest Sequence Theorem was proved by the authors in [25], but in fact the theorem is little more than a reformulation and generalization of former results by Yen [77].

Murata [66] and Kumagai, Kodama and Kitawaga [57] have obtained some extensions of the reachability results of the chapter. A survey of these results and others on the synthesis of live and 1-bounded T-systems can be found in [67]. Teruel, Chrzistowski-Wachtel, Colom and Silva [72] have studied weighted T-systems, a generalization of T-systems in which the arcs are labelled with natural numbers (weights); these numbers indicate how many tokens are removed from or added to a place when a transition occurs. Conflict-free systems are another generalization of T-systems; a system is *conflict-free* if $s^\bullet \subseteq {}^\bullet s$ for every place s with more than one output transition. Conflict-free systems have been thoroughly studied by Landweber and Robertson [58], Howell and Rosier [47, 48, 49], Yen [77], Esparza [29], and Yen, Wang and Yang [78].

The presentation of this chapter has been inspired by Best's and Thiagarajan's survey on some classes of live and 1-bounded net systems [10].

Chapter 4

Liveness in free-choice systems

In this chapter we start the study of free-choice systems. The main result of the chapter is Commoner's structural characterization of liveness. The first section contains the formal definition of free-choice systems and some basic properties. The second section introduces siphons and traps, the notions on which Commoner's result is based. This result itself is proved in Section 4.3, which also introduces allocations, a central notion in the theory of free-choice nets.

An easy corollary of Commoner's theorem is that the non-liveness problem of free-choice systems (i.e., the problem of deciding if a given free-choice system is not live) belongs to the class NP. In Section 4.4 we show that this problem is NP-complete.

The last two sections of the chapter contain some results that will be useful later. Section 4.5 studies minimal siphons, and Section 4.6 shows that, under certain conditions, liveness and deadlock-freedom coincide for free-choice systems.

4.1 Free-choice systems

Definition 4.1   *Free-choice nets, free-choice systems*

A net $N = (S, T, F)$ is free-choice if $(s, t) \in F$ implies ${}^\bullet t \times s^\bullet \subseteq F$ for every place s and every transition t.

A system (N, M_0) is free-choice if its underlying net N is free-choice.

There exist other equivalent definitions of free-choice nets. The following proposition gives three examples.

Fig. 4.1   Illustration of Proposition 4.2(1)

Proposition 4.2   *Characterizations of free-choice nets*

(1) A net (S, T, F) is free-choice iff for every two places s and r and every two transitions t and u

$$\{(s, t), (r, t), (s, u)\} \subseteq F \implies (r, u) \in F.$$

(2) A net is free-choice iff for every two places s and r either $s^\bullet \cap r^\bullet = \emptyset$ or $s^\bullet = r^\bullet$.

(3) A net is free-choice iff for every two transitions t and u either $^\bullet t \cap {}^\bullet u = \emptyset$ or $^\bullet t = {}^\bullet u$.

Proof:

(1) Follows easily from the definition of free-choice nets.

(2) ($\Rightarrow$): Let $N = (S, T, F)$ be a free-choice net, and let s and r be two places of N such that $s^\bullet \cap r^\bullet \neq \emptyset$. Then there exists a transition $t \in s^\bullet \cap r^\bullet$, and therefore arcs (s, t) and (r, t). Now, let u be an output transition of s. By (1), u is an output transition of r. This proves $s^\bullet \subseteq r^\bullet$. The converse inclusion can be similarly proved.

($\Leftarrow$): Let $N = (S, T, F)$ be a non-free-choice net. Then there is an arc (s, t), a place $r \in {}^\bullet t$, and a transition $u \in s^\bullet$ such that $(r, u) \notin F$. Since t belongs to both $s^\bullet$ and $r^\bullet$, we have $s^\bullet \cap r^\bullet \neq \emptyset$. Since u belongs to $s^\bullet$, but not to $r^\bullet$, we have $s^\bullet \neq r^\bullet$.

(3) Similar to the proof of (2). $\square$

The first characterization of this proposition is illustrated in Figure 4.1: the net on the left is not free-choice whereas the net on the right is free-choice.

Proposition 4.3   *Fundamental property of free-choice nets*

Let s be a place of a free-choice net N. If a marking of N enables some transition of $s^\bullet$, then it enables every transition of $s^\bullet$.

Proof:

Immediate consequence of Proposition 4.2(3). $\square$

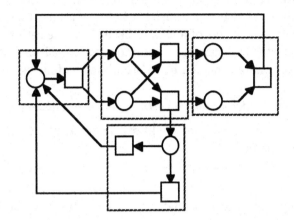

Fig. 4.2 Partition of the nodes of a free-choice net into clusters

We shall frequently use the notion of cluster. Although we define it for arbitrary nets, it is particularly useful for free-choice nets.

Definition 4.4   *Clusters*

Let x be a node of a net. The cluster of x, denoted by $[x]$, is the minimal set of nodes such that

- $x \in [x]$,
- if a place s belongs to x then $s^\bullet$ is included in $[x]$, and
- if a transition t belongs to $[x]$ then $^\bullet t$ is included in $[x]$.

Figure 4.2 shows a free-choice net together with the partition of its nodes into clusters. Clusters have the following property:

Proposition 4.5   *A property of clusters*

Let N be a net. The set $\{[x] \mid x$ is a node of $N\}$ is a partition of the nodes of N.

Proof:

Let $N = (S, T, F)$. It follows easily from the definition of the cluster $[x]$ of a node x that $y \in [x]$ iff the pair (x, y) belongs to the relation

$$E = (\, (F \cap (S \times T)) \cup (F \cap (S \times T))^{-1}\,)^*$$

E is the reflexive, symmetric and transitive closure of $F \cap (S \times T)$, and therefore an equivalence relation. Since the equivalence class of x is $[x]$, the result follows.   □

The clusters of a free-choice net have a particularly simple structure: each place s of a cluster c is connected to every transition t of c by an arc (s,t) (see Figure 4.2). It follows that all the transitions of a cluster have the same set of input places, and all the places of a cluster have the same set of output transitions. The fundamental property of free-choice nets can then be reformulated as follows:

Proposition 4.6   *Fundamental property in terms of clusters*

If a marking of a free-choice net enables a transition t, then it enables every transition of the cluster $[t]$.

Proof:

Follows immediately from the fact that all the transitions of the cluster have the same input places.   □

4.2   Stable predicates: siphons and traps

Let $\mathcal{M}$ be the set of markings M of a net N such that the system (N, M) is live. By the definition of liveness, if (N, M) is live and L is reachable from M, then the system (N, L) is also live. Therefore, every marking reachable from a marking in $\mathcal{M}$ is still in $\mathcal{M}$. We call the sets of markings satisfying this property *stable*.

Definition 4.7   *Stable sets, stable predicates*

A set $\mathcal{M}$ of markings of a net is stable if $M \in \mathcal{M}$ implies $[M\rangle \subseteq \mathcal{M}$. The membership predicate of a stable set is called a stable predicate.

It follows easily from the definition that in order to determine if a predicate is stable, it suffices to check the following condition for every transition t

$$(M \in \mathcal{M} \wedge M \xrightarrow{t} L) \implies L \in \mathcal{M}$$

We study in this chapter some interesting stable predicates which can be derived from the structure of a net. Consider the set of places $\{s_1, s_2\}$ of the net shown in Figure 4.3. It is easy to see that for every transition t the following holds:

$$(M(\{s_1, s_2\}) = 0 \wedge M \xrightarrow{t} L) \implies L(\{s_1, s_2\}) = 0$$

We have thus found an example of a stable predicate for N, namely $M(\{s_1, s_2\}) = 0$. It corresponds to the stable set of markings that mark neither s_1 nor s_2. This

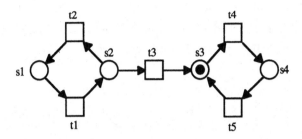

Fig. 4.3 The set $\{s_1, s_2\}$ is a siphon; the set $\{s_3, s_4\}$ is a trap

predicate provides important information about liveness: if there exists a reachable marking M that does not mark $\{s_1, s_2\}$ – like the one shown in the figure – then no marking of the set $[M\rangle$ enables t_1 nor t_2. This implies that the system is not live. The predicate $M(\{s_1, s_2\}) = 0$ is stable because the transitions t_1 and t_2, which could put a token onto s_2 and s_1 respectively, need a token from s_1 or s_2 to occur. In other words,

$$^\bullet\{s_1, s_2\} \subseteq \{s_1, s_2\}^\bullet$$

Sets of places satisfying this property are called *siphons*.

Definition 4.8   *Siphons, proper siphons*

A set R of places of a net is a siphon if $^\bullet R \subseteq R^\bullet$. A siphon is called proper if it is not the empty set.

Proposition 4.9   *Unmarked siphons remain unmarked*

If R is a siphon then the set of markings M satisfying $M(R) = 0$ is stable.

Proof:

Follows easily from the definition.   □

The following propositions state two connections between siphons and the behaviour of a system.

Proposition 4.10   *Live systems have no unmarked proper siphons*

Every proper siphon of a live system is initially marked (marked at the initial marking).

Proof:

Let R be a proper siphon and let $s \in R$. Since liveness implies place-liveness (Proposition 2.17), s is marked at some reachable marking, and therefore so is R. By Proposition 4.9, R was never unmarked before. In particular, the initial marking marks R.   □

Proposition 4.11   *Deadlocked systems have an unmarked proper siphon*

Let (N, M_0) be a deadlocked system, i.e., M_0 is a dead marking of N. Then the set R of places of N unmarked at M_0 is a proper siphon.

Proof:

Since M_0 is a dead marking, every transition has an unmarked input place at M_0, and therefore $R^\bullet$ contains every transition of the net. In particular, we have $^\bullet R \subseteq R^\bullet$. Hence R is a siphon. Since the net has at least one transition by the definition of a system, R is not the empty set.   □

The last proposition shows that if all proper siphons of a system are marked at every reachable marking, then the system is deadlock-free. This property of proper siphons can be enforced using the notion of a trap, which is defined next.

Consider again the system of Figure 4.3. We have:

$$(M(\{s_3, s_4\}) > 0 \wedge M \xrightarrow{t} L) \implies L(\{s_3, s_4\}) > 0$$

So the predicate $M(\{s_3, s_4\}) > 0$ is stable. The reason is that the transitions t_4 and t_5, which remove tokens from s_3 or s_4, return tokens to s_4 or s_3 respectively. In other words,

$$\{s_3, s_4\}^\bullet \subseteq {}^\bullet\{s_3, s_4\}$$

Sets of places satisfying this property are called *traps*.

Definition 4.12   *Traps, proper traps*

A set R of places of a net is a trap if $R^\bullet \subseteq {}^\bullet R$. A trap is called proper if it is not the empty set.

Proposition 4.13   *Marked traps remain marked*

If R is a trap then the set of markings M satisfying $M(R) > 0$ is stable.

Proof:

Follows easily from the definition.   □

In order to prevent a siphon from becoming unmarked, it suffices to guarantee that it includes an *initially marked trap* – a trap marked at the initial marking. Since such a trap remains marked, the siphon does too.

Proposition 4.14   *A sufficient condition for deadlock-freedom*

If every proper siphon of a system includes an initially marked trap, then the system is deadlock-free.

Proof:

Assume that some reachable marking M is dead. By Proposition 4.11, the set of places which are not marked at M, say R, is a proper siphon. Since R is not marked at M, it includes no trap marked at M. Since marked traps remain marked, R does not include any initially marked trap.   □

We finish this section with some important structural properties of siphons and traps.

Proposition 4.15   *Structural properties of siphons and traps*

(1) The union of siphons (traps) is a siphon (trap).

(2) Every siphon includes a unique maximal trap with respect to set inclusion (which may be empty).

(3) A siphon includes a marked trap iff its maximal trap is marked.

Proof:

(1) follows immediately from the definitions of siphons and traps. (2) and (3) are consequences of (1).   □

4.3   Commoner's Theorem

In the previous section we have obtained properties of siphons and traps valid for any system. In particular, Proposition 4.14 gives a sufficient condition for a system to be deadlock-free. In this section we prove a result, known as Commoner's Theorem, which shows that this condition becomes more interesting for free-choice systems:

> *A free-choice system is live if and only if every proper siphon includes an initially marked trap.*

We shall prove the 'if' and 'only if' directions separately. For the proof of the 'if' direction we first introduce the notions of dead transition and dead place, and briefly discuss their properties. Then, we obtain some preliminary results, among them the fact that liveness and place-liveness coincide for free-choice systems.

Definition 4.16   *Dead nodes*

A transition of a net is dead at a marking M if it is not enabled at any marking reachable from M. A place of a net is dead at a marking M if it is not marked at any marking reachable from M.

Proposition 4.17   *Elementary properties of dead nodes*

(1) If a system is not live, then a transition is dead at some reachable marking. If a system is not place-live, then a place is dead at some reachable marking.

(2) If a node is dead at a marking M, then it remains dead at any marking reachable from M. In other words, if $M \xrightarrow{*} L$, then the set of nodes dead at M is included in the set of nodes dead at L.

(3) Every transition in the pre-set or post-set of a dead place is also dead.

(4) In a free-choice system, if an output transition of a place s is dead at a marking M, then every output transition of s is dead at M.

Proof:

(1), (2) and (3) follow easily from the definitions. To prove (4), recall that, by the fundamental property of free-choice nets, a marking enables some output transition of a place iff it enables all its output transitions. $\qquad\square$

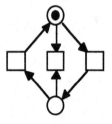

Fig. 4.4 A system that is place-live but not live

A consequence of Part (3) of this proposition is that the existence of dead places in a system implies the existence of dead transitions. The converse does not hold in general: in Figure 4.4, the transition at the center of the net is dead at the initial marking, but no place is dead at any reachable marking. The following lemma states that dead places and dead transitions are more tightly related in free-choice systems.

Lemma 4.18

If a transition t of a free-choice net is dead at a marking M, then some input place of t is dead at some marking reachable from M.

Proof:

We prove the contraposition: if no input place of t is dead at any marking reachable from M, then t is not dead at M.

Let $\bullet t = \{s_1, \ldots, s_n\}$ be the pre-set of t. By Proposition 4.2(2), all the places of $\bullet t$ have the same set of output transitions.

Since no input place of t is dead at any marking reachable from M, there exists an occurrence sequence

$$M \xrightarrow{\sigma_1} M_1 \ldots M_{n-1} \xrightarrow{\sigma_n} M_n$$

such that $M_i(s_i) > 0$ for $1 \leq i \leq n$.

If this sequence contains a transition of the cluster $[t]$, say u, then some intermediate marking of the occurrence sequence enables u. Since t and u belong to the same cluster, the same marking enables t (fundamental property of free-choice systems). Then t is not dead at M.

If this sequence does not contain any transition of the cluster $[t]$, then the number of tokens in the places of $\bullet t$ does not decrease during its execution. Therefore, we have $M_n(s_i) > 0$ for $1 \leq i \leq n$. Then M_n enables t, and so t is not dead at M.   □

An easy consequence of this lemma is that the converse of Proposition 2.17 (liveness implies place-liveness) holds for free-choice systems.

Proposition 4.19   *Place-liveness and liveness coincide in free-choice systems*

A free-choice system is live iff it is place-live.

Proof:

A live free-choice system is place-live by Proposition 2.17. To prove the converse, observe that a non-live free-choice system has a reachable marking M and a transition t such that t is dead at M. By the previous lemma, some input place of t is dead at some marking reachable from M. So the system is not place-live.   □

Lemma 4.20

Every non-live free-choice system has a proper siphon R and a reachable marking M such that R is unmarked at M.

Proof:

Since, by Proposition 4.19, place-liveness and liveness coincide for free-choice systems, a non-live system is not place-live either. Therefore, some place s is dead at some reachable marking L.

Let $M \in [L\rangle$ be a marking such that every place not dead at M is not dead at any marking of $[M\rangle$. Such a marking exists, because dead places remain dead (so the set of dead places can only increase when transitions occur), and the set of places is finite. It follows that all markings of $[M\rangle$ have the same set of dead places, say R.

We claim that R is a proper siphon, and that R is unmarked at M. We first prove the following three claims:

(i) $R \neq \emptyset$.

   The place s is dead at L. Since dead places remain dead, s is dead at M. So $s \in R$.

(ii) $^\bullet R$ contains only transitions dead at M.

   Let $s \in R$. Then s is dead at M. So every transition in $^\bullet s$ is dead at M.

(iii) Every transition t dead at M has an input place in R.

   By Lemma 4.18, some place $s \in {}^\bullet t$ is dead at a marking reachable from M. By the definition of M, this place is already dead at M, and therefore in R.

R is a siphon by (ii) and (iii). R is unmarked at M because, by the definition of dead places, every place dead at M is in particular unmarked at M.   □

The 'if' direction of Commoner's Theorem is now easy to prove:

Theorem 4.21   *'If' direction of Commoner's Theorem*

   If every proper siphon of a free-choice system includes an initially marked trap, then the system is live.

Proof:

By Lemma 4.20, a non-live free-choice system contains a proper siphon R such that $M(R) = 0$ for some reachable marking M. So every trap included in R is unmarked at M. Since marked traps remain marked, every trap included in R is initially unmarked.   □

The proof of the 'only if' direction of Commoner's Theorem is more involved. It is organized as follows. First, we introduce *allocations*, a proof technique which plays an important role in this book, and prove the Allocation Lemma, which states a general property of allocations in free-choice systems. Then, we consider a particular class of allocations, called circuit-free, and prove the Circuit-free Allocation Lemma. Finally, we use these results to prove the 'only if' direction of Commoner's Theorem.

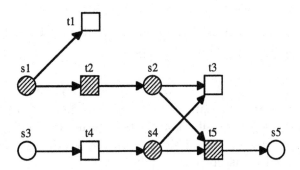

Fig. 4.5   Illustration of an allocation

Definition 4.22   *Allocations, total allocations*

Let C be a set of clusters of a net $N = (S, T, F)$ such that every cluster of C contains at least one transition. An allocation is a function $\alpha \colon C \to T$ satisfying $\alpha(c) \in c$ for every $c \in C$.

A transition t is said to be allocated by α (or α-allocated) if $t = \alpha(c)$ for some cluster c.

The set of transitions allocated by α is denoted by $\alpha(C)$.

If C is the set of all clusters of N which contain at least one transition, then α is called total.

An allocation specifies a strategy to resolve conflicts between the transitions of a cluster. Let c be a cluster in the domain of an allocation α, and assume that a transition of c is enabled at a marking. The free-choice property implies that all the transitions of c are enabled at this marking, and are therefore in conflict with each other. The allocation α specifies the strategy in which only the transition $\alpha(c)$ is allowed to occur.

Figure 4.5 shows a graphical representation of the allocation $\alpha \colon C \to T$ given by

$$C = \{\{s_1, t_1, t_2\}, \{s_2, s_4, t_3, t_5\}\}$$
$$\alpha(\{s_1, t_1, t_2\}) = t_2$$
$$\alpha(\{s_2, s_4, t_3, t_5\}) = t_5$$

The places contained in the clusters of C are shaded, as well as the allocated transitions.

An allocation of a set of clusters C defines a set of paths, formed by places of clusters of C and allocated transitions. For the allocation α given above, these paths are $s_1\, t_2\, s_2\, t_5$ and $s_4\, t_5$. The occurrence sequences that resolve conflicts according to the strategy specified by α make tokens flow along these paths. We say that these occurrence sequences *agree* with α.

Definition 4.23   *Sequences that agree with an allocation*

A sequence σ of transitions agrees with an allocation $\alpha\colon C \to T$ if it contains no transition t satisfying $[t] \in C$ and $t \neq \alpha(c)$.

Let α be an allocation of a live free-choice system having a nonempty domain. Then, from any reachable marking it is possible to find an occurrence sequence which enables an allocated transition, and lets it occur. By concatenating infinitely many of these sequences, we get infinite occurrence sequences which agree with α, and in which allocated transitions occur infinitely often.

Lemma 4.24   *Allocation Lemma*

Let α be an allocation of a live free-choice system having a nonempty domain C. Then the initial marking enables an infinite occurrence sequence σ such that

(1) σ agrees with α, and

(2) $\sigma|_{\alpha(C)}$ is infinite.

Proof:

We define inductively sequences $\sigma_0, \sigma_1, \sigma_2, \ldots$ such that $M_i \xrightarrow{\sigma_i} M_{i+1}$, where M_0 is the initial marking of the system.

Given M_i, let τ_i be a minimal sequence such that $M_i \xrightarrow{\tau_i} L_i$ and L_i enables some transition t_i allocated by α. Define $\sigma_i = \tau_i t_i$. Since the system is live and $C \neq \emptyset$, there is at least one α-allocated transition. So σ_i exists for every $i \in I\!N$.

By the free-choice property, a transition of a cluster $c \in C$ is enabled at a marking M if and only if the allocated transition $\alpha(c)$ is enabled at M. Since τ_i is minimal, it contains no transition allocated by α. The transition t_i is allocated. So, σ_i agrees with α.

Define σ as the infinite sequence $\sigma_1 \sigma_2 \sigma_3 \ldots$. This sequence σ agrees with α, because every σ_i agrees with α. Moreover, $\sigma|_{\alpha(C)}$ is infinite, because every σ_i contains a transition of $\alpha(C)$. $\square$

Figure 4.6 shows an allocation of a set of clusters C. The places contained in the clusters of C are represented by shaded circles, and the allocated transitions by shaded boxes. For this allocation, take $\sigma = (t_2 \, t_3 \, t_6 \, t_4 \, t_1)^\omega$ (with the notions of the above proof, we have e.g. $\sigma_0 = t_2, \sigma_1 = t_3, \sigma_2 = t_6, \sigma_3 = t_4 \, t_1 \, t_2, \ldots$).

Our goal is to prove that in a live free-choice system every siphon includes an initially marked trap. We first outline the proof in an informal way.

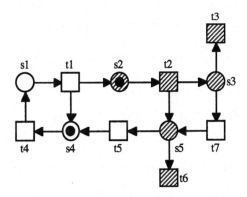

Fig. 4.6 Illustration of Lemma 4.24

Let R be a siphon which is not a trap and let Q be the maximal trap included in R. The proof will show that Q is initially marked. For that, it constructs an allocation α and an infinite occurrence sequence σ enjoying properties (1) and (2) of the Allocation Lemma, and additionally the following two conditions:

(3) σ continuously 'pumps' tokens out of the set $D = R \setminus Q$ (D stands for 'difference').

In order to understand what this means, consider again the system of Figure 4.6, with the allocation given there. The system is live, and its set of places is a siphon R. The maximal trap included in R is $Q = \{s_1, s_4\}$. We take again $\sigma = (t_2\, t_3\, t_6\, t_4\, t_1)^\omega$. This sequence makes tokens flow along the paths defined by the allocation and, in this way, it pumps tokens out of $D = \{s_2, s_3, s_5\}$.

(4) Q cannot become marked by the occurrence of a transition of σ.

To ensure this property, every transition of $^\bullet Q$ which occurs in σ belongs to $Q^\bullet$. In our example, this means that σ does not contain the transition t_5.

The sequence σ makes tokens flow continuously along the paths defined by α. Therefore, σ must also contain a transition that does not belong to these paths but puts tokens in their places. The proof shows that these transitions belong to $Q^\bullet$.

In our example, $s_2\, t_2\, s_5\, t_6$ is one of the paths defined by the allocation. Since t_2 occurs infinitely often in σ, so does the transition t_1. This transition is an output transition of the maximal trap $\{s_1, s_4\}$.

Since σ contains a transition of $Q^\bullet$, the trap Q is marked at some point during the occurrence of σ. Then, Q must be initially marked because of (4), which is the result we are after.

In order to pump tokens out of D, the net cannot contain a circuit containing only places of D and allocated transitions, because the tokens contained in such circuits are not extracted. The purpose of the next definition and lemma is to prove that there exists an allocation satisfying this property.

Definition 4.25   *Circuit-free allocations*

Let R be a set of places of a net. Define $C = \{[t] \mid t \in R^{\bullet}\}$ (C is the set of all clusters containing at least one place of R and at least one transition). An allocation with domain C is circuit-free for R if no circuit of the net contains only places of R and allocated transitions.

The allocation shown in Figure 4.6 is circuit-free. With the graphical conventions used in the figure, an allocation is circuit-free if no circuit contains only shaded nodes.

The following lemma shows that there exists a circuit-free allocation for the set D. Moreover, no allocated transition belongs to $^{\bullet}Q$. Note that the lemma holds for arbitrary sets of places, not only for siphons.

Lemma 4.26   *Circuit-free Allocation Lemma*

Let N be a free-choice net, let R be a set of places of N, and let Q be the maximal trap included in R (which can be the empty set). Let $D = R \setminus Q$, and let $C = \{[t] \mid t \in D^{\bullet}\}$. Then there exists an allocation α with domain C, circuit-free for D, such that $\alpha(C) \cap {}^{\bullet}Q = \emptyset$.

Proof:

The proof is by induction on $|R|$.

Base. $|R| = 0$. Take α as the unique allocation with empty domain.

Step. $|R| > 0$.

We can assume that R is not a trap since otherwise $D = \emptyset$, and we can take α as the unique allocation with empty domain.

Since R is not a trap, there exists a transition $t \in R^{\bullet}$ such that $t \notin {}^{\bullet}R$. Define $R' = R \setminus {}^{\bullet}t$. Since $t \in R^{\bullet}$ we have $R' \subset R$. Therefore, we can apply the induction hypothesis to R'.

Let Q' be the maximal trap included in R'. Let $D' = R' \setminus Q'$ and $C' = \{[u] \mid u \in D'^{\bullet}\}$. By the induction hypothesis there exists an allocation $\alpha' \colon C' \to T$, circuit-free for D', such that $\alpha'(C') \cap {}^{\bullet}Q' = \emptyset$ (where T is the set of transitions of N). Define $\alpha \colon C \to T$ as follows:

$$\alpha(c) = \begin{cases} \alpha'(c) & \text{if } c \neq [t] \\ t & \text{if } c = [t] \end{cases}$$

First we have to show that α is well-defined. For that we prove in three steps that every cluster of C except $[t]$ is contained in the domain of α', or, equivalently, $C \subseteq C' \cup \{[t]\}$.

(i) $Q' = Q$.

We have to show that Q is the maximal trap included in R'. Since Q is a trap and $Q \subset R$, we have $Q^\bullet \subseteq {}^\bullet Q \subseteq {}^\bullet R$. Since $t \notin {}^\bullet R$, we have $t \notin Q^\bullet$. In other words, no place in ${}^\bullet t$ belongs to Q. Therefore, $Q \subseteq R'$. Since Q is the maximal trap included in R, Q is also the maximal trap included in R'.

(ii) $D \subseteq D' \cup {}^\bullet t$.

$$
\begin{aligned}
D &= R \setminus Q \\
&\subseteq (R' \cup {}^\bullet t) \setminus Q && \text{(definition of } R') \\
&\subseteq (R' \setminus Q) \cup {}^\bullet t \\
&= (R' \setminus Q') \cup {}^\bullet t && \text{(i)} \\
&= D' \cup {}^\bullet t && \text{(definition of } D')
\end{aligned}
$$

(iii) $C \subseteq C' \cup \{[t]\}$.

$$
\begin{aligned}
C &= \{[u] \mid u \in D^\bullet\} && \text{(definition of } C) \\
&\subseteq \{[u] \mid u \in D'^\bullet \cup ({}^\bullet t)^\bullet\} && \text{(ii)} \\
&= \{[u] \mid u \in D'^\bullet\} \cup [t] && (({}^\bullet t)^\bullet \subseteq \{[t]\}) \\
&= C' \cup \{[t]\} && \text{(definition of } C')
\end{aligned}
$$

We now prove that α is circuit-free for t and $\alpha(C) \cap {}^\bullet Q = \emptyset$.

(iv) $\alpha(C) \subseteq \alpha'(C') \cup \{t\}$.

$$
\begin{aligned}
\alpha(C) &\subseteq \alpha(C' \cup \{[t]\}) && \text{(iii)} \\
&= \alpha((C' \setminus \{[t]\}) \cup \{[t]\}) \\
&= \alpha(C' \setminus \{[t]\}) \cup \alpha([t]) \\
&= \alpha(C' \setminus \{[t]\}) \cup \{t\} && \text{(definition of } \alpha) \\
&= \alpha'(C' \setminus \{[t]\}) \cup \{t\} && \text{(definition of } \alpha') \\
&\subseteq \alpha'(C') \cup \{t\}
\end{aligned}
$$

(v) α is circuit-free for D.

Assume there exists a circuit γ contained in $D \cup \alpha(C)$. By (ii) and (iv), we have

$$
D \cup \alpha(C) \subseteq D' \cup \alpha'(C') \cup \{t\} \cup {}^\bullet t
$$

By the induction hypothesis, $D' \cup \alpha'(C')$ contains no circuits. So γ contains an element of $\{t\} \cup {}^\bullet t$. Since $\{t\} \cup {}^\bullet t \subseteq [t]$, γ contains a transition of $[t]$. Since γ only contains allocated transitions, it contains t.

All places appearing in γ are contained in R by the definition of γ and because $D \subseteq R$. Since $t \notin {}^\bullet R$, γ contains no place in $t^\bullet$, in contradiction to the assumption that γ is a circuit.

(vi) $\alpha(C) \cap {}^\bullet Q = \emptyset$.

$$
\begin{aligned}
\alpha(C) \cap {}^\bullet Q \ &\subseteq\ (\alpha'(C') \cup \{t\}) \cap {}^\bullet Q && \text{(iv)} \\
&=\ (\alpha'(C') \cap {}^\bullet Q) \cup (\{t\} \cap {}^\bullet Q) \\
&=\ \emptyset \cup (\{t\} \cap {}^\bullet Q) && \text{(induction hypothesis and (i))} \\
&=\ \emptyset && (t \notin {}^\bullet R \text{ and } {}^\bullet Q \subseteq {}^\bullet R)
\end{aligned}
$$

$\square$

Theorem 4.27   *'Only if' direction of Commoner's Theorem*

Every proper siphon of a live free-choice system includes an initially marked trap.

Proof:

Let (N, M_0) be a live free-choice system. Let R be a proper siphon of N and let Q be the maximal trap included in R. We prove that Q is initially marked, i.e., $M_0(Q) > 0$.

Since (N, M_0) is live, we have $M_0(R) > 0$ by Proposition 4.10. Define $D = R \setminus Q$. If $D^\bullet = \emptyset$, then D is a trap included in R. By the maximality of Q, we have $D \subseteq Q$. By the definition of D, we have $D = \emptyset$. So $Q = R$ and $M_0(Q) = M_0(R) > 0$.

Now we consider the case $D^\bullet \neq \emptyset$. Define $C = \{[t] \mid t \in D^\bullet\}$. By Lemma 4.26, there exists an allocation α with domain C, circuit-free for D, satisfying

(a) $\alpha(C) \cap {}^\bullet Q = \emptyset$.

The Allocation Lemma (Lemma 4.24) can be applied to α. So there exists an infinite occurrence sequence $M_0 \xrightarrow{\sigma}$ satisfying

(b) σ agrees with α, which implies $\mathcal{A}(\sigma) \cap D^\bullet \subseteq \alpha(C)$ by the definition of C, and

(c) $\sigma|_{\alpha(C)}$ is infinite.

Loosely speaking, the sequence σ "pumps" tokens out of the set D.

We prove the following:

(i) $\mathcal{A}(\sigma) \cap {}^{\bullet}Q \subseteq Q^{\bullet}$.

   (Q cannot become marked during the occurrence of σ)

   We have

$$
\begin{aligned}
\mathcal{A}(\sigma) \cap {}^{\bullet}Q \ &\subseteq \ \mathcal{A}(\sigma) \cap {}^{\bullet}R && (Q \subseteq R) \\
&\subseteq \ \mathcal{A}(\sigma) \cap R^{\bullet} && (R \text{ is a siphon}) \\
&= \ \mathcal{A}(\sigma) \cap (Q^{\bullet} \cup D^{\bullet}) && (R = Q \cup D) \\
&\subseteq \ (\mathcal{A}(\sigma) \cap Q^{\bullet}) \cup \alpha(C) && (b)
\end{aligned}
$$

By (a), $(\mathcal{A}(\sigma) \cap {}^{\bullet}Q) \cap \alpha(C) = \emptyset$. So $\mathcal{A}(\sigma) \cap {}^{\bullet}Q \subseteq \mathcal{A}(\sigma) \cap Q^{\bullet} \subseteq Q^{\bullet}$.

(ii) A transition of $Q^{\bullet}$ occurs in σ.

   (Q is marked at some point during the occurrence of σ)

   Define the relation $\lhd \subseteq \alpha(C) \times \alpha(C)$ as follows:

   $t \lhd t'$ if there exists a path $t \ldots t'$ containing only nodes of $D \cup \alpha(C)$.

   We have $t \lhd t'$ if t precedes t' in some path defined by the allocation α. The circuit-freeness of α implies that $\lhd$ is a partial order.

   By (c), the set of α-allocated transitions that occur infinitely often in σ is nonempty. Let u be a minimal transition of this set with respect to $\lhd$, and let s be a place of ${}^{\bullet}u \cap D$ (such a place s exists by the definition of C). Since u occurs infinitely often in σ, some transition $v \in {}^{\bullet}s$ occurs infinitely often in σ. We have

$$
\begin{aligned}
v \ &\in \ {}^{\bullet}D && (v \in {}^{\bullet}s \text{ and } s \in D) \\
&\subseteq \ {}^{\bullet}R && (D \subseteq R) \\
&\subseteq \ R^{\bullet} && (R \text{ is a siphon}) \\
&= \ Q^{\bullet} \cup D^{\bullet} && (R = Q \cup D)
\end{aligned}
$$

   By the minimality of u, $v \notin \alpha(C)$. By (b), $v \notin D^{\bullet}$. So $v \in Q^{\bullet}$.

By (i) and (ii), σ can be split in the following way: $\sigma = \sigma_1 \, t \, \sigma_2$ with $t \in Q^{\bullet}$ and $\mathcal{A}(\sigma_1) \cap ({}^{\bullet}Q \cup Q^{\bullet}) = \emptyset$. Let $M_0 \xrightarrow{\sigma_1} M$. Then $M_0(Q) = M(Q)$. Since M enables $t \in Q^{\bullet}$, $M(Q) > 0$. So we also have $M_0(Q) > 0$, and therefore Q is an initially marked trap. $\qquad \square$

4.4   The non-liveness problem is NP-complete

Commoner's Theorem leads to the following nondeterministic algorithm for deciding
if a free choice system is *not* live:

(1) guess a set of places R;

(2) check if R is a siphon;

(3) if R is a siphon, compute the maximal trap Q included in R;

(4) if $M_0(Q) = 0$, then answer "non-live".

Steps (2) and (4) can be performed in polynomial time in the size of the system.
Exercise 4.5 gives an algorithm for step (3); the reader can prove its correctness and
show that its complexity is polynomial as well. It follows from these results that the
non-liveness problem for free-choice systems is in NP.

The obvious corresponding deterministic algorithm consists of an exhaustive search
through all subsets of places. However, since the number of these subsets is 2^n for
a net with n places, the algorithm has exponential complexity.

We now show that the non-liveness problem is NP-complete. As a consequence, no
polynomial algorithm to decide liveness of a free-choice system exists unless P=NP.

Theorem 4.28   *Complexity of the non-liveness problem of free-choice systems*

The following problem is NP-complete:

Given a free-choice system, to decide if it is not live.

Proof:

Commoner's Theorem shows that the problem is in NP. The hardness is proved by
a reduction from the satisfiability problem for propositional formulas in conjunctive
normal form (CNF-SAT).

A formula ϕ is a conjunction of clauses $C_1, \ldots, C_m$ over variables $x_1, \ldots, x_n$. A
literal l_i is either a variable x_i or its negation $\overline{x_i}$. The negation of l_i is denoted by
$\overline{l_i}$. A clause is a disjunction of literals.

Let ϕ be a formula. We construct a free-choice system (N, M_0) in several stages,
and show that ϕ is satisfiable iff (N, M_0) is not live.

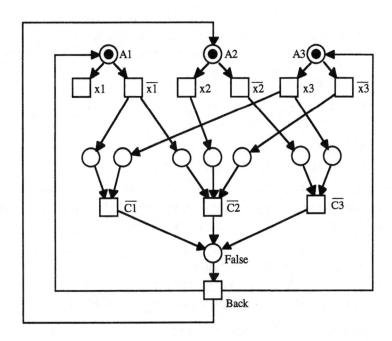

Fig. 4.7 The free-choice system corresponding to ϕ

- For every variable x_i, define a place A_i, two transitions x_i and $\overline{x}_i$ and arcs (A_i, x_i) and $(A_i, \overline{x}_i)$. Let A denote the set $\{A_1, \ldots, A_n\}$.

- For every clause C_j, define a transition $\overline{C_j}$. For every clause C_j and for every literal l_i appearing in C_j define a place $(\overline{l_i}, \overline{C_j})$, an arc leading from the transition $\overline{l_i}$ to the place $(\overline{l_i}, \overline{C_j})$, and an arc leading from $(\overline{l_i}, \overline{C_j})$ to the transition $\overline{C_j}$.

- Define a place *False* and, for every clause C_j, an arc $(\overline{C_j}, \textit{False})$. Define a transition *Back*, an arc $(\textit{False}, \textit{Back})$ and, for every variable x_i, an arc $(\textit{Back}, A_i)$.

- Define M_0 as the marking that puts one token in all and only the places of A.

It is easy to see that N is a connected free-choice net, and hence (N, M_0) a free-choice system. Moreover, (N, M_0) can be constructed in polynomial time in the length of ϕ. Figure 4.7 shows the system obtained from the formula

$$\phi = (x_1 \vee \overline{x_3}) \wedge (x_1 \vee \overline{x_2} \vee x_3) \wedge (x_2 \vee \overline{x_3}).$$

We can freely choose at every place A_i between letting the transition x_i or $\overline{x}_i$ occur. The occurrences of the selected transitions correspond to the choice of a truth assignment. After these occurrences, a transition $\overline{C_j}$ is enabled if and only if the truth assignment does not satisfy the clause C_j. If $\overline{C_j}$ is enabled, then it can occur and put a token in the place *False*, which corresponds to the fact that, since the clause C_j is false under this assignment, the whole formula ϕ is false. We now prove:

($\Rightarrow$) If ϕ is satisfiable, then (N, M_0) is not live.

> Let f be a truth assignment satisfying ϕ, and let $l_1, \ldots, l_n$ be the literals mapped to *true* by f. Let $\sigma_f = l_1 \ldots l_n$.
>
> By the construction of (N, M_0), σ_f is an occurrence sequence (in our example, we can take $\sigma_f = x_1\, x_2\, x_3$). Let $M_0 \xrightarrow{\sigma_f} M$.
>
> We show that no transition of N is enabled at M, which proves the result. By the construction of (N, M_0) and σ_f, only $\overline{C_j}$ transitions can be enabled at M. So it suffices to prove that no transition $\overline{C_j}$ is enabled at M.
>
> Consider a clause C_j. Since f satisfies ϕ, there exists a literal l_i in C_j such that $f(l_i) = true$. By the definition of σ_f, we have $l_i \in \sigma_f$ and $\overline{l_i} \notin \sigma_f$. Since $\overline{l_i} \notin \sigma_f$, the place $(\overline{l_i}, \overline{C_j})$ is not marked at M. By the construction of N, $(\overline{l_i}, \overline{C_j})$ is an input place of $\overline{C_j}$. So $\overline{C_j}$ is not enabled at M.

($\Leftarrow$) If (N, M_0) is not live, then ϕ is satisfiable.

> We start with the following observation: if a transition x_i has an output place $(x_i, \overline{C_j})$ and $\overline{x_i}$ has an output place $(\overline{x_i}, \overline{C_k})$, then the set
>
> $$Q = \{False, A_i, (x_i, \overline{C_j}), (\overline{x_i}, \overline{C_k})\}$$
>
> is a trap. Moreover, Q is initially marked because $M_0(A_i) = 1$.
>
> Now, assume that (N, M_0) is not live. By Commoner's Theorem, there exists a proper siphon R of N which includes no initially marked trap. By the construction of N, R contains *False* and at least one place A_i of A. Moreover, R contains either no place of $x_i^\bullet$ or no place of $\overline{x_i}^\bullet$; otherwise we would have $Q \subseteq R$ for the initially marked trap Q defined above.
>
> This last property of R allows us to construct a truth assignment f satisfying the following for every place $A_i \in R$: if $x_i^\bullet \cap R \neq \emptyset$ then $f(\overline{x_i}) = true$ and if $\overline{x_i}^\bullet \cap R \neq \emptyset$ then $f(x_i) = true$.
>
> We show that f satisfies ϕ. Let C_j be an arbitrary clause of ϕ. Since *False* is a place of R, the set R contains some input place $(\overline{l_i}, \overline{C_j})$ of $\overline{C_j}$ and hence it also contains the place A_i, which belongs to $^\bullet \overline{l_i}$. So $\overline{l_i}^\bullet \cap R \neq \emptyset$.
>
> By the definition of f, we have $f(l_i) = true$. Since, by construction of N, l_i is a literal of C_j, the assignment f satisfies C_j. Finally, f satisfies ϕ because C_j was arbitrarily chosen. $\square$

Exercise 4.7 contains more information about other complexity results.

4.5 Minimal siphons

The so-called minimal siphons have particularly interesting properties.

Definition 4.29 *Minimal siphons*

A siphon is minimal if it is proper and does not include any other proper siphon.

Notice that every proper siphon includes a minimal one (which is not necessarily unique).

It follows easily from Commoner's Theorem that a free-choice system is live if and only if every *minimal* siphon includes an initially marked trap. The following theorem gives a characterization of minimal siphons.

Theorem 4.30 *Characterization of minimal siphons*

A nonempty set of places R of a free-choice net N is a minimal siphon iff:

(a) every cluster c of N contains at most one place of R, and

(b) the subnet generated by $R \cup {}^\bullet R$ is strongly connected.

Proof:

Let $N_R = (R, {}^\bullet R, F_R)$ be the subnet generated by $R \cup {}^\bullet R$.

$(\Rightarrow)$ (a): Assume that N has a cluster c such that two distinct places s and s' of c belong to R. Since N is free-choice, we have $s^\bullet = s'^\bullet$. Then

$$
\begin{aligned}
{}^\bullet(R \setminus \{s\}) &\subseteq {}^\bullet R && (R \setminus \{s\} \subseteq R) \\
&\subseteq R^\bullet && (R \text{ is a siphon}) \\
&= (R \setminus \{s\})^\bullet && (s' \in R \setminus \{s\} \text{ and } s'^\bullet = s^\bullet)
\end{aligned}
$$

Therefore, $R \setminus \{s\}$ is a siphon. Moreover, it is proper because it contains s'. So R is not a minimal siphon.

$(\Rightarrow)$ (b): Observe first that N_R is connected; otherwise, N_R has two different connected components, and the set of places of each of them is a proper siphon included in R.

Let (x, y) be an arbitrary arc of N_R. We prove in four steps that N_R contains a path from y to x. Define

$$
Q = \{ s \in R \mid \text{ there exists a path from } s \text{ to } x \text{ in } N_R \}.
$$

(i) $Q \neq \emptyset$.

Since x is a node of N_R, $x \in R \cup {}^\bullet R$.

If $x \in R$, then $x \in Q$ by the definition of Q, and hence $Q \neq \emptyset$.

If $x \in {}^\bullet R$ then $x \in R^\bullet$ since R is a siphon. So $x \in s^\bullet$ for some place $s \in R$. By the definition of Q, $s \in Q$ and hence $Q \neq \emptyset$.

(ii) Q is a siphon.

Let t be a transition of ${}^\bullet Q$. We show $t \in Q^\bullet$. Since $t \in {}^\bullet Q$, we have $t \in {}^\bullet s$ for some place $s \in Q$. By the definition of Q, the subnet N_R contains a path π leading from s to x. Since $Q \subseteq R$, and R is a siphon, t is an output transition of some place $s' \in R$. So the path $\pi' = s' \, t \, \pi$ leads from s' to x. Since $t \in {}^\bullet Q \subseteq {}^\bullet R$, the path π' only contains elements of $R \cup {}^\bullet R$, and is therefore a path of N_R. Then, $s' \in Q$ by the definition of Q. Since $t \in s'^\bullet$, we get $t \in Q^\bullet$.

(iii) $Q = R$.

By (i) and (ii), Q is a proper siphon. Since Q is included in the minimal siphon Q, we have $Q = R$.

(iv) N_R contains a path from y to x.

Since y is a node of N_R, we have $y \in R \cup {}^\bullet R$.

Assume $y \in R$. Then $y \in Q$ by (iii) and, by the definition of Q, N_R contains a path from y to x.

Assume $y \in {}^\bullet R$. Then $y \in {}^\bullet Q$ by (iii). So $y \in {}^\bullet s$ for some $s \in Q$. By the definition of Q, there exists a path π of N_R from s to x. Since $s \in Q \subseteq R$, the path $y \, \pi$ is contained in N_R, and leads from y to x.

($\Leftarrow$): The proof is divided into two steps.

(i) R is a siphon.

Let t be a transition of ${}^\bullet R$. By the definition of N_R, t is a node of N_R. By (b), N_R is strongly connected. Therefore, t has at least one input place s in N_R. By the definition of N_R, s belongs to R. So $t \in R^\bullet$.

(ii) R is minimal.

Let Q be a nonempty proper subset of R. We show that Q is not a siphon. Since N_R is strongly connected by (b) and $\emptyset \neq Q \neq R$, there exists a path $r \, t \, s$ of N_R such that $s \in Q$ and $r \in R \setminus Q$. By (a), r is the only place of R in the pre-set of t. Hence, since $r \notin Q$ and $Q \subseteq R$, we have $t \notin Q^\bullet$. Since $t \in {}^\bullet s \subseteq {}^\bullet Q$, the set Q is not a siphon. $\qquad \square$

4.6 Liveness and deadlock-freedom

In this final section we prove that liveness and deadlock-freedom coincide for bounded and strongly connected free-choice systems.

Theorem 4.31 *Relationship between liveness and deadlock-freedom*

A bounded and strongly connected free-choice system is live iff it is deadlock-free.

Proof:

($\Rightarrow$): Holds for arbitrary systems by Proposition 2.18.

($\Leftarrow$): Let (N, M_0) be a bounded, strongly connected and deadlock-free free-choice system.

Let K be a reachable marking such that the number of transitions dead at K is maximal; i.e., no marking $M \in [M_0\rangle$ has more dead transitions than K. We show that this number is 0. This implies that no transition can ever become dead and hence that the system is live.

Since (N, M_0) is deadlock-free, some transition t is not dead at K. Since N is strongly connected, there exists a path of N starting at t which contains all transitions of N. We show that if u and v are two consecutive transitions of this path and u is not dead at K, then neither is v. This proves that no transition of N is dead at K.

There exists an infinite occurrence sequence $K \xrightarrow{\sigma}$ which contains u infinitely often; otherwise u is dead at some marking L reachable from K, and – since dead transitions remain dead – L has more dead transitions than K, which contradicts the definition of K. Since u and v are consecutive transitions of the path, there is a place s such that (u, s) and (s, v) are arcs of the net. Since s is bounded, some transition $v' \in s^\bullet$ occurs infinitely often in σ. In particular, v' is not dead at K. By the free-choice property, v and v' are enabled at the same markings. So v is not dead at K. $\quad\square$

None of the three conditions of the theorem (boundedness, strong connectedness, free-choice property) can be dropped. Figure 4.3 shows this for the strong connectedness condition. Exercise 4.10 asks the reader to show it for the other two conditions.

Exercises

Exercise 4.1

1) Show that the intersection of two stable sets of markings is stable.

2) Which is the minimal stable set containing a given marking M?

3) A marking M of a net N is live (bounded) if (N, M) is live (bounded). Show that the set of live markings of a net is stable. Idem for the sets of bounded markings.

4) Show that the set of non-live markings of a net is not necessarily stable.

5) * Let N be a net bounded for every marking. Is the set of non-live markings of N stable?

Exercise 4.2

Transform the proof of Lemma 4.26 into an algorithm for the construction of the circuit-free allocation.

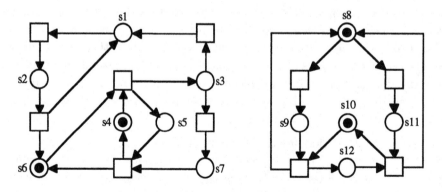

Fig. 4.8   Two free-choice systems

Exercise 4.3

Compute all siphons of the free-choice systems of Figure 4.8. Check if every siphon includes an initially marked trap.

Exercise 4.4

Let (N, M_0) be an arbitrary system. Exhibit counterexamples for the following conjectures:

1) If every proper siphon of N includes an initially marked trap at M_0, then (N, M_0) is live.

2) If (N, M_0) is live, then every proper siphon of N includes an initially marked trap.

Exercise 4.5

Consider the following algorithm:

> **Input:** A net $N = (S, T, F)$ and $R \subseteq S$.
> **Output:** $Q \subseteq R$.
> **Initialization:** $Q = R$.
>
> **begin**
>   **while** there exists $s \in Q$ and $t \in s^\bullet$ such that $t \notin {}^\bullet Q$ **do**
> $Q := Q \setminus \{s\}$
>   **endwhile**
> **end**

Prove that the output Q is the maximal trap included in R. Estimate the complexity of the algorithm. Transform it into an algorithm that computes the maximal siphon included in R.

Exercise 4.6   *

Show that Commoner's Theorem implies the Liveness Theorems for S- and T-systems given in Chapter 3.

Exercise 4.7

Prove the following:

1) Deciding if a given free-choice net is structurally live is NP-complete.

2) Deciding if a given bounded free-choice system is deadlock-free is NP-hard.

3) * The problem of (2) is also NP-complete.

Exercise 4.8

A system (N, M_0) is *monotonously live* if every marking $M \geq M_0$ is live.

1) Prove that live free-choice systems are monotonously live.

2) Exhibit a live system which is not monotonously live.

Exercise 4.9

1) Exhibit a net having a minimal siphon R and a transition t such that $|{}^\bullet t \cap R| \geq 2$.

2) Construct for each $i \in I\!N$ a net with at most $2i$ places and at least 2^i minimal siphons.

Exercise 4.10

1) Exhibit a bounded, strongly connected, deadlock-free system which is not live.

2) Exhibit a strongly connected and deadlock-free free-choice system which is not live.

Bibliographic Notes

Siphons and traps were introduced by Commoner in [18]. He used the name 'deadlocks' instead of siphons, due to Proposition 4.11 (which states that in any deadlocked system the set of unmarked places is a siphon). We prefer the name siphon to avoid confusions. Lautenbach [62] and Ezpeleta, Couvreur and Silva [36] have given linear algebraic techniques to compute siphons and traps of arbitrary nets. Minoux and Barkaoui describe in [65] another technique based on a resolution algorithm for Horn clauses. Kemper shows in [53] how to efficiently compute siphons and traps of free-choice nets.

Commoner's Theorem was first published in Hack's Master Thesis at M.I.T. [42]. The proof of [42] contains some mistakes, which have been corrected here.

The NP-completeness of the non-liveness problem was proved by Jones, Landweber and Lien in [51]. The characterization of minimal siphons in free-choice nets was obtained by Esparza, Best and Silva in [35], and can also be found in [34]. Barkaoui and Lemaire give a characterization of minimal siphons for arbitrary nets in [2]. Hillen proved Theorem 4.31 in [45].

The algorithm of Exercise 4.5 is due to Starke [71]. The results of Parts (2) and (3) of Exercise 4.7 are due to Cheng, Esparza and Palsberg [14]. Exercise 4.8 is a well-known result, first published by Döpp [26].

Chapter 5 —————————————————————

The Coverability Theorems

Throughout the rest of the book we study the properties of live and bounded free-choice systems. In this chapter, we prove the S-coverability Theorem and the T-coverability Theorem, which state that well-formed free-choice nets can be decomposed in two different ways into simpler nets. Together with Commoner's Theorem, the Coverability Theorems are part of what can be called classical free-choice net theory, developed in the early seventies.

5.1 The S-coverability Theorem

Figure 5.1 shows a live and bounded (even 1-bounded) free-choice system that we shall frequently use to illustrate the results of this and the next chapters. Its underlying well-formed free-choice net can be decomposed into the two S-nets shown at the bottom of the figure. Observe that they are connected to the rest of the net only through transitions. We prove in this section that every well-formed free-choice net can be decomposed in this way[1].

Definition 5.1   *S-components*

Let N' be the subnet of a net N generated by a nonempty set X of nodes. N' is an S-component of N if

- ${}^\bullet s \cup s^\bullet \subseteq X$ for every place s of X, and
- N' is a strongly connected S-net.

The two nets at the bottom of Figure 5.1 are S-components of the net at the top. The subnet generated by $\{s_1, t_1, s_3, t_3, s_7, t_7\}$ is not an S-component; it satisfies the second condition of Definition 5.1, but not the first. Neither is the subnet generated by all nodes (i.e., the net of Figure 5.1 itself), because it satisfies the first condition, but not the second.

Observe that, by the first condition of Definition 5.1, an S-component is determined by its set of places, i.e., two different S-components have different sets of places.

---

[1]In Figure 5.1 the subnets have disjoint sets of places, which in general need not be the case.

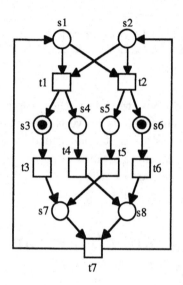

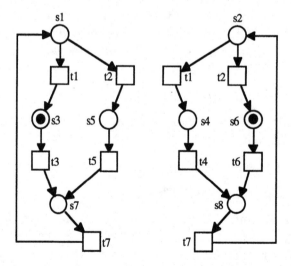

Fig. 5.1   A live and bounded free-choice system and its decomposition into S-components

The following proposition contains some elementary properties of S-components. Its proof is left for an exercise.

Proposition 5.2 *Elementary properties of S-components*

Let $N_1 = (S_1, T_1, F_1)$ be an S-component of a net N.

(1) For every $t \in T_1$, $|{}^\bullet t \cap S_1| = 1 = |t^\bullet \cap S_1|$.

(2) If M and M' are markings of N such that $M' \in [M\rangle$, then $M'(S_1) = M(S_1)$.

(3) S_1 is a minimal siphon and a minimal trap of N. $\qquad\qquad\qquad\square$

We now introduce the notion of S-cover and net covered by S-components.

Definition 5.3 *S-covers, nets covered by S-components*

Let $\mathcal{C}$ be a set of S-components of a net. $\mathcal{C}$ is an S-cover if every place of the net belongs to an S-component of $\mathcal{C}$. A net is covered by S-components if it has an S-cover.

The two nets at the bottom of Figure 5.1 are an S-cover of the net at the top.

The name S-cover is particularly adequate for nets in which every transition has some input place or some output place (notice that a net underlying a system always satisfies this condition). In this case, by the definition of an S-component, not only every place, but also every transition and every arc of a net covered by S-components belongs to an element of an S-cover.

The main result we shall prove in this section is the S-coverability Theorem:

Well-formed free-choice nets are covered by S-components.

In the proof we make use of the properties of siphons and traps. In particular, we show that there exists a very tight connection between the S-components and the minimal siphons of well-formed free-choice nets.

Proposition 5.4 *Properties of minimal siphons in well-formed free-choice nets*

Let R be a minimal siphon of a well-formed free-choice net. Then:

(1) R is a trap.

(2) The subnet generated by $R \cup {}^\bullet R$ is an S-component.

Proof:

Let N be a well-formed free-choice net, and let R be a minimal siphon of N.

(1) Let Q be the maximal trap contained in R. We show $Q = R$, which proves that R is a trap. The proof is divided into five parts:

(i) Q is a proper trap.

Let M_0 be a marking of N such that (N, M_0) is live (M_0 exists by the well-formedness of N). By Commoner's Theorem, R contains a trap marked at M_0. This trap is proper, because only proper traps can be marked, and it is included in Q, because Q is maximal. So Q is proper.

(ii) For every transition t of $Q^\bullet$, $|{}^\bullet t \cap Q| = 1$.

Let $t \in Q^\bullet$. Then, $|{}^\bullet t \cap Q| \geq 1$. Since $Q \subseteq R$, we have $|{}^\bullet t \cap Q| \leq |{}^\bullet t \cap R|$. By the characterization of minimal siphons given in Theorem 4.30, $|{}^\bullet t \cap R| \leq 1$. So $|{}^\bullet t \cap Q| \leq 1$.

(iii) For every transition t of $Q^\bullet$, $|t^\bullet \cap Q| \geq 1$.

Since Q is a trap, $t \in Q^\bullet$ implies $t \in {}^\bullet Q$, which is equivalent to $|t^\bullet \cap Q| \geq 1$.

(iv) For every transition t of ${}^\bullet Q$, $|{}^\bullet t \cap Q| \geq |t^\bullet \cap Q|$.

Assume there exists a transition $u \in {}^\bullet Q$ such that $|{}^\bullet u \cap Q| < |u^\bullet \cap Q|$. Then, we have

$$M \xrightarrow{u} L \implies L(Q) > M(Q)$$

Moreover, it follows from (ii) and (iii) that for every transition t,

$$M \xrightarrow{t} L \implies L(Q) \geq M(Q)$$

Let M_0 be a marking of N such that (N, M_0) is live. Then, for every number n there exists an occurrence sequence of (N, M_0) containing the transition u at least n times. By the two above implications, this sequence leads to a marking that puts at least n tokens in Q. Therefore, (N, M_0) is not bounded. Since M_0 is an arbitrary live marking, N has no live and bounded markings, which contradicts its well-formedness.

(v) $Q = R$.

Let t be a transition of ${}^\bullet Q$. Then $|t^\bullet \cap Q| \geq 1$ and, by (iv), $|{}^\bullet t \cap Q| \geq 1$. So $t \in Q^\bullet$. Therefore, Q is a siphon. By (i) and the minimality of R, we get $Q = R$.

(2) Let N_R be the subnet generated by $R \cup {}^\bullet R$. By the definition of S-component, it suffices to show:

(i) For every place s of R, ${}^\bullet s \cup s^\bullet \subseteq {}^\bullet R$.

   For every place s of R, we have ${}^\bullet s \subseteq {}^\bullet R$. To prove $s^\bullet \subseteq {}^\bullet R$, observe that $s^\bullet \subseteq R^\bullet$, and $R^\bullet \subseteq {}^\bullet R$ because, by (1), R is a trap.

(ii) N_R is an S-net.

   Let t be a transition of N_R. We have to show that t has exactly one input place and one output place in N_R. Since N_R is generated by the set $R \cup {}^\bullet R$, the set of places of N_R is R. Therefore, it suffices to show $|{}^\bullet t \cap R| = 1 = |t^\bullet \cap R|$.

   Since N_R is generated by $R \cup {}^\bullet R$, we have $t \in R^\bullet$, and, since R is a trap by (1), we also have $t \in {}^\bullet R$. Moreover, since $Q = R$, (1)(ii) – (1)(iv) hold after substituting R for Q. So t satisfies $|{}^\bullet t \cap R| = 1$ by (1)(ii). For the other equality, observe that

$$\begin{aligned}
1 &\leq |t^\bullet \cap R| & \text{(1)(iii)} \\
&\leq |{}^\bullet t \cap R| & \text{(1)(iv)} \\
&\leq 1 & \text{(1)(ii)}
\end{aligned}$$

(iii) N_R is strongly connected.

   R is a minimal siphon and N_R is the subnet generated by $R \cup {}^\bullet R$. Apply the characterization of minimal siphons given in Theorem 4.30.   □

Recall that our goal is to prove that every place of a well-formed free-choice net is contained in an S-component. Using the second part of Proposition 5.4, it suffices to prove that every place is contained in a minimal siphon. This is done in the following lemma.

Lemma 5.5

   Every place of a well-formed free-choice net is contained in a minimal siphon.

Proof:

Let N be a well-formed free-choice net and let s be a place. We show that s is contained in a minimal siphon of N.

Let $N_1 = (S_1, T_1, F_1)$ be a maximal subnet of N (with respect to set inclusion) satisfying the following three properties:

(a) $s \in S_1$,

(b) $|S_1 \cap c| \leq 1$ for every cluster c of N, and

(c) N_1 is strongly connected.

Since the subnet $(\{s\}, \emptyset, \emptyset)$ satisfies (a), (b), and (c), such a maximal subnet exists.

We prove that S_1 is a minimal siphon of N by means of the characterization of minimal siphons given in Theorem 4.30. The first condition of the characterization coincides with (b), and therefore holds. We now prove the second condition, namely that the subnet generated by $S_1 \cup {}^\bullet S_1$ is strongly connected. For that, we show that this subnet is in fact N_1, which is strongly connected by definition.

Since two subnets containing the same nodes coincide, it suffices to prove that $S_1 \cup {}^\bullet S_1$ is equal to $S_1 \cup T_1$, the set of nodes of N_1. This reduces to proving ${}^\bullet S_1 = T_1$, which we do in two steps.

(i) $T_1 \subseteq {}^\bullet S_1$.

Let t be a transition of T_1. By (a), N_1 contains at least the place s. Since N_1 is strongly connected, it contains a path from t to s. Since all the places of this path belong to S_1, we have $t \in {}^\bullet S_1$.

(ii) ${}^\bullet S_1 \subseteq T_1$.

Let t be a transition of ${}^\bullet S_1$. We show that t belongs to T_1. N is strongly connected because it is well-formed (Theorem 2.25). Therefore, it contains a path leading from an element of N_1 to the transition t. Let $\pi = x_1 \ldots x_k$ be such a path (i.e., $x_1 \in S_1 \cup T_1$ and $x_k = t$). Assume moreover that π has minimal length (no shorter path leads from an element of N_1 to t). Let $N_2 = (S_2, T_2, F_2)$ be the subnet of N generated by the union of S_1, T_1, and the nodes appearing in π. We show that N_2 satisfies conditions (a) to (c). We are then finished, because, by the maximality of N_1, we have $N_1 = N_2$, which implies in particular that t belongs to T_1.

N_2 satisfies condition (a) because $s \in S_1$ and $S_1 \subseteq S_2$.

To prove that N_2 satisfies (c), observe that N_1 is strongly connected by definition, and that the addition of π does not spoil this property because $x_1 \in S_1 \cup T_1$ and, since $x_k = t$, we also have $x_k \in {}^\bullet S_1$. So N_2 is strongly connected.

We prove indirectly that N_2 satisfies (b). Assume that there exists a cluster c such that $|S_2 \cap c| \geq 2$, and let s_1, s_2 be two different places of $S_2 \cap c$. By the free-choice property, we have $s_1^\bullet = s_2^\bullet$. Since N_1 contains at most one place of a cluster, at least one of the places s_1 and s_2 does not belong to S_1. Consider two cases:

Case 1. Neither s_1 nor s_2 belong to S_1.

Then they both appear in the path π. Assume without loss of generality that $s_1 = x_i$ and $s_2 = x_j$, where $1 \leq i < j < k$ ($j = k$ is impossible because $x_k = t$ and t is a transition). Since x_i and x_j are places that belong to the same cluster, they have the same post-sets, and therefore $x_{j+1} \in x_i^\bullet$. So $x_1 \ldots x_i \, x_{j+1} \ldots x_k$ is a path of N, shorter than π, which leads from a node of N_1 to t. This contradicts the minimality of π.

Case 2. Exactly one of s_1 and s_2 belongs to S_1.

Assume without loss of generality that $s_1 \in S_1$ and $s_2 \notin S_1$. Then s_2 appears in π, and hence $s_2 = x_i$ for some $1 \leq i \leq k$. We have $1 < i$ because $x_i \notin S_1$, and $i < k$ because $x_k = t$ is a transition. Since $x_{i+1} \in s_2^\bullet$ and $s_1^\bullet = s_2^\bullet$, the path $s_1 x_{i+1} \ldots x_k$ is contained in N, leads from a node of N_1 to t, and is shorter than π. This contradicts the minimality of π.

Since we reach a contradiction in both cases, N_2 satisfies condition (b).   □

Theorem 5.6   *S-coverability Theorem*

Well-formed free-choice nets are covered by S-components.

Proof:

Let s be a place of a well-formed free-choice net. By Lemma 5.5, some minimal siphon R contains s. By Proposition 5.4(2), the subnet generated by $R \cup {}^\bullet R$ is an S-component. This S-component contains s, which proves the result.   □

5.2   Derived results

In this section, we show some consequences of Proposition 5.4 and the S-coverability Theorem. We will make use of the following proposition, which shows that the characteristic function of the places of an S-component is a semi-positive S-invariant. On this occasion, we also prove that this S-invariant is minimal.

Proposition 5.7　　*S-components induce minimal S-invariants*

Let $N_1 = (S_1, T_1, F_1)$ be an S-component of a net N. Then $\chi[S_1]$ is a minimal S-invariant of N.

Proof:

The proof is divided into two parts:

(i) $\chi[S_1]$ is an S-invariant of N.

Let t be an arbitrary transition of N. Then

$$\sum_{s \in \bullet t} \chi[S_1](s) = |\bullet t \cap S_1| \quad \text{and} \quad \sum_{s \in t\bullet} \chi[S_1](s) = |t^\bullet \cap S_1|$$

By the definition of an S-invariant, we only have to prove $|\bullet t \cap S_1| = |t^\bullet \cap S_1|$.

If $t \notin T_1$ then $|\bullet t \cap S_1| = |t^\bullet \cap S_1| = 0$ because $T_1 = {}^\bullet S_1 \cup S_1{}^\bullet$.

If $t \in T_1$, then $|\bullet t \cap S_1| = |t^\bullet \cap S_1| = 1$ because N_1 is an S-net.

(ii) $\chi[S_1]$ is minimal.

By the definition of a characteristic function, the support $\langle \chi[S_1] \rangle$ of $\chi[S_1]$ is S_1. Let I be an arbitrary semi-positive S-invariant of N satisfying $\langle I \rangle \subseteq S_1$. We prove $\langle I \rangle = S_1$, which implies that $\chi[S_1]$ is minimal.

Let s_1 and s_2 be two arbitrary places of N_1. Since N_1 is strongly connected, a path of N_1 leads from s_1 to s_2. Let $s\,t\,r$ be three consecutive nodes of this path, where s and r are places. We claim $I(s) = I(r)$.

$$
\begin{aligned}
I(s) &= \sum_{q \in \bullet t \cap S_1} I(q) & (N_1 \text{ is an S-net}) \\
&= \sum_{q \in \bullet t} I(q) & (\langle I \rangle \subseteq S_1) \\
&= \sum_{q \in t^\bullet} I(q) & (I \text{ is an S-invariant}) \\
&= \sum_{q \in t^\bullet \cap S_1} I(q) & (\langle I \rangle \subseteq S_1) \\
&= I(r) & (N_1 \text{ is an S-net})
\end{aligned}
$$

By repeated application of the claim, we get $I(s_1) = I(s_2)$. Since s_1 and s_2 are two arbitrary places of S_1, we have either $\langle I \rangle = S_1$ or $\langle I \rangle = \emptyset$. Since I is semi-positive, its support is nonempty, and so $\langle I \rangle = S_1$.　　　□

We say that an S-component is marked at a marking M if at least one of its places is marked at M. With the help of Proposition 5.7, we prove the following results:

Theorem 5.8   *Consequences of the S-coverability Theorem*

Let N be a well-formed free-choice net.

(1) N has a positive S-invariant.

(2) Every system (N, M) is bounded.

(3) A system (N, M) is live iff every S-component of N is marked at M.

Proof:

(1) Let $\{N_1, N_2, \ldots, N_k\}$ be an S-cover of N, and let S_i be the set of places of N_i for $1 \le i \le k$. By Proposition 5.7, every characteristic function $\chi[S_i]$ is a semi-positive S-invariant of N. Define $I = \chi[S_1] + \chi[S_2] + \cdots + \chi[S_k]$. Since S-invariants are closed under sum, I is an S-invariant. Moreover, we have $I(s) \ge 1$ for every place s, because every place of N is contained in an S-component of the S-cover. So I is positive.

(2) Follows from (1) (Theorem 2.31).

(3) ($\Rightarrow$): By Proposition 5.2(3), the set of places of an S-component is a proper siphon. By Commoner's Theorem, this siphon contains a trap marked at M and is thus marked itself.

($\Leftarrow$): Let R be a minimal siphon of N. By Proposition 5.4, R is a trap, and also the set of places of an S-component of N. Since all S-components are marked at M, the siphon R contains a trap marked at M, namely R itself. By Commoner's Theorem, the system (N, M) is live.   □

None of the three parts of this theorem holds if N is well-formed, but not a free-choice net (see Exercise 5.4).

We now study the place bounds of live and bounded free-choice systems. The results turn out to be completely analogous to those obtained in Chapter 3 on the place bounds of live T-systems. The role played by circuits in the case of T-systems is now played by S-components.

Theorem 5.9   *Place bounds in live and bounded free-choice systems*

Let s be a place of a live and bounded free-choice system (N, M_0). The bound of s is equal to

$$\min\{M_0(S_1) \mid (S_1, T_1, F_1) \text{ is an S-component of } N \text{ containing } s\}.$$

Proof:

The proof of this theorem is almost identical to the proof of of Corollary 3.19(2). Let M be a reachable marking such that $M(s)$ is equal to the bound of s. For every S-component (S_1, T_1, F_1), we have $M(s) \leq M(S_1)$ and, by Proposition 5.2(2), $M(S_1) = M_0(S_1)$. It remains to prove that $M(s) = M(S_1)$ holds for some S-component (S_1, T_1, F_1).

Define the marking L of N as follows:

$$L(r) = \begin{cases} M(r) & \text{if } r \neq s \\ 0 & \text{if } r = s \end{cases}$$

We claim that (N, L) is not live. Assume the contrary.

Then, since liveness implies place-liveness (Proposition 2.17), there exists an occurrence sequence $L \xrightarrow{\sigma} L'$ such that $L'(s) > 0$. Since $M \geq L$, the sequence σ is also enabled at M (Monotonicity Lemma). Let $M \xrightarrow{\sigma} M'$. Since $L(s) = 0$ we have $M'(s) = L'(s) + M(s) > M(s)$, which contradicts the assumption that $M(s)$ is equal to the bound of s. This finishes the proof of the claim.

Since (N, L) is not live but N is well-formed, some S-component N_1 is unmarked at L (Theorem 5.8(3)). Since (N, M) is live, N_1 is marked at M. As L and M only differ in the place s, the S-component N_1 contains s. Moreover, s is the only place of N_1 marked at M, and therefore $M(S_1) = M(s)$.   □

This theorem implies that the live and 1-bounded free-choice systems are those which are live and bounded, and, moreover, can be covered by S-components containing exactly one token. These S-components can be seen as finite automata: the places are the states, and the place which holds the token is the initial state.

Finally, we show that every well-formed free-choice net has a live and 1-bounded marking. This result is analogous to Genrich's Theorem for T-systems (Theorem 3.20).

Theorem 5.10   *Well-formed free-choice nets have live and 1-bounded markings*

Let N be a well-formed free-choice net. There exists a marking M_0 of N such that (N, M_0) is a live and 1-bounded system.

Proof:

Throughout this proof, we use N_1 as a variable ranging over S-components, and S_1 as the set of places of N_1.

Since N is well-formed, there exists a marking M such that the system (N, M) is live and bounded. If (N, M) is 1-bounded, we are done. So assume that it is not 1-bounded. We construct another marking L such that (N, L) is also live and bounded, and satisfies the following two conditions:

- for every S-component N_1, $L(S_1) \leq M(S_1)$, and

- for some S-component N_1, $L(S_1) < M(S_1)$.

An exhaustive application of this construction yields a live and 1-bounded system.

To construct L, let s be a place which is not 1-bounded in (N, M). Then, there exists a marking M' reachable from M satisfying $M'(s) \geq 2$. Let L be the marking that coincides with M' everywhere except in s, where it puts only one token.

Since (N, M) is live, (N, M') is live. So every S-component of N is marked at M', and, by the construction of L, every S-component of N is marked at L. Therefore (N, L) is live. By Theorem 5.8(2), (N, L) is also bounded.

By Proposition 5.2(2), we have $M(S_1) = M'(S_1)$ for every S-component N_1. By the construction of L, we also have $L(S_1) \leq M'(S_1)$. Moreover, if an S-component N_1 contains s (and some S-component does, because N is covered by S-components), then $L(S_1) < M'(S_1)$. $\square$

5.3   The T-coverability Theorem

Figure 5.2 shows the live and bounded free-choice system of Figure 5.1, together with a decomposition of its underlying net into strongly connected T-nets. Observe that the T-nets are connected to the rest of the net only through places. We show in this section that all well-formed free-choice nets can be decomposed in this way.

We introduce the definitions of T-component and T-cover. They are obtained from the definitions of S-component and S-cover by interchanging places and transitions.

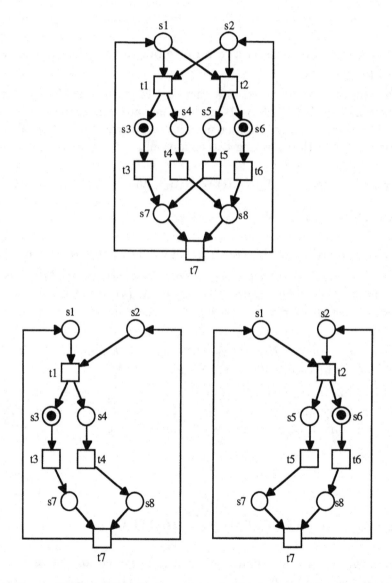

Fig. 5.2 A live and bounded free-choice system and its decomposition into T-components

Definition 5.11   *T-components*

Let N' be the subnet of a net N generated by a nonempty set X of nodes. N' is a T-component of N if:

- $^\bullet t \cup t^\bullet \subseteq X$ for every transition t of X, and

- N' is a strongly connected T-net.

As we did for S-components, we state some elementary properties of T-components, whose proofs are left for exercises.

Proposition 5.12   *Elementary properties of T-components*

Let $N_1 = (S_1, T_1, F_1)$ be a T-component of a net N.

(1) For every place s of N_1, $|^\bullet s \cap T_1| = 1 = |s^\bullet \cap T_1|$.

(2) Let M_0 be a marking of N, and let σ be a sequence of transitions of T_1. Then, $M_0 \xrightarrow{\sigma} M$ in N iff $M_0|_{S_1} \xrightarrow{\sigma} M|_{S_1}$ in N_1.   □

Loosely speaking, part (2) of this proposition states that the behaviour of a T-component is not restricted by the rest of the system.

Definition 5.13   *T-covers, nets covered by T-components*

Let $\mathcal{C}$ be a set of T-components of a net. $\mathcal{C}$ is a T-cover if every transition of the net belongs to a T-component of $\mathcal{C}$. A net is covered by T-components if it has a T-cover.

Similarly to the case of S-covers, if every place of a net covered by T-components has some input transition or some output transition, then not only every transition, but also every place and every arc belong to some T-component of a T-cover.

The main result of this section is the T-coverability Theorem:

Well-formed free-choice nets are covered by T-components.

The proof of this result is very different from that of the S-coverability Theorem. It starts by studying the relationship between T-components and minimal T-invariants. A first connection is easily derived from Proposition 5.7 by interchanging the role of places and transitions.

Proposition 5.14   *T-components induce minimal T-invariants*

Let $N_1 = (S_1, T_1, F_1)$ be a T-component of a net N. Then $\chi[T_1]$ is a minimal T-invariant of N. $\square$

We prove that for well-formed free-choice nets a sort of converse of this proposition also holds: given a minimal T-invariant J, the subnet generated by $\,^\bullet\langle J\rangle \cup \langle J\rangle \cup \langle J\rangle^\bullet$ is a T-component. Let us first see an example. The vectors

$$J_1 = (1, 0, 1, 1, 0, 0, 1)   \quad J_2 = (0, 1, 0, 0, 1, 1, 1)$$

are minimal T-invariants of the well-formed free-choice net of Figure 5.2. The net generated by $\,^\bullet\langle J_1\rangle \cup \langle J_1\rangle \cup \langle J_1\rangle^\bullet$ is the T-component on the left hand side, at the bottom of the figure, whereas $\,^\bullet\langle J_2\rangle \cup \langle J_2\rangle \cup \langle J_2\rangle^\bullet$ generates the T-component on the right.

For the proof of this result we introduce so-called cyclic allocations, and prove the Cyclic Allocation Lemma.

Definition 5.15   *Cyclic allocations*

An allocation α is cyclic if, for every cluster c of its domain C, the set $\alpha(c)^\bullet$ contains only places of C^2.

The name 'cyclic allocation' is due to the fact that every infinite path which contains only places and allocated transitions includes a circuit.

Lemma 5.16   *Cyclic Allocation Lemma*

Let (N, M_0) be a live and bounded free-choice system. Let α be a cyclic allocation of N with a nonempty domain C. There exists an occurrence sequence $M_0 \xrightarrow{\tau\,\sigma}$ such that:

   (i) τ is finite and contains no transition of C, and

   (ii) σ is infinite and contains only α-allocated transitions.

Before proving this lemma, let us consider the example of Figure 5.3. Let C be the set of clusters shown in the figure by dashed rectangles and let t_1, t_2 and t_3 be the allocated transitions. To verify that the Cyclic Allocation Lemma holds, we can choose $\sigma = (t_1\, t_2\, t_3)^\omega$ and $\tau = t_5$.

---

[2]We abuse language, and say 'places of C' instead of 'places of the clusters of C', and similarly for transitions.

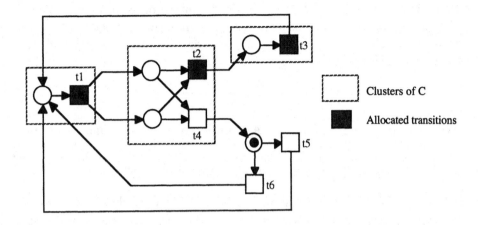

Fig. 5.3   Illustration of the proof of the Cyclic Allocation Lemma

Proof of Lemma 5.16:

By the Allocation Lemma (Lemma 4.24), there exists an infinite occurrence sequence $M_0 \xrightarrow{\sigma'}$ which agrees with α and contains α-allocated transitions infinitely often. It is easy to see that there exists a finite sequence σ_1 and an infinite sequence σ_2 such that $\sigma' = \sigma_1 \sigma_2$, and every transition in the alphabet $\mathcal{A}(\sigma_2)$ occurs infinitely often in σ_2.

Define $U = \mathcal{A}(\sigma') \setminus \alpha(C)$ and $V = \mathcal{A}(\sigma') \cap \alpha(C)$. Clearly, U and V are a partition of $\mathcal{A}(\sigma')$. Notice that U contains no transitions of C, because $U \subseteq \mathcal{A}(\sigma')$ and σ' agrees with α.

If $U = \emptyset$ then σ' contains only α-allocated transitions. We can then take $\tau = \epsilon$ and $\sigma = \sigma'$.

Assume now $U \neq \emptyset$. We show that we can take $\tau = \sigma_1|_U$ and $\sigma = \sigma_1|_V \sigma_2|_V$. We have to prove the following four properties:

(i) $\tau \sigma$ is an occurrence sequence enabled at M_0.

Let $M_0 \xrightarrow{\sigma_1} M_1 \xrightarrow{\sigma_2}$.

We claim $^\bullet U \cap V^\bullet = \emptyset$, which allows us to apply the Exchange Lemma (Lemma 2.14) to both $M_0 \xrightarrow{\sigma_1} M_1$ and $M_1 \xrightarrow{\sigma_2}$. Since α is cyclic and V contains only α-allocated transitions, $V^\bullet$ contains only places of C. On the other hand, $^\bullet U$ contains no places of C, because U contains no transitions of C. So $^\bullet U \cap V^\bullet = \emptyset$.

Since every transition in $\mathcal{A}(\sigma_2)$ occurs infinitely often in σ_2 and $V \neq \emptyset$ by the definition of σ', the sequence $\sigma_2|_V$ is infinite. Therefore, the application of the Exchange Lemma to $M_0 \xrightarrow{\sigma_1} M_1$ (Lemma 2.14(1)) and $M_1 \xrightarrow{\sigma_2}$ (Lemma 2.14(3)) yields

$$M_0 \xrightarrow{\sigma_1|_U \; \sigma_1|_V} M_1 \xrightarrow{\sigma_2|_U}$$

We prove $M_1 \xrightarrow{\sigma_2|_V}$, which, by the definition of τ and σ, completes the proof.

We apply once more the Exchange Lemma to $M_1 \xrightarrow{\sigma_2}$. Consider the partition of $\mathcal{A}(\sigma_2)$ given by $U_2 = \mathcal{A}(\sigma_2) \cap U$ and $V_2 = \mathcal{A}(\sigma_2) \cap V$.

We claim $^\bullet V_2 \cap U_2^\bullet = \emptyset$. Assume $^\bullet V_2 \cap U_2^\bullet$ contains a place s. We prove that s is not bounded in (N, M_0), which contradicts the hypothesis of the lemma.

Since $s \in {}^\bullet V_2$ and V_2 is included in V, we have $s \in {}^\bullet V$. Since V contains only α-allocated transitions, the cluster $[s]$ belongs to C.

Since U contains no transitions of C, it contains no transition of the cluster $[s]$. Therefore, the number of tokens of s does not decrease during the occurrence of $\sigma_2|_U$. On the other hand, U_2 does contain some transition t of $^\bullet s$ because $s \in U_2^\bullet$. So the number of tokens of s increases with each occurrence of t in $\sigma_2|_U$. By the definition of σ_2, the transition t occurs infinitely often in σ_2, and hence t occurs infinitely often in $\sigma_2|_U$. So s is not bounded, which proves the claim.

The claim makes it possible to apply the Exchange Lemma to $M_1 \xrightarrow{\sigma_2}$, using the sets V_2 and U_2. We obtain $M_1 \xrightarrow{\sigma_2|_{V_2}}$ (Lemma 2.14(3)). Since $\sigma_2|_V = \sigma_2|_{V_2}$ by the definition of V_2, we get $M_1 \xrightarrow{\sigma_2|_V}$.

(ii) τ is finite and contains no transition of C.

Since $\tau = \sigma_1|_U$ and σ_1 is finite, τ is finite. Since U contains no transitions of C, neither does τ.

(iii) σ is infinite.

Follows from the definition of σ and the fact that $\sigma_2|_V$ is infinite, as shown in the proof of (i).

(iv) σ contains only α-allocated transitions.

Follows from $\mathcal{A}(\sigma) \subseteq V$ (definition of σ) and $V \subseteq \alpha(C)$ (definition of V).

□

Theorem 5.17   *Minimal T-invariants induce T-components*

Let N be a well-formed free-choice net and let J be a minimal T-invariant of N. The subnet generated by $^{\bullet}\langle J \rangle \cup \langle J \rangle \cup \langle J \rangle^{\bullet}$ is a T-component of N.

Proof:

Let N_J be the subnet generated by $^{\bullet}\langle J \rangle \cup \langle J \rangle \cup \langle J \rangle^{\bullet}$. According to the definition of a T-component, we first have to show for every transition t of N_J that its input and output places are places of N_J. This is immediate, because the set of transitions of N_J is $\langle J \rangle$. It remains to prove that N_J is a strongly connected T-net. We will use several times $^{\bullet}\langle J \rangle = \langle J \rangle^{\bullet}$, which follows from the fact that minimal invariants are semi-positive and Proposition 2.41.

The net N_J has $\langle J \rangle$ as set of transitions. Therefore, in order to show that it is a strongly connected T-net, it suffices to prove the following three properties:

(i) For every place s of N_J, $|s^{\bullet} \cap \langle J \rangle| = 1$.

Since $^{\bullet}\langle J \rangle = \langle J \rangle^{\bullet}$, we have $s \in {}^{\bullet}\langle J \rangle$ and therefore $|s^{\bullet} \cap \langle J \rangle| \geq 1$. We prove $|s^{\bullet} \cap \langle J \rangle| \leq 1$ by means of the Cyclic Allocation Lemma.

Let C_J be the set of clusters of N which contain transitions of $\langle J \rangle$. Let α be an allocation with domain C_J, such that every α-allocated transition belongs to $\langle J \rangle$. We show that α is cyclic, i.e., that for every cluster c of C_J the set $\alpha(c)^{\bullet}$ contains only places of C_J. Let c be a cluster of C_J. Since $\alpha(c)$ belongs to $\langle J \rangle$, we have $\alpha(c)^{\bullet} \subseteq \langle J \rangle^{\bullet}$. Since $^{\bullet}\langle J \rangle = \langle J \rangle^{\bullet}$, $\alpha(c)^{\bullet} \subseteq {}^{\bullet}\langle J \rangle$. So every place of $\alpha(c)^{\bullet}$ has an output transition in $\langle J \rangle$, which, by the definition of C_J, implies that it belongs to C_J.

By the Cyclic Allocation Lemma, there exists an occurrence sequence $M_0 \xrightarrow{\tau\sigma}$ such that σ is infinite and contains only α-allocated transitions, i.e. we have $\mathcal{A}(\sigma) \subseteq \langle J \rangle$. By the Reproduction Lemma (Lemma 2.39), the alphabet $\mathcal{A}(\sigma)$ includes the support of some semi-positive T-invariant. By the minimality of J, this support is $\langle J \rangle$ itself, and hence $\langle J \rangle \subseteq \mathcal{A}(\sigma)$. So we have $\mathcal{A}(\sigma) = \langle J \rangle$.

Now, since σ contains only α-allocated transitions, we have $|s^{\bullet} \cap \mathcal{A}(\sigma)| \leq 1$ for every place s. Since $\mathcal{A}(\sigma) = \langle J \rangle$, we also have $|s^{\bullet} \cap \langle J \rangle| \leq 1$.

(ii) For every place s of N_J, $|^{\bullet}s \cap \langle J \rangle| = 1$.

Let $\langle J \rangle = \{t_1, t_2, \ldots, t_n\}$ and let L be an arbitrary marking of N (not necessarily reachable from M_0) which enables the occurrence sequence $\sigma = t_1\, t_2 \ldots t_n$ (notice that, since L can be arbitrarily large, it always exists).

Let $L \xrightarrow{\sigma} L'$. For every place s of N we have

$$L'(s) = L(s) + |^{\bullet}s \cap \langle J \rangle| - |s^{\bullet} \cap \langle J \rangle|$$

We show $L' = L$, which implies $|{}^\bullet s \cap \langle J \rangle| = |s^\bullet \cap \langle J \rangle|$, and, by (i), the result we wish to prove.

If s does not belong to N_J, then it does not belong to ${}^\bullet \langle J \rangle$ or $\langle J \rangle^\bullet$. Therefore, $|{}^\bullet s \cap \langle J \rangle| = 0 = |s^\bullet \cap \langle J \rangle|$, which implies $L'(s) = L(s)$. If s belongs to N_J, then it also belongs to $\langle J \rangle^\bullet$ because ${}^\bullet \langle J \rangle = \langle J \rangle^\bullet$. By (i), it has exactly one output transition in $\langle J \rangle$. So $L'(s) \geq L(s)$.

Therefore, we have $L' \geq L$. Since N is bounded for any marking by Theorem 5.8(2), the system (N, L) is bounded. By the Boundedness Lemma (Lemma 2.22), $L' = L$.

(iii) N_J is strongly connected.

Let t be a transition of N_J, and let U be the set of transitions u of N_J such that some path of N_J leads from u to t. We claim that U contains every transition of N_J.

Let $U = \{u_1, u_2, \ldots, u_n\}$ and let L be an arbitrary marking of N (not necessarily reachable from M_0) which enables the occurrence sequence $\sigma = u_1 u_2 \ldots u_n$. Define L' as the marking reached by the occurrence of σ from L, i.e., $L \xrightarrow{\sigma} L'$.

Let s be an arbitrary place of N_J. By the definition of U, if the unique output transition of s in N_J occurs in σ, then so does the unique input transition of s in N_J. Therefore, the occurrence of σ adds at least as many tokens to a place as it takes from it, i.e., $L' \geq L$. The same argument used in (ii) proves $L' = L$. By the fundamental property of T-invariants (Proposition 2.37), the Parikh vector of σ is a semi-positive T-invariant. By the definition of σ, the support of this T-invariant is the set U. Now, recall that the set of transitions of N_J is $\langle J \rangle$. Since J is a minimal T-invariant, we cannot have $U \subset \langle J \rangle$, and therefore $U = \langle J \rangle$, which proves the claim.

So every transition of N_J is connected to the transition t by a path. Since t was chosen arbitrarily, every two transitions of N_J are connected by a path. Since N_J is a T-net, any two of its nodes are connected by a path.   □

Theorem 5.18   *T-coverability Theorem*

Well-formed free-choice nets are covered by T-components.

Proof:

Let N be a well-formed free-choice net. N has a positive T-invariant J by Theorem 2.38, which is the sum of minimal T-invariants by Theorem 2.43(1). Therefore, every transition is contained in the support of a minimal T-invariant. By Theorem 5.17, this support is the set of transitions of a T-component. So every transition belongs to a T-component of N.   □

5.4   Derived results

Although the relevance of Theorem 5.17 and the T-coverability Theorem will become clearer in the next chapters, we can already derive an interesting consequence.

The transitions of the vending machine model we considered in the Introduction can be divided into *observable* and *internal* transitions. The observable transitions, like `dispense candy`, model actions that can be perceived outside the system, while the internal transitions, like `refill`, model actions that have no visible effect.

A net system is *divergent* for a certain division of its transitions into observable and internal if some reachable marking enables an infinite occurrence sequence of internal transitions. A divergent system is not well designed, because it may engage in an infinite useless behaviour. Using Theorem 5.17, we characterize the divisions for which a given live and bounded free-choice system is divergent.

Before we can apply Theorem 5.17, we introduce activated T-components.

Definition 5.19   *Activation of T-components*

Let $N_1 = (S_1, T_1, F_1)$ be a T-component of a net N. A marking M of N activates N_1 if the system $(N_1, M|_{S_1})$ is live.

Not every reachable marking activates a given T-component. In fact, there exist live and bounded free-choice systems in which no T-component at all is activated. An example is the initial marking of the system of Figure 5.2. However, the following result holds:

Theorem 5.20   *T-components can become activated*

Let N_1 be a T-component of a live and bounded free-choice system (N, M_0). Then there exists an occurrence sequence $M_0 \xrightarrow{\tau} M$ such that M activates N_1 and no transition of N_1 occurs in τ.

Proof:

Let C_1 be the set of clusters containing transitions of N_1. Define an allocation α of N with domain C_1 such that for every cluster c of C_1, the transition $\alpha(c)$ is the unique transition of c contained in N_1. There is at least one such transition because N_1 is strongly connected, and there is at most one such transition because N_1 is a T-net.

We claim that α is a cyclic allocation. Let c be a cluster of C. Since $\alpha(c)$ is a transition of N_1, and N_1 is a T-component, $\alpha(c)^\bullet$ is a set of places of N_1. Since every place of N_1 has an output transition in N_1, every place of $\alpha(c)^\bullet$ belongs to a cluster of C_1, which proves the claim.

By the Cyclic Allocation Lemma, there exists an occurrence sequence $M_0 \xrightarrow{\tau\sigma}$ such that no transition of N_1 occurs in τ and, moreover, σ is an infinite sequence containing only α-allocated transitions. We prove that M activates N_1. Since only transitions of N_1 occur in σ, the marking $M|_{S_1}$ enables σ in the net N_1. Theorem 3.17 states that a strongly connected T-system is live iff it has an infinite occurrence sequence. So, since N_1 is strongly connected, the system $(N_1, M|_{S_1})$ is live, and therefore M activates N_1. □

Theorem 5.21 *A characterization of divergence*

Let (N, M_0) be a live and bounded free-choice system and let T_I, T_O be a partition of the transitions of N into internal and observable transitions, respectively. (N, M_0) is divergent for this partition iff there exists a T-component (S_1, T_1, F_1) of N such that $T_1 \subseteq T_I$.

Proof:

($\Rightarrow$): Since (N, M_0) is divergent, there exists a reachable marking M and an infinite sequence σ such that $\mathcal{A}(\sigma) \subseteq T_I$ and $M \xrightarrow{\sigma}$. By the Reproduction Lemma (Lemma 2.39), there exists a semi-positive T-invariant J of N such that $\langle J \rangle \subseteq \mathcal{A}(\sigma)$. By the definition of minimality, some minimal T-invariant J' satisfies $\langle J' \rangle \subseteq \langle J \rangle$. By Theorem 5.17, there exists a T-component (S_1, T_1, F_1) of N such that $T_1 = \langle J' \rangle$. Altogether we have

$$T_1 = \langle J' \rangle \subseteq \langle J \rangle \subseteq \mathcal{A}(\sigma) \subseteq T_I,$$

and so $T_1 \subseteq T_I$.

($\Leftarrow$): By Theorem 5.20, some reachable marking M activates N_1, i.e., the system $(N_1, M|_{S_1})$ is live. So the marking $M|_{S_1}$ enables some infinite sequence σ in the net N_1. Since N_1 is a T-component, the marking M enables σ in the net N. □

Exercises

Exercise 5.1
    Prove Propositions 5.2 and 5.12.

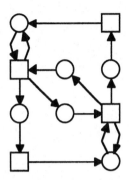

Fig. 5.4 A net which is not well-formed

Exercise 5.2
Prove or disprove:

1) A bounded free-choice system is live iff every minimal siphon is an initially marked trap.

2) A live free-choice system is bounded iff every minimal siphon is an initially marked trap.

Exercise 5.3

1) A trap is minimal if it is proper and includes no smaller proper trap. Exhibit a live and bounded free-choice system in which not every minimal trap is a siphon.

2) Exhibit a strongly connected net in which not every place belongs to a minimal siphon.
   Hint: Four nodes suffice.

Exercise 5.4
Prove that the net of Figure 5.4 is not well-formed. Add two arcs to transform it into a well-formed net (non free-choice) which does not satisfy any of the three properties of Theorem 5.8.

Exercise 5.5
Specialize the S- and T-coverability Theorems for both S- and T-systems.

Exercise 5.6

Give an algorithm that accepts as input a live and bounded free-choice system and returns a live and 1-bounded free-choice system with the same underlying net.

Exercise 5.7 *

Exhibit a live and bounded system containing a T-component that cannot become activated.

Bibliographic Notes

The Coverability Theorems were proved by Hack in his Master Thesis [42], which can be considered as the first and one of the main pieces of work on free-choice systems. Unfortunately, some proofs in Hack's Thesis contain mistakes. Corrections and new proofs were published by Hack himself [43], Best and Thiagarajan [10], and Döpp [26].

Proposition 5.5 (every place of a free-choice system is contained in a minimal siphon) was proved by Esparza, Best and Silva in [35]. Theorem 5.9 (place bounds in live and bounded free-choice systems) is due to Best and Desel [7].

Best and Desel proved Theorem 5.17 (relationship between minimal T-invariants and T-components) in [7]. Theorem 5.21 (characterization of divergent systems) is due to Thiagarajan and Voss [75]. They call the sets of observable transitions for which the system is not divergent *prompt interfaces*.

Solutions to the Exercises 5.7 and 5.4 can be found in [70] by Reisig and in [50] by Jantzen and Valk, respectively.

Chapter 6 ———————

The Rank Theorem

In this chapter, we provide a result which characterizes well-formedness of free-choice nets in a very suitable way for verification purposes. All the conditions of the characterization are decidable in polynomial time in the size of the net. The most interesting feature of the result is that it exhibits a tight relation between the well-formedness of a free-choice net and the rank of its incidence matrix. Accordingly, it is known as the Rank Theorem. It will be an extremely useful lemma in the proof of many results of this chapter and of the next ones.

We also provide a characterization of the live and bounded markings of a well-formed free-choice net. Again, the conditions of the characterization can be checked in polynomial time. Together with the Rank Theorem, this result yields a polynomial time algorithm to decide if a given free-choice system is live and bounded.

In the last section of the chapter we use the Rank Theorem to prove the Duality Theorem. This result states that the class of well-formed free-choice nets is invariant under the transformation that interchanges places and transitions and reverses the arcs of the net.

6.1 Characterizations of well-formedness

Using the results of Chapter 4 and Chapter 5, it is easy to obtain the following characterization of well-formed free-choice nets.

Proposition 6.1 *A first characterization of well-formedness*

Let N be a connected free-choice net with at least one place and at least one transition.

(1) N is structurally live iff every proper siphon contains a proper trap.

(2) N is well-formed iff it is structurally live and has a positive S-invariant.

Proof:

(1) ($\Rightarrow$): By Commoner's Theorem, if M is a live marking of N then every proper siphon of N contains a trap marked at M. So, in particular, every proper siphon contains a proper trap.

($\Leftarrow$): Let M_0 be the marking that puts a token in every place of N. Clearly, every proper trap is marked at M_0. Since every proper siphon contains a proper trap by the hypothesis, every proper siphon contains a trap marked at M_0. By Commoner's Theorem, (N, M_0) is a live system, which implies that N is structurally live.

(2) ($\Rightarrow$): Every well-formed net is, by definition, structurally live. The existence of a positive S-invariant follows from Theorem 5.8(1).

($\Leftarrow$): Let M_0 be a live marking of N. Since N has a positive S-invariant, every marking of N is bounded. Hence, M_0 is a live and bounded marking, and therefore N is well-formed.   □

Unfortunately, this proposition does not easily lead to an efficient verification algorithm, because deciding if a free-choice net is structurally live is an NP-complete problem (Exercise 4.7). We shall prove a different characterization whose conditions can be checked in polynomial time. It relates the well-formedness of a free-choice net to the rank of its incidence matrix (i.e., the maximum number of linearly independent rows or columns), and is called the Rank Theorem. In order to state it, we introduce the following notations. Given a net N,

- Rank(**N**) denotes the rank of the incidence matrix of N, and

- C_N denotes the set of clusters of N.

Now, the Rank Theorem looks as follows:

> *A free-choice net N is well-formed if and only if*
>
>   (a) *it is connected, and has at least one place and one transition,*
>
>   (b) *it has a positive S-invariant,*
>
>   (c) *it has a positive T-invariant, and*
>
>   (d) Rank(**N**) $= |C_N| - 1$.

Condition (d) is called the Rank Equation in the sequel.

We present the proof of the Rank Theorem in a top-down style. Given two statements A and B, we say that A reduces to B if B implies A. We obtain a chain of statements, starting with the Rank Theorem, such that each element of the chain reduces to its successor. Then we prove the last statement of the chain.

For the first reduction, we have already proved a good part of the 'only if' direction in the previous chapters: a well-formed net satisfies Condition (a) by definition; by Theorem 5.8(1), every well-formed free-choice net has a positive S-invariant (Condition (b)); moreover, by Theorem 2.38, every well-formed net has a positive T-invariant (Condition (c)).

Using these results, we can reduce the Rank Theorem to the conjunction of the two following statements:

(A) *A free-choice net satisfying Conditions (a) to (d) is well-formed.*

(B) *Every well-formed free-choice net satisfies Condition (d).*

These two assertions are proved in the next sections. Let us first consider an example. The net N_1 on the left hand side of Figure 6.1 is known from the previous chapter. The following facts can be easily checked:

$(1, 1, 1, 1, 1, 1, 1, 1)$ is a positive S-invariant of N_1.

$(1, 1, 1, 1, 1, 1, 2)$ is a positive T-invariant of N_1.

N_1 has 6 clusters, and $\text{Rank}(N_1) = 5$.

Therefore, N_1 satisfies the conditions of the Rank Theorem, and so it should be well-formed. This is in fact the case, because, for instance, the marking that puts one token in the places s_1 and s_2 is live and bounded.

Consider now the net N_2 on the right hand side of the figure. It is obtained by reversing the direction of the arcs of the net N_1, and happens to be a free-choice net.[1] By the definition of incidence matrix, we obtain $\mathbf{N_2} = -\mathbf{N_1}$. Hence $\text{Rank}(\mathbf{N_2}) = \text{Rank}(\mathbf{N_1}) = 5$. Moreover, both nets have the same S- and T-invariants, and so N_2 has a positive S-invariant and a positive T-invariant. However, N_2 has only 5 clusters, one less than N_1, and therefore the Rank Equation does not hold. According to the Rank Theorem, N_2 should not be well-formed, and this is the case. In fact, N_2 is not even structurally live: the set

$$\{s_1, s_2, s_4, s_5, s_7, s_8\}$$

is a proper siphon of N_2 that does not include any proper trap. It follows from Commoner's Theorem that N_2 has no live markings.

---

[1] The net obtained from a free-choice net by reversing the arcs need not be free-choice.

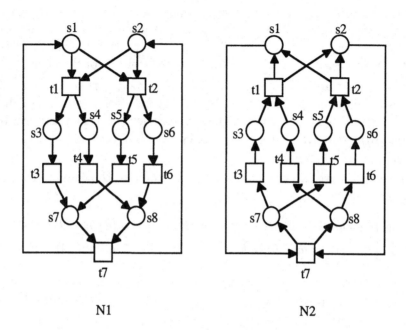

N1   N2

Fig. 6.1 N_1 is well-formed, N_2 is not well-formed

6.2   The non-well-formed case

In this section we prove the following assertion, which implies (A).

> *If a free-choice net N satisfying Conditions* (a), (b) *and* (c) *is not well-formed, then* Rank($\mathbf{N}$) $\geq |C_N|$.

Throughout this section, N_p denotes a net satisfying Conditions (a), (b) and (c), i.e., N_p is connected, has at least one place and one transition, and it also has a positive S-invariant and a positive T-invariant.

Since N_p has a positive S-invariant, all its markings are bounded. Therefore, by the definition of well-formedness, N_p is well-formed if and only if it has a live marking, i.e., if and only if it is structurally live. So we can reduce (A) further to:

> *If N_p is not structurally live then* Rank($\mathbf{N}_p$) $\geq |C_{N_p}|$.

The rank of a matrix is equal to its maximum number of linearly independent column vectors. Therefore, for proving a lower bound on the rank of the incidence matrix, it suffices to find a set of transitions whose corresponding column vectors are linearly independent. Abusing language, we will also call the transitions of such a set linearly independent. The transitions we will prove to be linearly independent will be those allocated by a certain allocation. Notice that an allocation whose domain has n clusters allocates n transitions. In particular, a total allocation of a strongly connected net N allocates $|C_N|$ transitions. Since N_p is strongly connected, we can reduce (A) to

> *If N_p is not structurally live, then there exists a total allocation such that the set of allocated transitions is linearly independent.*

The linear independence of a set of transitions is closely related to the notion of a T-invariant. Assume that a set of transitions U is not linearly independent. Then, there exist transitions $t_1, \ldots, t_n \in U$ and nonzero rational numbers $a_1, \ldots, a_n$ such that

$$a_1 \mathbf{t}_1 + \ldots + a_n \mathbf{t}_n = \mathbf{0}.$$

These numbers are the nonzero entries of a T-invariant. The following lemma shows that, for the net N_p, this T-invariant can be chosen semi-positive.

Lemma 6.2

For every allocation of N_p, either the set of allocated transitions is linearly independent, or it contains the support of a semi-positive T-invariant.

Proof:

Let α be an allocation of N_p and assume that the set of α-allocated transitions is not linearly independent. Then there exists a T-invariant J_α satisfying $J_\alpha \neq 0$ and $J_\alpha(t) = 0$ for every transition t which is not allocated. We show that there exists a semi-positive T-invariant J such that its support $\langle J \rangle$ contains only allocated transitions.

By the definition of a T-invariant, the entries of J_α are rational numbers. They can be multiplied by a suitable constant to obtain an integer-valued T-invariant; so we can assume without loss of generality that J_α is integer-valued. Moreover, we can assume that at least one entry of J_α is greater than zero; otherwise J_α can be multiplied by (-1).

Let J denote the positive part of J_α, defined by

$$J(t) = \begin{cases} J_\alpha(t) & \text{if } J_\alpha(t) > 0 \\ 0 & \text{otherwise} \end{cases}$$

By its definition, and since J_α has at least one positive entry by the assumption, the vector J is semi-positive. We show that it is a T-invariant.

Since J_α is integer-valued, J is also integer-valued. Hence we can find a sequence of transitions σ such that $\vec{\sigma} = J$. Let M be an arbitrary marking of N which enables σ, and let $M \xrightarrow{\sigma} M'$. For proving that J is a T-invariant we show that $M' = M$. Let s be a place of N and let $t = \alpha([s])$. We have $t \in s^\bullet$ because N_p is free-choice. Every transition $u \in s^\bullet \setminus \{t\}$ is not allocated, and therefore satisfies $J_\alpha(u) = J(u) = 0$ by the definitions of J_α and J.

Case 1. $J(t) = 0$.

Then $M'(s) \geq M(s)$ because neither t nor any other transition of $s^\bullet$ occurs in σ.

Case 2. $J(t) > 0$.

By the definition of J, we have $J(t) = J_\alpha(t)$, and $J(u) \geq J_\alpha(u)$ for every transition $u \in {}^\bullet s$. Since J_α is a T-invariant we get

$$\sum_{u \in {}^\bullet s} J(u) \geq \sum_{u \in {}^\bullet s} J_\alpha(u) = \sum_{u \in s^\bullet} J_\alpha(u) = J_\alpha(t) = J(t)$$

Since $M'(s) = M(s) + \sum_{u \in {}^\bullet s} J(u) - J(t)$, we obtain $M'(s) \geq M(s)$.

Since s was chosen arbitrarily we get $M' \geq M$. Since N_p has a positive S-invariant, M is a bounded marking of N_p. Finally, the Boundedness Lemma (Lemma 2.22) implies $M' = M$.   □

Using this result, we further reduce (A) to:

> *If N_p is not structurally live, then there exists a total allocation such that the set of allocated transitions does not contain the support of any semi-positive T-invariant.*

We wish to transform this condition on semi-positive T-invariants into a condition on the set of all possible infinite occurrence sequences of N_p, i.e., all the infinite occurrence sequences $M \xrightarrow{\sigma}$ for arbitrary markings M of N_p.

Lemma 6.3

Let J be a semi-positive T-invariant of a net. There exists a marking M and an infinite occurrence sequence $M \xrightarrow{\sigma}$ such that $\mathcal{A}(\sigma) = \langle J \rangle$.

Proof:

As in the proof of the previous lemma we can assume without loss of generality that J is integer-valued. Then, there exists a sequence τ such that $\vec{\tau} = J$ (and therefore $\mathcal{A}(\tau) = \langle J \rangle$).

Let M be a marking that enables τ. Since J is a T-invariant we have $M \xrightarrow{\tau} M$. So M enables the infinite sequence $\sigma = \tau^\omega$.   □

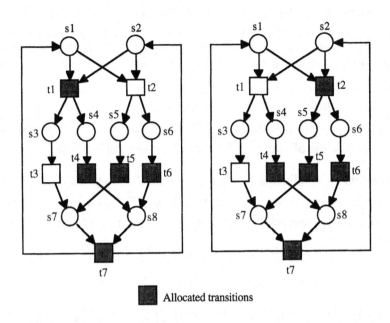

Allocated transitions

Fig. 6.2 Illustration of the definition of a pointing allocation

By this lemma, if no infinite occurrence sequence of N_p contains only α-allocated transitions, then the set of α-allocated transitions does not contain the support of any semi-positive T-invariant. So we can finally reduce (A) to:

If N_p is not structurally live, then there exists a total allocation α such that no infinite occurrence sequence contains only α-allocated transitions.

In the rest of this section we prove this statement by finding a suitable allocation.

Definition 6.4 *Allocations pointing to a set of clusters*

Let C be a set of clusters of a net N. An allocation of N points to C if for every place s of N there exists a path π from s to a place of C such that all the transitions of π are allocated.[2]

Figure 6.2 shows two allocations of the net N_1 of Figure 6.1. Both of them have the same domain, namely all the clusters of the net except $c = \{s_3, t_3\}$. The allocation on the left points to $\{c\}$. The allocation on the right does not point to $\{c\}$, because no path containing only allocated transitions leads from s_1 to s_3. Observe, however, that this allocation does point to the set $\{\{s_3, t_3\}, \{s_1, s_2, t_1, t_2\}\}$.

---

[2]Recall that we call a place of a cluster of C simply a place of C.

Intuitively, an allocation that points to a set C of clusters directs the tokens towards clusters of C. It is easy to see that the domain of such an allocation need not contain any cluster of C because for every place s of C the path s itself satisfies the requirement of Definition 6.4.

Lemma 6.5   *Pointing Allocation Lemma*

Let C be a nonempty set of clusters of a strongly connected free-choice net N and let $\overline{C}$ be the set of clusters of N which do not belong to C.

(1) There exists an allocation α with domain $\overline{C}$ that points to C.

(2) If M is a bounded marking of N and $M \xrightarrow{\sigma}$ is an infinite occurrence sequence that agrees with α, then some transition of C occurs infinitely often in σ.

Proof:

(1) Assume $N = (S, T, F)$. Define the function $\phi: T \to I\!N$ as follows:

$$\phi(t) \; = \; \text{minimum length of the paths leading from } t \text{ to a place of } C$$

Since N is strongly connected and $C \neq \emptyset$, the function ϕ is well-defined. The value $\phi(t)$ can be interpreted as the minimal distance from t to the set C. Figure 6.3(a) shows the function ϕ for an example.

Let $\alpha: \overline{C} \to T$ be an allocation which allocates only transitions with minimal distance to C. In other words, α satisfies, for every cluster $c \in \overline{C}$,

$$\phi(\alpha(c)) = \min\{\phi(t) \mid t \in c \cap T\}$$

Such an allocation α exists, because, by the strong connectedness of N, every cluster contains at least one transition. Figure 6.3(b) shows such an allocation.

We prove that α points to C. Let s be an arbitrary place of S. We construct a path $\pi = s \ldots s'$ such that s' belongs to C and all the transitions of π are α-allocated.

If s belongs to C, define $\pi = s$.

Assume that s belongs to $\overline{C}$. We proceed by induction on $\phi(\alpha([s]))$. Define $t = \alpha([s])$. We have $t \in s^\bullet$ since N is free-choice.

Base. $\phi(t) = 2$.

Then some place of $t^\bullet$, say s', belongs to C. Define $\pi = s\, t\, s'$.

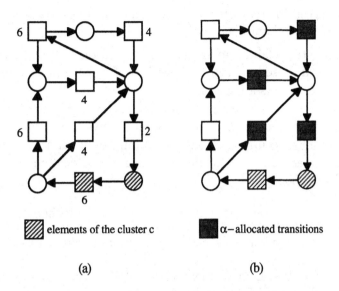

Fig. 6.3 Illustration of the proof of Lemma 6.5(1) for $C = \{c\}$. The numbers indicate the values of ϕ

Step. $\phi(t) > 2$.

By the definition of ϕ there exists a path $t \ldots r$ of length $\phi(t)$ such that r belongs to C. Let q be the successor of t in this path. By the definition of α, we have $\phi(\alpha([q])) < \phi(t)$. By the induction hypothesis, there exists a path π' leading from q to a place of a cluster of C such that all the transitions of π' are α-allocated. Define $\pi = s\, t\, \pi'$.

(2) Let U be the set of transitions that occur in σ infinitely often. Since σ is an infinite sequence, U is nonempty. Let t_1 be an arbitrary transition in U.

If t_1 belongs to C, then we are finished.

Assume that t_1 belongs to $\overline{C}$. Let s_0 be an arbitrary input place of t_1. We have $t_1 = \alpha([s_0])$ because σ agrees with α. Since α points to C, there exists a path $\pi = s_0\, t_1\, s_1\, t_2 \ldots t_k\, s_k$ such that $t_i = \alpha([s_{i-1}])$ for $0 \leq i \leq k - 1$, and moreover $s_0, \ldots, s_{k-1}$ belong to $\overline{C}$ and s_k belongs to C.

We claim that every transition of π belongs to U. Since $t_1 \in U$, it suffices to show that, for an arbitrary number $1 \leq i \leq k - 1$, if $t_i \in U$ then also $t_{i+1} \in U$. So assume that $t_i \in U$ for some index $i \leq k - 1$. Since π is a path, t_i is an input transition of s_i. The cluster $[s_i]$ is in $\overline{C}$ because $i \leq k-1$. So $[s_i]$ is in the domain of α, and $t_{i+1} = \alpha([s_i])$. Since M is a bounded marking and $t_i \in U$, some output transition of s_i also belongs to U. Since σ agrees with α, the transition t_{i+1} is the only output transition of s_i that occurs in σ. Therefore, $t_{i+1} \in U$, and the claim is proved.

In particular, this claim implies that the transition t_k is in U. Since M is a bounded marking, some output transition t of s_k belongs to U as well. Since s_k is a place of C, t is a transition of C. $\square$

We have to show that in case N_p is not structurally live there is a total allocation α such that no infinite occurrence sequence contains only allocated transitions (or, since α is total, agrees with α). Roughly speaking, the allocation α will be defined as the union of two allocations:

- a circuit-free allocation that 'pumps' tokens out of a siphon R, and

- an allocation that points to the clusters containing places of R.

By the Pointing Allocation Lemma, any infinite sequence that agrees with α contains transitions of the clusters of R infinitely often. We will show that, due to our choice of R and α, this leads to a contradiction.

Proposition 6.6   *A lower bound for not structurally live nets*

If N_p is not structurally live, then there exists a total allocation α such that no infinite occurrence sequence contains only α-allocated transitions.

Proof:

By Commoner's Theorem there is a proper siphon R of N which does not include a proper trap; otherwise any marking which marks all places and hence all proper traps would be live.

Let C be the set of clusters that contain places of R. Every place in R has an output transition because N is strongly connected. Since the maximal trap in R is the empty set, we can apply Lemma 4.26 to R and get an allocation β, circuit-free for R, with domain C.

By the first part of the Pointing Allocation Lemma there is an allocation γ with domain $\overline{C}$ that points to C (where $\overline{C}$ is the set of clusters of N which are not in C). Define the total allocation $\alpha = \beta \cup \gamma$ (i.e., $\alpha(c) = \beta(c)$ for $c \in C$ and $\alpha(c) = \gamma(c)$ for $c \in \overline{C}$).

Assume that $M \stackrel{\sigma}{\longrightarrow}$ is an infinite occurrence sequence containing only α-allocated transitions. Then, in particular, σ agrees with α. Since γ points to C and since $\alpha(\overline{C}) = \gamma(\overline{C})$, the allocation α also points to C. Moreover, M is a bounded marking because N_p has a positive S-invariant. So the second part of the Pointing Allocation Lemma applies to $M \stackrel{\sigma}{\longrightarrow}$, and therefore a transition t of C occurs in σ infinitely often. Since σ only contains α-allocated transitions, the transition t is α-allocated. It is also β-allocated because $\alpha(C) = \beta(C)$ by the definition of α.

Define a binary relation $\lhd \subseteq \beta(C) \times \beta(C)$:

> $t_1 \lhd t_2$ if there exists a path from t_1 to t_2 which contains only places of R and β-allocated transitions.

Since β is circuit-free for R, the relation $\lhd$ is a partial order.

Let u be a β-allocated transition that belongs to C, minimal with respect to $\lhd$, and occurs in σ infinitely often (u exists because the transition t is β-allocated and occurs in σ infinitely often). Since u belongs to C, some place s of $[u]$ is contained in R. Moreover, since N is free-choice, s is an input place of u. Since u occurs infinitely often in σ, some input transition v of s occurs infinitely often in σ as well. We now have

$$
\begin{aligned}
v \in {}^\bullet s &\Rightarrow v \in {}^\bullet R && (s \in R) \\
&\Rightarrow v \in R^\bullet && (R \text{ is a siphon}) \\
&\Rightarrow [v] \in C && (\text{definition of } C) \\
&\Rightarrow v \in \alpha(C) && (\sigma \text{ agrees with } \alpha) \\
&\Rightarrow v \in \beta(C) && (\alpha \text{ and } \beta \text{ coincide on } C)
\end{aligned}
$$

Then $v\,s\,u$ is a path that contains only places of R and β-allocated transitions. So $v \lhd u$, which contradicts the minimality of u. $\qquad\square$

The net N_2 of Figure 6.1 is not structurally live. Figure 6.4 shows a total allocation of N_2 such that no infinite occurrence sequence contains only allocated transitions.

6.3 The well-formed case

In this section we prove statement (B):

> (B) *If N is a well-formed free-choice net then* $\mathrm{Rank}(\mathbf{N}) = |C_N| - 1$.

As we did in the previous section, we fix a notation for a net satisfying a particular property: let throughout this section N_w denote a well-formed free-choice net. We prove $\mathrm{Rank}(\mathbf{N}_w) \geq |C_{N_w}| - 1$ and $\mathrm{Rank}(\mathbf{N}_w) \leq |C_{N_w}| - 1$ separately.

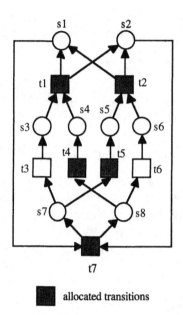

Fig. 6.4 A total allocation α of N_2 such that no infinite occurrence sequence agrees with α

Proposition 6.7   *A lower bound for well-formed free-choice nets*

$$\operatorname{Rank}(\mathbf{N}_w) \geq |C_{N_w}| - 1.$$

Proof:

It suffices to prove that N_w has $|C_{N_w}| - 1$ linearly independent transitions. Similarly to the case of (A), we do it by defining an allocation α with a domain of size $|C_{N_w}| - 1$, and proving that the set of α-allocated transitions is linearly independent.

The net N_w has a place and a transition since it is well-formed. By Theorem 5.8(1) and since N_w is free-choice, it has a positive S-invariant. Moreover, by Theorem 2.38, it has a positive T-invariant. So we can apply Lemma 6.2 and Lemma 6.3 of the previous section to N_w. Using these results, it suffices to show that no infinite occurrence sequence of N_w contains only α-allocated transitions.

Let c be an arbitrary cluster of N. Recall that N_w is strongly connected because it is well-formed. By the first part of the Pointing Allocation Lemma, there exists an allocation α that points to $\{c\}$ and whose domain does not contain c. Now, let $M \xrightarrow{\sigma}$ be an arbitrary infinite occurrence sequence. If σ does not agree with α, then it contains a non-allocated transition, and we are done. If σ agrees with α, then, by the second part of the Pointing Allocation Lemma, it contains a transition of c infinitely often. This transition is not α-allocated. $\square$

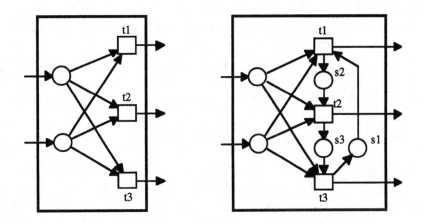

Fig. 6.5   A regulation circuit of the transitions of a cluster

We now prove that $\text{Rank}(\mathbf{N}_w) \leq |C_{N_w}| - 1$. Let $\mathcal{J}$ be the space of T-invariants of N_w. By the definition of a T-invariant, $\mathcal{J}$ is the *right kernel* of the matrix $\mathbf{N}_w$. A well-known theorem of linear algebra states

$$\text{Rank}(\mathbf{N}_w) + \dim(\mathcal{J}) = \text{number of columns of } \mathbf{N}_w$$

where $\dim(\mathcal{J})$ denotes the dimension of $\mathcal{J}$.

Since the number of columns of $\mathbf{N}_w$ is equal to the number of transitions of N_w, it suffices to prove that $\dim(\mathcal{J}) \geq |T| - |C_{N_w}| + 1$, where T is the set of transitions of N_w. We shall do it by constructing $|T| - |C_{N_w}| + 1$ linearly independent T-invariants of N_w. The construction is based on the following notion:

Definition 6.8   *Regulation circuits of sets of transitions*

Let $U = \{t_1, \ldots, t_m\}$ be a set of transitions of a net (where $t_1 \ldots t_m$ is an arbitrary fixed order). For every transition t_i of U, we define a new place s_i. The net

$$N_U = (\{s_1, \ldots, s_m\}, U, \{(s_1, t_1), (t_1, s_2), \ldots, (s_m, t_m), (t_m, s_1)\})$$

is called a regulation circuit of U.

We say that the net obtained from N and N_U by componentwise union of places, transition and arcs is the result of adding N_U to N.

We will regulate the sets of transitions of a free-choice net that belong to the same cluster, i.e., for each cluster c, we add a regulation circuit of the transitions of c. Figure 6.5 shows an example. Notice that, after the addition of such a circuit, the resulting net is non-free-choice (unless the cluster contains only one transition).

The following proposition contains two elementary properties of regulation circuits. The proof is left for an exercise.

Proposition 6.9   *Elementary properties of regulation circuits*

Let N be a net and let U be a nonempty set of transitions of N. Let N' be the net obtained by adding to N a regulation circuit N_U of U.

Given a marking M' of N', define M as the projection of M' on the places of N.

(1) If $L'_1 \xrightarrow{\sigma} L'_2$ is an occurrence sequence of N', then $L_1 \xrightarrow{\sigma} L_2$ is an occurrence sequence of N.

(2) The regulation circuit N_U is an S-component of N'.   □

We construct a set of $|T| - |C_{N_w}| + 1$ linearly independent T-invariants. The first element of this set, say J, satisfies $J(t) = J(u)$ for every two transitions t and u of the same cluster. The other T-invariants satisfy this same condition for all clusters *but one*. Moreover, the cluster that does not satisfy the condition is different for each T-invariant, which will guarantee linear independence.

Lemma 6.10

The net N_w has a positive T-invariant J such that for every two transitions t and u, if $[t] = [u]$, then $J(t) = J(u)$.

Proof:

Let M_0 be a live and bounded marking of N_w. Let N'_w be the net obtained from N_w by adding, for each cluster c, a regulation circuit of the transitions of c. Choose a marking M'_0 of N'_w which coincides with M_0 on all places of N_w and marks one place of each regulation circuit. We make the following two claims:

(i) (N'_w, M'_0) is bounded.

By the S-coverability Theorem, N_w is covered by S-components. Since both the S-components of N_w and the added regulation circuits are S-components of N'_w, the net N'_w is also covered by S-components, which proves the claim.

(ii) (N'_w, M'_0) is deadlock-free.

Let M' be a reachable marking of (N'_w, M'_0), and let M be its restriction to the places of N_w. By Proposition 6.9, M is a reachable marking of (N_w, M_0). We prove that M' enables some transition.

Since (N_w, M_0) is live and M is reachable, M enables a transition t. Since N_w is free-choice, M enables every transition of the cluster $[t]$. Since the regulation circuit of the transitions of $[t]$ is an S-component of N'_w, the total number of tokens in its set of places remains constant, and so M' marks one of its places. This place belongs to the pre-set of some transition in $[t]$, say u. Then M' enables u, and the claim is proved.

By (ii), there exists an infinite occurrence sequence $M_0' \xrightarrow{\sigma}$. By the Reproduction Lemma (Lemma 2.39), N_w' has a semi-positive T-invariant J. J is also a T-invariant of N_w because the pre- and post-set of a place of N_w coincides with its pre- and post-set in N_w'. We prove that $[t] = [u]$ implies $J(t) = J(u)$, and that J is positive.

(iii) $[t] = [u]$ implies $J(t) = J(u)$.

Since $[t] = [u]$, there exists a path $t\, s_1 t_1 \ldots t_{k-1} s_k u$ inside the regulation circuit of the transitions of $[t]$ leading from t to u. Since J is a T-invariant of N_w', and the places $s_1, \ldots, s_k$ have exactly one input and one output transition, we have

$$J(t) = J(t_1) = \ldots = J(t_{k-1}) = J(u)$$

(iv) J is positive.

Let t be a transition of $\langle J \rangle$. Since N_w is strongly connected, t has an output place s in N_w. Since J is a semi-positive T-invariant, we have ${}^\bullet\langle J \rangle = \langle J \rangle^\bullet$, and therefore $s^\bullet$ contains a transition u of $\langle J \rangle$. By (iii), $\langle J \rangle$ includes every transition of the cluster $[u]$. Since N_w is free-choice, this set is $s^\bullet$. Hence, $(\langle J \rangle^\bullet)^\bullet \subseteq \langle J \rangle$. Since $\langle J \rangle$ is non-empty and N_w is strongly connected, the set $\langle J \rangle$ contains all transitions of N_w, which implies that J is positive. $\square$

Lemma 6.11

Let t be an arbitrary transition of N_w. Then there exists a positive T-invariant J_t of N_w such that

- for every two transitions u and v, if $[u] = [v]$ and $u \neq t \neq v$, then $J_t(u) = J_t(v)$;

- for every transition u, if $[t] = [u]$ and $t \neq u$, then $J_t(t) > J_t(u)$.

Proof:

Assume $N_w = (S, T, F)$. We introduce an auxiliary net $N_w' = (S', T', F')$, defined as follows:

$S' = S$,

$T' = T \cup \{t'\}$, where t' is a new transition, and

$F' = F \cup \{(s, t') \mid s \in {}^\bullet t\} \cup \{(t', s) \mid s \in t^\bullet\}$.

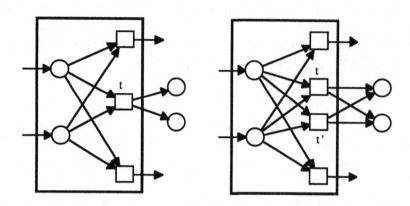

Fig. 6.6 Illustration of the proof of Lemma 6.11

Loosely speaking, N'_w is constructed by 'replicating' the transition t in N_w, i.e., t and t' have identical pre- and post-sets (see Figure 6.6). By construction, N'_w is a free-choice net.

It is easy to see that if (N_w, M_0) is live and bounded then (N'_w, M_0) is also live and bounded. So N'_w is well-formed. By Lemma 6.10 there exists a positive T-invariant J of N'_w satisfying $J(u) = J(v)$ for every two transitions u and v of the same cluster. Define the vector J' of N'_w as follows:

$$
J'(u) = \begin{cases} J(u) & \text{if } t \neq u \neq t' \\ 2 \cdot J(u) & \text{if } u = t \\ 0 & \text{if } u = t' \end{cases}
$$

Since t and t' have the same pre- and post-sets, J' is also a T-invariant of N'_w.

Let J_t be the restriction of J' to transitions of N_w. Since the pre- and post-set of a place s of N_w differ from its pre- and post-set in N'_w only with respect to t', and $J'(t') = 0$, the vector J_t is a T-invariant of N_w.

J_t is positive because every entry of J' except $J'(t')$ is positive. Moreover, if u and v are two transitions of the same cluster, different from t, then $J_t(u) = J_t(v)$ (J_t inherits this property from J'). For a transition u of the cluster $[t]$, different from t, we have

$$
J_t(t) = J'(t) = 2 \cdot J(t) = 2 \cdot J(u) = 2 \cdot J'(u) = 2 \cdot J_t(u)
$$

Since J_t is positive we have $J_t(u) > 0$. So $J_t(t) > J_t(u)$.   □

We can now prove that our set of T-invariants is linearly independent and has the required cardinality.

Proposition 6.12

Let T be the set of transitions and $\mathcal{J}$ the space of T-invariants of N_w. Then $\dim(\mathcal{J}) \geq |T| - |C_{N_w}| + 1$.

Proof:

Choose an arbitrary total allocation, and let U be the set of transitions which are *not* allocated. Since a total allocation of a well-formed free-choice net allocates $|C_{N_w}|$ transitions, we have $|U| = |T| - |C_{N_w}|$.

If $U = \emptyset$ then we only have to prove $\dim(\mathcal{J}) \geq 1$, which follows from the fact that well-formed nets have nonzero T-invariants (Theorem 2.38). So assume in the sequel $U \neq \emptyset$.

Let J be a positive T-invariant as in Lemma 6.10. Then $J(t) = J(u)$ for every two transitions t and u satisfying $[t] = [u]$. For every transition $t \in U$ define a positive T-invariant J_t as in Lemma 6.11. Then $J_t(u) = J_t(v)$ for every two transitions u and v, different from t, satisfying $[u] = [v]$. Moreover, $J_t(t) > J_t(u)$ for every transition u, different from t, satisfying $[t] = [u]$.

We show that the set $\{J\} \cup \{J_t\}_{t \in U}$ is linearly independent. The result then follows, because the cardinality of this set is $|T| - |C_{N_w}| + 1$.

Take a linear combination of the vectors of the set, with rational coefficients, equal to the null vector

$$k \cdot J + \sum_{t \in U} k_t \cdot J_t = \mathbf{0}$$

We show that all the coefficients are 0, which proves the result.

Let u be an arbitrary transition of U. By the definition of U, the cluster $[u]$ also contains a transition v that does not belong to U. We have

$$k\, J(u) + \sum_{t \in U \backslash \{u\}} k_t\, J_t(u) + k_u\, J_u(u) = 0$$

$$k\, J(v) + \sum_{t \in U \backslash \{u\}} k_t\, J_t(v) + k_u\, J_u(v) = 0$$

We also have $J(u) = J(v)$ and $J_t(u) = J_t(v)$ for every transition t of $U \backslash \{u\}$. Therefore, subtracting the second equation from the first, we get

$$k_u(J_u(u) - J_u(v)) = 0$$

Since $J_u(u) > J_u(v)$ by the definition of J_u, we obtain $k_u = 0$.

Finally, $k \neq 0$ because $J \neq \mathbf{0}$. $\square$

As discussed before, we finally get:

Proposition 6.13   *An upper bound for well-formed free-choice nets*

$\mathrm{Rank}(\mathbf{N}_w) \leq |C_{N_w}| - 1$.

Proof:

Follows from Proposition 6.12 because

$$\mathrm{Rank}(\mathbf{N}_w) = |T| + \dim(\mathcal{J})$$

where T is the set of transitions of N_w and $\mathcal{J}$ is the space of its T-invariants.   □

This result concludes the proof of the Rank Theorem.

Theorem 6.14   *The Rank Theorem*

Let N be a free-choice net. Let $\mathbf{N}$ be the incidence matrix of N and C_N the set of clusters of N. The net N is well-formed iff

  (a) it is connected, and has at least one place and one transition,

  (b) it has a positive S-invariant,

  (c) it has a positive T-invariant, and

  (d) $\mathrm{Rank}(\mathbf{N}) = |C_N| - 1$.   □

Actually, along the way we have also proved the following result (statement (A)):

Proposition 6.15   *Rank for non-well-formed free-choice nets*

Let N be a free-choice net satisfying Conditions (a), (b) and (c) of the Rank Theorem. If N is not well-formed then $\mathrm{Rank}(\mathbf{N}) \geq |C_N|$.   □

6.4   Derived results

The first interesting consequence of the Rank Theorem is that we can decide in polynomial time if a free-choice net is well-formed. The bibliographic notes contain references to papers which carry out a more detailed complexity analysis.

Corollary 6.16   *Complexity of the well-formedness problem*

The following problem can be solved in polynomial time:

    Given a free-choice net, to decide if it is well-formed.

Proof:

Let $N = (S, T, F)$ be a free-choice net. It is easy to decide if N is connected, and has at least one place and one transition. The existence of a positive S-invariant can be decided by solving the system of linear inequations

$$I \cdot \mathbf{N} = 0$$
$$I \geq (1, \dots, 1)$$

in the field of the rational numbers. Since all the elements of $\mathbf{N}$ belong to the set $\{-1, 0, 1\}$, the size of this problem is $O(|S| \cdot |T|)$. It is well-known that systems of linear inequations can be solved in polynomial time using linear programming algorithms (see the bibliographic notes). So the existence of a positive S-invariant can be decided in polynomial time in the size on N. The same result holds for the existence of a positive T-invariant. The rank of $\mathbf{N}$ can also be computed in polynomial time using well-known methods of linear algebra. Finally, the clusters of N can be counted in polynomial time in the size of N. □

Now, we can easily prove that deciding if a free-choice system (N, M_0) is live and bounded is also a polynomial problem. We characterize in the next theorem the live and bounded markings of a well-formed free-choice net.

Theorem 6.17 *Characterization of live and bounded free-choice systems*

A free-choice system (N, M_0) is live and bounded iff

  (i) N is well-formed, and

  (ii) M_0 marks every proper siphon of N.

Proof:

($\Rightarrow$): N is well-formed because it has a live and bounded marking. By Commoner's Theorem, every proper siphon of N includes a marked trap and is thus marked itself.

($\Leftarrow$): Since N is well-formed by (i), it is covered by S-components and therefore (N, M_0) is bounded (Theorem 5.8(2)).

We show that (N, M_0) is live. Let R be an arbitrary siphon of N. Then R includes a minimal siphon Q which, by (ii), is marked at M_0. Since minimal siphons of well-formed free-choice nets are traps (Proposition 5.4), Q is a trap. Therefore, R includes an initially marked trap. By Commoner's Theorem, (N, M_0) is live. □

Corollary 6.18   *Complexity of the liveness and boundedness problem*

The following problem can be solved in polynomial time:

Given a free-choice system, to decide if it is live and bounded.

Proof:

Let (N, M_0) be a free-choice system. We show that Conditions (i) and (ii) of Theorem 6.17 can be checked in polynomial time in the size of the net N. By the definition of a system, N is connected, and has at least one place and at least one transition. By Corollary 6.16, we can decide in polynomial time if N is well-formed. Let R be the set of places of N which are not marked by M_0. Every proper siphon of N is marked at M_0 iff the only siphon included in R is the empty siphon. The algorithm given in Exercise 4.5 computes the maximal trap included in a given set of places. By exchanging pre- and post-sets, it can be easily transformed into an algorithm that computes the maximal siphon. Therefore, every proper siphon of N is marked at M_0 iff this transformed algorithm, applied to the set R, yields the empty set as output. Since the algorithm runs in polynomial time in the size of N, the result follows.   □

Free-choice nets are invariant under the transformation consisting of interchanging places and transitions and reversing the arcs of the net (a proof is given below). We study this transformation in the remainder of this section.

Definition 6.19   *Dual nets*

Let $N = (S, T, F)$ be a net. The net $N^d = (T, S, F^{-1})$ is the dual net of N.[3]

Proposition 6.20   *Elementary properties of dual nets*

(1) The dual net of N^d is N.

(2) If N is a free-choice net then so is N^d.

(3) Every cluster of N is a cluster of N^d.

(4) The incidence matrix of N^d is the transposed of $\mathbf{N}$.

(5) Every S-invariant of N is a T-invariant of N^d, and every T-invariant of N is an S-invariant of N^d.

(6) Every S-component of N is a T-component of N^d, and every T-component of N is an S-component of N^d.

_____

[3]In some texts N^d is called the *reverse-dual* of N.

Proof:

Let $N = (S, T, F)$ and $N^d = (S^d, T^d, F^d)$. We have $S^d = T$, $T^d = S$ and $F^d = F^{-1}$ by the definition of N^d.

(1), (3), (5) and (6) follow easily from the definitions.

(2) We denote by ${}^\bullet(x)_N$ the pre-set of a node x in N and by ${}^\bullet(x)_{N^d}$ the pre-set of x in N^d, and use the corresponding notation for post-sets. By the definition of N^d we have ${}^\bullet(x)_N = (x)^\bullet_{N^d}$ and $(x)^\bullet_N = {}^\bullet(x)_{N^d}$.

Assume that N is a free-choice net. Let (x, y) be an arbitrary element of $F^d \cap (S^d \times T^d)$. By the definition of N^d, we have $(y, x) \in F \cap (S \times T)$. Since N is free-choice, ${}^\bullet(x)_N \times (y)^\bullet_N \subseteq F$. Then, $(x)^\bullet_{N^d} \times {}^\bullet(y)_{N^d} \subseteq F$. This is equivalent to ${}^\bullet(y)_{N^d} \times (x)^\bullet_{N^d} \subseteq F^d$, which proves that N^d is free-choice.

(4) Let $\mathbf{N}^d$ be the incidence matrix of N^d, and let s and t be a place and a transition of N, respectively. We have

$$
\begin{aligned}
\mathbf{N}^d(t, s) &= |(t, s) \cap F^d| - |(s, t) \cap F^d| \\
&= |(s, t) \cap F| - |(t, s) \cap F| \\
&= \mathbf{N}(s, t)
\end{aligned}
$$

$\square$

When we add a notion of behaviour to nets – through the introduction of markings and the occurrence rule – the symmetry between places and transitions is broken: only places can contain tokens, and only transitions can occur. Therefore, one does not expect to find general relationships between behavioural properties of a net and behavioural properties of its dual net. However, such a relationship turns out to exist for free-choice nets.

Theorem 6.21   *Duality Theorem*

N is a well-formed free-choice net iff N^d is a well-formed free-choice net.

Proof:

By Proposition 6.20(1) and (2), N is a free-choice net iff N^d is a free-choice net. By Proposition 6.20(5), N has a positive S-invariant iff N^d has a positive T-invariant, and N has a positive T-invariant iff N^d has a positive S-invariant. By Proposition 6.20(4), the rank of $\mathbf{N}$ is equal to the rank of $\mathbf{N}^d$. By Proposition 6.20(3), the number of clusters of N is equal to the number of clusters of N^d.

Then, by the Rank Theorem, N is a well-formed free-choice net iff N^d is a well-formed free-choice net.

$\square$

Any of the two Coverability Theorems is a consequence of the other one and the Duality Theorem, because a net is covered by S-components if and only if its dual is covered by T-components.

The major interest of the Duality Theorem – as it happens with results of similar flavour in other branches of Mathematics – is its use as a 'metatheorem'. In the following chapters, we will use the Duality Theorem to prove dual versions of several propositions on well-formed free-choice nets.

Exercises

Exercise 6.1

Give an algorithm that accepts a strongly connected free-choice net N and a nonempty set C of clusters of N as input, and returns a total allocation that points to C.

Exercise 6.2

Prove Proposition 6.9.

Exercise 6.3

Prove that none of the conditions of the Rank Theorem can be dropped by exhibiting suitable counterexamples.

Exercise 6.4

Prove that the rank of the incidence matrix of an *arbitrary* S-system is equal to its number of places minus 1. Prove that the rank of the incidence matrix of an arbitrary T-system is equal to its number of transitions minus 1.

Exercise 6.5

1) Prove an analogon of Theorem 5.17 for minimal S-invariants: Let I be a minimal S-invariant of a well-formed free-choice net N, and let N_I be the subnet generated by $^\bullet\langle I\rangle \cup \langle I\rangle \cup \langle I\rangle^\bullet$. Then N_I is an S-component of N.
   Hint: Use the Duality Theorem.

2) * Prove the same result *without* appeal to the Duality Theorem.
   Hint: Prove first that the support of a minimal S-invariant is a minimal siphon.

Exercise 6.6

Exhibit a well-formed, non-free-choice net whose dual net is not well-formed.

Exercise 6.7   * Let $N = (S, T, F)$ be a well-formed free-choice net, and M_0 a marking of N. Let N^d be the dual net of N. Consider the following partition of the set S of transitions of N^d into internal and observable transitions:

$$S_O = \{s \in S \mid M_0(s) \geq 1\}$$
$$S_I = S \setminus S_O$$

Show that (N, M_0) is live and bounded iff N^d with the given partition is non-divergent.

Bibliographic Notes

The basic notions of linear algebra used in the chapter (e.g. linear independence or rank of a matrix) can be found in any introductory textbook on algebra. A good reference is the book of Cohn [16].

The Rank Theorem was stated by Campos, Chiola and Silva in [13]. Unfortunately, the proof of [13] contains a major gap (see [22]). Using results of the following chapter, Esparza proved a slightly weaker version of the theorem in [28]. The proof given in the text is an improved version of that presented by Desel in [21, 22].

The proof of Corollary 6.16 (polynomiality of the well-formedness problem) given in the text relies on the fact that systems of linear inequations can be solved in polynomial time. This was first shown by Khachiyan [55], and a more efficient algorithm was later presented by Karmarkar [52]. The simplex algorithm is still the most popular to solve these systems, because, even though it needs exponential time in the worst case, it has an excellent average complexity. A good reference on the simplex algorithm is the book of Chvatal [15].

Corollary 6.16 can also be proved without resorting to sophisticated results about systems of linear inequations. Using the version of the Rank Theorem presented in [28], Kemper and Bause [54] and Kemper [53] have developed an algorithm to recognize well-formed free-choice nets in $O(|S|^2|T|)$ time, where S and T are the sets of places and transitions of the net.

The Duality Theorem was proved by Hack in [42]. Other proofs were given by Desel in [21] and Esparza and Silva [31]. Silva observed that the Duality Theorem is a corollary of the Rank Theorem.

Besides Proposition 6.1 and the Rank Theorem, there exist other characterizations of well-formed free-choice nets. Esparza and Silva present a graph-theoretic characterization in [31], and a compositional characterization in [33] (see also [27]).

Chapter 7 ————————————————

Reduction and synthesis

We present in this chapter an alternative method for the analysis of well-formedness. The method makes use of a kit of so called *reduction rules*. A reduction rule transforms a free-choice net into a simpler one while preserving well-formedness; more precisely, the reduced net is well-formed if and only if the original net is well-formed. The kit of rules we present reduces all and only well-formed free-choice nets to the net of this picture:

It follows that well-formedness of a free-choice net can be decided by applying the rules of the kit as long as possible, and then checking if the final result is the net of the picture. This new algorithm is not as efficient as the one derived from the Rank Theorem. However, it is interesting for two reasons. First, it provides more information about *why* a certain net is not well-formed. Second, and more important, the reduction rules can be "reversed" to obtain *synthesis rules*. The kit of inverse rules generates all and only well-formed free-choice nets starting from the net of the picture.

The reduction algorithm for well-formedness can be easily transformed into an algorithm to check liveness and boundedness of free-choice systems. It suffices to use the characterization of live and bounded markings given in Theorem 6.17, which states that a free-choice system (N, M_0) is live and bounded iff N is well-formed, and M_0 marks every proper siphon of N. Then, to decide if a free-choice system is live and bounded, we first check if every proper siphon is marked. If the system passes this test, we apply the reduction algorithm to its underlying net.

The chapter is organized as follows. Section 7.1 introduces the basic vocabulary we use to speak about reductions. Section 7.2 describes the reduction rules and shows that they preserve well-formedness. Section 7.3 exhibits an example of reduction. Section 7.4 contains the completeness result. So-called CP-subnets play an important role in the proof of this result, and they are introduced and studied in this section. Finally, Section 7.5 shows how to derive a synthesis procedure from the reduction rules.

7.1   Basic notions

A *transformation rule* (or just a *rule*) ϕ is a binary relation on the class of all free-choice nets[1]. Given $(N, \tilde{N}) \in \phi$, the net N is called *source net* and $\tilde{N}$ is called *target net*. $(N, \tilde{N}) \in \phi$ is read "the rule ϕ can transform N into $\tilde{N}$".

A rule ϕ is *applicable* to a net N if there exists another net $\tilde{N}$ such that $(N, \tilde{N}) \in \phi$. A set Φ of rules is called a *kit*. A net N can be transformed into $\tilde{N}$ by the kit Φ if the successive application of rules of Φ can transform N into $\tilde{N}$.

We reserve the name *reduction rule* for rules which transform a source net into a target net with *fewer* nodes. The rules which *increase* the number of nodes are called *synthesis rules*.

We are interested in rules that preserve well-formedness.

A rule ϕ is *sound* if it satisfies for every $(N, \tilde{N}) \in \phi$

>   if N is well-formed then $\tilde{N}$ is well-formed,

A rule ϕ is *strongly sound* if it satisfies for every $(N, \tilde{N}) \in \phi$

> N is well-formed if and only if $\tilde{N}$ is well-formed.

A kit of rules is (strongly) sound if all its elements are (strongly) sound. Clearly, strong soundness implies soundness.

A net is *atomic* if it is isomorphic to the net $(\{s\}, \{t\}, \{(s, t), (t, s)\})$, or, equivalently, if it has two nodes and is strongly connected). Essentially, there exists one atomic net, namely the net shown in the introduction to this chapter. It is easy to see that the atomic nets are the well-formed free-choice nets with the smallest possible number of nodes. A kit of reduction rules is *complete* if it can reduce all well-formed free-choice nets to atomic nets.

A strongly sound and complete kit of reduction rules reduces all and only the well-formed free-choice nets to atomic nets. Therefore, in order to verify if a free-choice net is well-formed, it suffices to exhaustively apply the rules of the kit, and then check if the final result is an atomic net. Notice that this procedure no longer works if the kit is only sound: such a kit may reduce not only well-formed, but also non-well-formed nets to atomic nets.

---

[1] We consider it conceptually convenient to define transformation rules in this generality, even though we shall only be interested in a small fragment of the possible rules (particularly, in those which are efficiently decidable).

If a sound synthesis rule ϕ is applied to a well-formed free-choice net, it yields a *larger* well-formed free-choice net. Therefore, when starting from an atomic net, a sound kit of synthesis rules generates only well-formed free-choice nets. It generates *all* well-formed free-choice nets if the kit of inverse rules, which are reduction rules, is complete.

7.2 The reduction rules

This section describes a set of reduction rules. For every rule, we first give the *conditions of application* which describe the nets to which the rule is applicable. Then, we explain how to transform the source net into the target net.

The abstraction rule

The abstraction rule is graphically described in Figure 7.1. In the figure, after the occurrence of an input transition of s the transition t can occur. Moreover, t can only be disabled by its own occurrence. The reduction hides the occurrence of t by merging t with the input transitions of s. A dual interpretation is that the local state s is hidden by merging the place s with the output places of t.

The textual description of the rule is as follows.

Rule 1 *The rule ϕ_A*

> *Let N and $\tilde{N}$ be two free-choice nets, where $N = (S, T, F)$ and $\tilde{N} = (\tilde{S}, \tilde{T}, \tilde{F})$. $(N, \tilde{N}) \in \phi_A$ if there exist a place $s \in S$ and a transition $t \in T$ such that:*

Conditions on N:

1. ${}^{\bullet}s \neq \emptyset$, $s^{\bullet} = \{t\}$
2. $t^{\bullet} \neq \emptyset$, ${}^{\bullet}t = \{s\}$
3. $({}^{\bullet}s \times t^{\bullet}) \cap F = \emptyset$

Construction of $\tilde{N}$:

4. $\tilde{S} = S \setminus \{s\}$
5. $\tilde{T} = T \setminus \{t\}$
6. $\tilde{F} = (\, F \cap ((\tilde{S} \times \tilde{T}) \cup (\tilde{T} \times \tilde{S}))\,) \cup ({}^{\bullet}s \times t^{\bullet})$

(where the dot-notation is taken with respect to N).

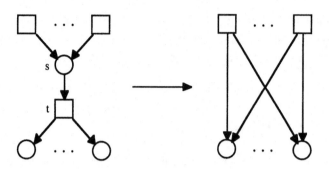

Fig. 7.1   The rule ϕ_A

Some rules similar to ϕ_A are discussed in the exercises.

The rule ϕ_A is strongly sound even if the source and target nets are allowed to be arbitrary nets, not necessarily free-choice. Exercise 7.2 provides a proof sketch of this fact. Here, we only prove strong soundness in the free-choice case, by means of the Rank Theorem.

Theorem 7.1   *Strong soundness of ϕ_A*

   ϕ_A is strongly sound.

Proof:

Let $(N, \tilde{N})$ be an arbitrary element of ϕ_A, where $N = (S, T, F)$ and $\tilde{N} = (\tilde{S}, \tilde{T}, \tilde{F})$. To prove strong soundness, we shall show that N satisfies the conditions for well-formedness given in the Rank Theorem if and only if $\tilde{N}$ satisfies them.

By the definition of ϕ_A, we have $\tilde{S} = S \setminus \{s\}$ and $\tilde{T} = T \setminus \{t\}$ for some s and t.

It is easy to see that the target net $\tilde{N}$ can be obtained from N in two steps as follows (along the proof, the pre-sets and post-sets always refer to the net N):

(a) For every transition $u \in {}^\bullet s$, remove the arc (u, s) and add arcs (u, r) for all places $r \in t^\bullet$ (these arcs did not exist before by Condition 3 of ϕ_A).

(b) Remove s, t, and their adjacent arcs.

We describe these two steps in terms of incidence matrices. For that, we first fix an order for the places and the transitions of N, and assume without loss of generality that the last row of the incidence matrix $\mathbf{N}$ of N is $\mathbf{s}$, and its last column is $\mathbf{t}$.

Let $N' = (S, T, F')$ be the net obtained after Step (a). We have

$$F' = F \setminus ({}^\bullet s \times \{s\}) \cup ({}^\bullet s \times t^\bullet)$$

Since $^\bullet t = \{s\}$ by Condition 2 and since $(^\bullet s \times t^\bullet) \cap F = \emptyset$ by Condition 3, the incidence matrix $\mathbf{N}'$ of N' is obtained from $\mathbf{N}$ by adding the column $\mathbf{t}$ to all the columns corresponding to the transitions of $^\bullet s$ (note that also by Condition 3, we have $t \notin {}^\bullet s$).

Define the $(T \times T)$-matrices A and A^{-1} as follows:

$$A(u, v) = \begin{cases} 1 & \text{if } u = v \\ 1 & \text{if } u = t \text{ and } v \in {}^\bullet s \\ 0 & \text{otherwise} \end{cases} \qquad A^{-1}(u, v) = \begin{cases} 1 & \text{if } u = v \\ -1 & \text{if } u = t \text{ and } v \in {}^\bullet s \\ 0 & \text{otherwise} \end{cases}$$

The matrix A^{-1} is well defined because $t \notin {}^\bullet s$ by Condition 3. Both A and A^{-1} coincide with the identity matrix everywhere except in the last row (recall that we assumed that the transition t corresponds to the last row).

It can be easily verified that A^{-1} is the inverse of A. Moreover, we have

$$\mathbf{N}' = \mathbf{N} \cdot A \qquad \mathbf{N} = \mathbf{N}' \cdot A^{-1}$$

In terms of incidence matrices, Step (b) corresponds to the deletion of the last row and the last column of $\mathbf{N}'$. Since the place s has an empty pre-set in the net N', the incidence matrix $\mathbf{N}'$ can be decomposed in the following way:

$$\mathbf{N}' = \begin{pmatrix} \tilde{\mathbf{N}} & B \\ 0 \ldots 0 & -1 \end{pmatrix} \quad \text{where} \quad \begin{pmatrix} B \\ -1 \end{pmatrix} \text{ is the last column of } \mathbf{N}.$$

We make the following four claims:

(i) N has a positive S-invariant iff $\tilde{N}$ has a positive S-invariant.

($\Rightarrow$): Let I be a positive S-invariant of N. Then $I \cdot \mathbf{N} = 0$, and so

$$I \cdot \mathbf{N} \cdot A = I \cdot \mathbf{N}' = 0.$$

Let $\tilde{I}$ be the vector composed by the first $|S| - 1$ components of I. By the matrix decomposition of $\mathbf{N}'$, we have $\tilde{I} \cdot \tilde{\mathbf{N}} = 0$. and therefore $\tilde{I}$ is a positive S-invariant of $\tilde{N}$.

($\Leftarrow$): Let $\tilde{I}$ be a positive S-invariant of $\tilde{N}$, and define $x = \tilde{I} \cdot B$. By Condition 2 of the rule ϕ_A, we have $^\bullet t = \{s\}$, which implies that no entry of B is negative, and $t^\bullet \neq \emptyset$, which implies that some entry of B is nonzero. Therefore, since $\tilde{I}$ is positive, we have $x > 0$. Define $I = (\tilde{I}\ x)$, i.e., I is the vector obtained by appending the entry x to the vector $\tilde{I}$. Since $x > 0$, the vector I is positive. By the matrix decomposition of $\mathbf{N}'$ and the construction of I we have $I \cdot \mathbf{N}' = 0$. Hence

$$I \cdot \mathbf{N} = I \cdot \mathbf{N}' \cdot A^{-1} = 0$$

which implies that I is a positive S-invariant of N.

(ii) N has a positive T-invariant iff $\tilde{N}$ has a positive T-invariant.

($\Rightarrow$): Let J be a positive T-invariant of N. Then $\mathbf{N} \cdot J = \mathbf{0}$, and therefore $\mathbf{N}' \cdot A^{-1} \cdot J = \mathbf{0}$. Define $J' = A^{-1} \cdot J$. Since, in the last row of $\mathbf{N}'$, only the last component is nonzero, the last entry of J' must be 0. Let $\tilde{J}$ be the vector composed by the first $|T| - 1$ components of J'. By the matrix decomposition of $\mathbf{N}'$, and since the last entry of J' is 0, we have $\tilde{\mathbf{N}} \cdot \tilde{J} = \mathbf{0}$, and so $\tilde{J}$ is a T-invariant of $\tilde{N}$. By the definition of A^{-1}, the vectors J and J' coincide in every component but the last one. Hence, since J is positive, so is $\tilde{J}$.

($\Leftarrow$): Let $\tilde{J}$ be a positive T-invariant of $\tilde{N}$. Define $J' = (\tilde{J}\ 0)$, i.e., J' is the result of appending a null entry to $\tilde{J}$. By the matrix decomposition of $\mathbf{N}'$, we have $\mathbf{N}' \cdot J' = \mathbf{0}$. Therefore, $\mathbf{N} \cdot A \cdot J' = \mathbf{0}$, i.e., $A \cdot J'$ is a T-invariant of N. By the definition of A, the vectors J' and $A \cdot J'$ coincide in every component but the last one. The last entry of $A \cdot J'$ is $\sum_{u \in {}^\bullet s} \tilde{J}(u)$. Since ${}^\bullet s \neq \emptyset$ by Condition 1 of ϕ_A, this last entry is positive. Since $\tilde{J}$ is positive, $A \cdot J'$ is positive.

(iii) $\mathrm{Rank}(\mathbf{N}) = \mathrm{Rank}(\tilde{\mathbf{N}}) + 1$.

We have $\mathrm{Rank}(\mathbf{N}) = \mathrm{Rank}(\mathbf{N}')$ since $\mathbf{N}' = \mathbf{N} \cdot A$ and A is an invertible matrix. $\mathrm{Rank}(\mathbf{N}') = \mathrm{Rank}(\tilde{\mathbf{N}}) + 1$ follows immediately from the matrix decomposition of $\mathbf{N}'$.

(iv) N has exactly one more cluster than $\tilde{N}$.

Every cluster of $\tilde{N}$ is a cluster of N. Additionally, N contains the cluster $\{s, t\}$.

By the definition of ϕ_A, the net N is connected and contains at least one place and one transition iff the target net $\tilde{N}$ satisfies these same conditions. So, by (i) to (iv), N satisfies the conditions of the Rank Theorem iff $\tilde{N}$ satisfies them. So the Rank Theorem implies that N is well-formed iff $\tilde{N}$ is well-formed. $\square$

Since the strong soundness of ϕ_A is intuitively rather obvious, the length of this proof may seem surprising. Notice that we have to prove not only that if the source net is well-formed the target net is well-formed, but also that if the source net is not well-formed the target net is not well-formed. This proof obligation is partially responsible of the complications. It is also worth mentioning that former versions of this theorem – in which the proof was considerably shorter because some steps were omitted – turned out to be wrong: we had forgotten to include a small but important condition in the rule.

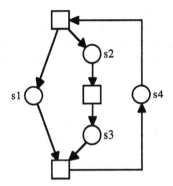

Fig. 7.2 s_1 is a nonnegative linearly dependent place

Linear dependency rules

The second and third rules consist in the removal of certain nodes of the net, places in the case of the second rule and transitions in the case of the third.

Definition 7.2 *Linearly dependent nodes*

Let N be a net, $N = (S, T, F)$. A place s of N is linearly dependent if there exists a vector $\Lambda \colon S \to \mathbb{Q}$ such that $\Lambda(s) = 0$ and $\Lambda \cdot \mathbf{N} = \mathbf{s}$.

A transition t of N is linearly dependent if there exists a vector $\Lambda \colon T \to \mathbb{Q}$ such that $\Lambda(t) = 0$ and $\mathbf{N} \cdot \Lambda = \mathbf{t}$.

The linearly dependent place s (respectively, transition t) is nonnegatively linearly dependent if moreover $\Lambda \geq 0$.

In the net of Figure 7.2, we have $\mathbf{s_1} = \mathbf{s_2} + \mathbf{s_3}$, and therefore s_1 is a linearly dependent place, even a nonnegative one.

Clearly, the removal of a linearly dependent place or transition does not change the rank of the incidence matrix. The Rank Theorem suggests that the removal of such a node might preserve well-formedness. We shall see that this is the case if the node is *nonnegative* linearly dependent.

A linearly dependent place enjoys an important property: the change of its number of tokens produced by an occurrence sequence is a linear function in the changes of the number of tokens in other places. To prove it, let s be a linearly dependent place of a net N, and let $M_1 \xrightarrow{\sigma} M_2$ be an occurrence sequence. Because of the Marking Equation, we have

$$M_2(s) - M_1(s) = \mathbf{s} \cdot \vec{\sigma} = \Lambda \cdot \mathbf{N} \cdot \vec{\sigma} = \Lambda \cdot (M_2 - M_1)$$

For the formulation of the second rule, we introduce the following notation. Given a net N and a node x of N, we denote by $N \backslash \{x\}$ the subnet of N obtained by removing the node x from N together with its adjacent arcs (equivalently, $N \backslash \{x\}$ is the subnet of N generated by all the nodes of N except x).

Rule 2 *The rule ϕ_S*

Let N and $\tilde{N}$ be two free-choice nets. $(N, \tilde{N}) \in \phi_S$ if:

Conditions on N:

1. N contains at least two places

2. N contains a nonnegative linearly dependent place s

3. ${}^{\bullet}s \cup s^{\bullet} \neq \emptyset$, i.e., s is not an isolated place

Construction of $\tilde{N}$:

4. $\tilde{N} = N \backslash \{s\}$

It could seem that Condition 2 and Condition 3 imply Condition 1, but this is not the case: every atomic net satisfies Condition 2 (take $\Lambda = 0$) and Condition 3, but contains only one place.

Theorem 7.3   *Strong soundness of ϕ_S*

ϕ_S is strongly sound.

Proof:

Let $(N, \tilde{N})$ be an arbitrary element of ϕ_S. To prove strong soundness, we shall show that N satisfies the conditions of the Rank Theorem iff $\tilde{N}$ satisfies them.

By the definition of ϕ_S, we have $\tilde{N} = N \backslash \{s\}$ for some nonnegative linearly dependent place s. Then, $\Lambda \cdot \tilde{\mathbf{N}} = \mathbf{s}$ for some nonnegative vector Λ. Assume without loss of generality that $\mathbf{s}$ is the last row of $\mathbf{N}$. We prove

(i) N has a positive S-invariant iff $\tilde{N}$ has a positive S-invariant.

($\Rightarrow$): Let I be a positive S-invariant of N, and let $\tilde{I}$ be the vector obtained by removing the last entry of I. Since the last row of $\mathbf{N}$ is equal to $\Lambda \cdot \tilde{\mathbf{N}}$, we have

$$\mathbf{0} = I \cdot \mathbf{N} = \tilde{I} \cdot \tilde{\mathbf{N}} + I(s) \cdot \Lambda \cdot \tilde{\mathbf{N}} = (\tilde{I} + I(s) \cdot \Lambda) \cdot \tilde{\mathbf{N}}$$

$(\tilde{I} + I(s) \cdot \Lambda)$ is a positive S-invariant of $\tilde{N}$ because $\tilde{I}$ is positive, $I(s) > 0$, and Λ is nonnegative.

($\Leftarrow$): Let $\tilde{I}$ be a positive S-invariant of $\tilde{N}$. Assume $\tilde{I} > \Lambda$ without loss of generality (if this is not the case, $\tilde{I}$ can be multiplied by an adequate positive constant). Let $I = ((\tilde{I} - \Lambda) \ 1)$, i.e., I coincides with $\tilde{I} - \Lambda$ on all places different from s, and $I(s) = 1$. By construction, I is positive. Since the last row of $\mathbf{N}$ is equal to $\Lambda \cdot \tilde{\mathbf{N}}$ we have

$$I \cdot \mathbf{N} = (\tilde{I} - \Lambda) \cdot \tilde{\mathbf{N}} + \Lambda \cdot \tilde{\mathbf{N}} = \tilde{I} \cdot \tilde{\mathbf{N}} = 0$$

which implies that I is a positive S-invariant of N.

(ii) N has a positive T-invariant iff $\tilde{N}$ has a positive T-invariant.

($\Rightarrow$): Let J be a positive T-invariant of N. Since every row of $\tilde{\mathbf{N}}$ is also a row of $\mathbf{N}$, J is also a positive T-invariant of $\tilde{N}$.

($\Leftarrow$): Let $\tilde{J}$ be a positive T-invariant of $\tilde{N}$. Since the last row of $\mathbf{N}$ is equal to $\Lambda \cdot \tilde{\mathbf{N}}$, we have:

$$\mathbf{N} \cdot \tilde{J} = \begin{pmatrix} \tilde{\mathbf{N}} \cdot \tilde{J} \\ \Lambda \cdot \tilde{\mathbf{N}} \cdot \tilde{J} \end{pmatrix} = 0$$

which implies that $\tilde{J}$ is a positive T-invariant of $\tilde{N}$.

(iii) $\mathrm{Rank}(\mathbf{N}) = \mathrm{Rank}(\tilde{\mathbf{N}})$.

This is obvious, because $\mathbf{s}$ is a linear combination of the rows of $\tilde{\mathbf{N}}$.

(iv) If $s^{\bullet} \neq \emptyset$ then N and $\tilde{N}$ have the same number of clusters.

Assume $s^{\bullet} \neq \emptyset$. Let c be a cluster of N, and consider two cases:

Case 1. $s \notin c$. Then c is also a cluster of $\tilde{N}$.

Case 2. $s \in c$. Since $s^{\bullet} \neq \emptyset$, we have $c \setminus \{s\} \neq \emptyset$. Since N is free-choice, every place of $c \setminus \{s\}$ is connected to all transitions of $c \setminus \{s\}$. Hence $c \setminus \{s\}$ is a cluster of $\tilde{N}$.

Since every node of $\tilde{N}$ is a node of N, a cluster c of $\tilde{N}$ is either itself a cluster of N or $c \cup \{s\}$ is a cluster of N. So N and $\tilde{N}$ have the same number of clusters.

We now show that N is well-formed iff $\tilde{N}$ is well-formed.

($\Rightarrow$): Assume that N is well-formed. Then, it satisfies the four conditions of the Rank Theorem. Moreover, it is strongly connected, which implies in particular $s^\bullet \neq \emptyset$. Therefore, using (i) to (iv), we get that $\tilde{N}$ satisfies the last three of these four conditions. For proving that $\tilde{N}$ is well-formed it remains to show that $\tilde{N}$ is weakly connected and contains at least one place and one transition (which is the first condition of the Rank Theorem). The net N has at least one transition because it is well-formed. It also has at least two places by Condition 1. So $\tilde{N}$ has at least one place and one transition. For showing that $\tilde{N}$ is weakly connected, we first claim that the cluster $[s]$ of N has more than one place.

Case 1: s = 0.

Then $^\bullet s = s^\bullet$. Since N is strongly connected and has more than one place, s has some input transition t which has some input place r different from s. Since t is also an output transition of s we get $[s] = [r]$.

Case 2: s $\neq$ 0.

The vector $\mathbf{s}$ cannot be semi-positive since otherwise some transition adds tokens to s whereas no transition reduces the number of tokens on s, and so no marking could be live and bounded. Therefore, $\mathbf{s}(t) < 0$ for some transition t, i.e., $t \in s^\bullet$. Since s is nonnegative linearly dependent, some place r different from s also satisfies $\mathbf{r}(t) < 0$. This implies $t \in r^\bullet$. So t is a common output transition of s and r and therefore $[s] = [r]$, which finishes the proof of the claim.

For every node x of N there is a path from s to x since N is strongly connected. Therefore, for every node x of $\tilde{N}$, there is a path in $\tilde{N}$ from an output transition of s to x. Since s and r have the same output transitions, $\tilde{N}$ is weakly connected.

We now apply the Rank Theorem to $\tilde{N}$. Since N is strongly connected, we have $s^\bullet \neq \emptyset$. By (iv), $\tilde{N}$ has the same number of clusters as N. By (i) to (iii) and the Rank Theorem, $\tilde{N}$ is well-formed.

($\Leftarrow$): Assume that $\tilde{N}$ is well-formed. By the Rank Theorem, it has a positive S-invariant and a positive T-invariant. Since N contains every node of $\tilde{N}$, it contains in particular one place and one transition. Since s is not an isolated place, N is at least weakly connected. By (i) and (ii), N has a positive S-invariant and a positive T-invariant. So N is strongly connected by Theorem 2.40. Therefore, the place s has at least one output transition. By (iii) and (iv), N satisfies the Rank Equation. By the Rank Theorem, N is well-formed.   □

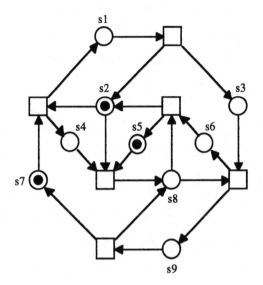

Fig. 7.3 The rule ϕ_S is not strongly sound for arbitrary nets

We point out two limitations of the rule ϕ_S:

- Loosely speaking, a rule is *local* if, in order to check its conditions of application, only the neighbourhood of the intended point of application has to be examined, and the changes affect only this neighbourhood. The rule ϕ_A is an example of a local rule: in order to check its conditions of application, it suffices to examine the pre-sets and post-sets of a place s and a transition t, the post-sets of the transitions in $\bullet s$ and the pre-sets of the places in $t\bullet$. On the contrary, the rule ϕ_S is non-local, because in order to find the linear combination proving that s is nonnegative linearly dependent it may be necessary to examine the whole net.

- The rule ϕ_S is not strongly sound for arbitrary nets. The non-free-choice net of Figure 7.3 is well-formed, because the marking shown in the figure is live and bounded. The place s_2 is nonnegative linearly dependent, because

$$s_2 = s_3 + s_5 + s_7 + s_9$$

However, after removing s_2, the remaining net is not well-formed. To prove it, observe that from any live marking it is possible to reach a marking which puts tokens on s_3 and s_8. From this marking, the transitions of the outer circuit can occur infinitely often, putting arbitrarily many tokens on s_4 and s_6.

Our last rule consists in the removal of nonnegative linearly dependent transitions.

Rule 3 *The rule ϕ_T*

Let N and $\tilde{N}$ be two free-choice nets. $(N, \tilde{N}) \in \phi_T$ if:

Conditions on N:

1. N contains at least two transitions

2. N contains a nonnegative linearly dependent transition t

3. ${}^\bullet t \cup t^\bullet \neq \emptyset$, i.e., t is not an isolated transition

Construction of $\tilde{N}$:

4. $\tilde{N} = N \backslash \{t\}$

Theorem 7.4   *Strong soundness of ϕ_T*

ϕ_T is strongly sound.

Proof:

Let $(N, \tilde{N})$ be an arbitrary element of ϕ_T. Then, $\tilde{N} = N \backslash \{t\}$ for some nonnegative linearly dependent transition t of N.

The dual net N^d is free-choice and contains at least two transitions, because N contains at least two places. Since the incidence matrix of N^d is the transposed of the incidence matrix of N, the transition t of N is a nonnegative linearly dependent place of N^d. Moreover, t is not an isolated place of N^d because it is not an isolated place of N. Therefore, $(N^d, \tilde{N}^d)$ belongs to ϕ_S. We now have

$$
\begin{aligned}
N \text{ is well-formed} \;\; &\Leftrightarrow \;\; N^d \text{ is well-formed} \quad &&\text{(Duality Theorem)} \\
&\Leftrightarrow \;\; \tilde{N}^d \text{ is well-formed} \quad &&\text{(Strong soundness of } \phi_S) \\
&\Leftrightarrow \;\; \tilde{N} \text{ is well-formed} \quad &&\text{(Duality Theorem)}
\end{aligned}
$$

□

We finish the section with an observation about the complexity of deciding if a rule of the kit $\{\phi_A, \phi_S, \phi_T\}$ is applicable.

Proposition 7.5   *Complexity of deciding if a rule is applicable*

The following problem can be solved in polynomial time:

Given a free-choice net, to decide if ϕ_A, ϕ_S or ϕ_T is applicable to it.

Proof:

In the case of ϕ_A, the result is obvious. Condition 1 and Condition 3 of ϕ_S can be easily checked in polynomial time. For Condition 2, we recall that a place s of a net N is nonnegative linearly dependent if the equation system $\Lambda \cdot \mathbf{N} = \mathbf{s}$ has a nonnegative solution satisfying $\Lambda(s) = 0$. Using linear programming, the existence of such a solution can be decided in polynomial time in the size of the equation system, which is polynomial in the size of the net. To decide if ϕ_S is applicable, at most $|S|$ equation systems have to be considered, where S is the set of places of the net. Therefore, deciding if ϕ_S is applicable is a polynomial problem. A similar argument proves the same result for ϕ_T. $\qquad\square$

Since the transformation caused by an applicable rule can also be performed in polynomial time, the kit of reduction rules provides a polynomial algorithm to decide well-formedness. However, the algorithm derived from the Rank Theorem is more efficient, because it requires to solve at most two systems of linear inequations (to determine if the net has a positive S-invariant and a positive T-invariant).

7.3   An example of reduction

We prove that the net of Figure 7.4(a) is not well-formed by means of our reduction rules. As before, we denote the row of a place s_i in the incidence matrix of the net by $\mathbf{s}_i$, and the column corresponding to a transition t_i by $\mathbf{t}_i$.

1. Apply ϕ_S to remove s_{11}: $\qquad \mathbf{s}_{11} = \mathbf{s}_7 + \mathbf{s}_{10}$
2. Apply ϕ_T to remove t_5: $\qquad\quad \mathbf{t}_5 = \mathbf{t}_1 + \mathbf{t}_2 + \mathbf{t}_6 + \mathbf{t}_7 + \mathbf{t}_8 + \mathbf{t}_9 + \mathbf{t}_{10}$
3. Apply ϕ_A to s_{10} and t_{10} (Figure 7.4(b))
4. Apply ϕ_T to remove t_3: $\qquad\quad \mathbf{t}_3 = \mathbf{0}$
5. Apply ϕ_A to s_2 and t_2, s_3 and t_4 (Figure 7.4(c))
6. Apply ϕ_S to remove s_5: $\qquad \mathbf{s}_5 = 2\,\mathbf{s}_1 + \mathbf{s}_4 + \mathbf{s}_6 + \mathbf{s}_8 + \mathbf{s}_9$
7. Apply ϕ_A to s_1 and t_1, s_4 and t_6, s_7 and t_8 (Figure 7.4(d)

The net of Figure 7.4(d) cannot be reduced anymore. Since it is not atomic, the net of Figure 7.4(a) is not well-formed.

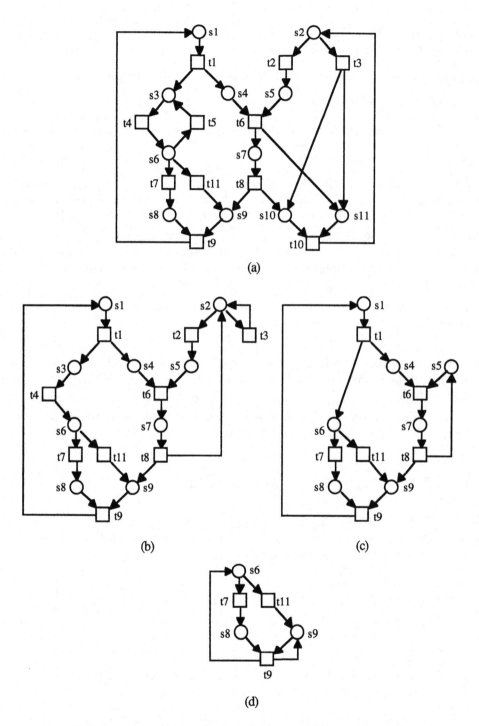

Fig. 7.4 Reduction of a non-well-formed free-choice net

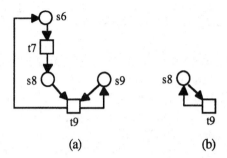

Fig. 7.5   Reduction of a well-formed free-choice net

The reduction procedure not only shows that this net is not well-formed, it also provides some information about *why* this is so. We observe in Figure 7.4(d) that the removal of t_{11} leads to a well-formed net. This makes us suspect that after removing t_{11} from the net of Figure 7.4(a) we get a well-formed net. To prove it, the reduction rules can be used again. The reader can easily check that the Steps 1. to 7. above can also be applied to the net without t_{11}, and yield the net of Figure 7.5(a). We can now proceed as follows:

8.   Apply ϕ_A to s_6 and t_7

9.   Apply ϕ_S to s_9: $\mathbf{s_9 = 0}$

We get the atomic net shown in Figure 7.5(b), and therefore the net of Figure 7.4(a) without the transition t_{11} is well-formed.

7.4   Completeness

We prove in this section that the kit of rules $\{\phi_A, \phi_S, \phi_T\}$ is complete. Recall from Section 7.1 that a kit of reduction rules is complete if it can reduce every well-formed free-choice net to an atomic net. The proof makes use of the properties of so-called CP-subnets[2]. The section is divided into two parts. In the first one, CP-subnets are introduced, and their properties studied. The second part contains the completeness proof itself.

CP-subnets

It is convenient to have some notations about subnets. The expression $N \backslash \{x\}$ was introduced in the previous section to denote the net generated by the nodes of N

---

[2]The name CP-subnet was chosen because these subnets are used in the completeness proof.

except x. We now generalize this notation: for a set X of nodes of N, we denote by $N \backslash X$ the subnet generated by the nodes of N which do not belong to X.

Given a subnet N' of a net N, a transition of N' is a *way-in transition* if its pre-set contains a node that does not belong to N' (through a way-in transition tokens can 'enter' the subnet N'). Similarly, a transition is a *way-out transition* if its post-set contains a node that does not belong to N'.

A subnet (S', T', F') of a net N is *transition-bordered* if ${}^\bullet s \cup s^\bullet \subseteq T'$ for every place $s \in S'$, and it is *place-bordered* if ${}^\bullet t \cup t^\bullet \subseteq S'$ for every transition $t \in T'$ (in both cases, the $\bullet$-notation refers to the net N). It is not difficult to see that a subnet of a net N generated by a set X of nodes is transition-bordered if and only if $N \backslash X$ is place-bordered (and vice versa). It follows easily from the definitions that the S-components of a net are transition-bordered and that its T-components are place-bordered. One of the essential properties of T-components (Proposition 5.12(2)) can be easily generalized to place-bordered subnets:

Proposition 7.6   *A property of place-bordered subnets*

> Let M_0 be a marking of a net N, and let σ be a sequence of transitions of a place-bordered subnet N' of N. Then $M_0 \xrightarrow{\sigma} M$ in N iff $M_0|_{S'} \xrightarrow{\sigma} M|_{S'}$ in N', where S' is the set of places of N'.

Proof:

Since N' is place-bordered, none of its transitions has input or output places outside N'. The result follows since all transitions of σ belong to N'.   □

After these preliminaries, we now define CP-subnets.

Definition 7.7   *CP-subnets*

> A subnet $N' = (S', T', F')$ of a net N is a CP-subnet if it is
>
> (i) nonempty and weakly connected,
> (ii) transition-bordered (i.e., contains pre- and post-sets of all its places),
> (iii) a T-net (i.e., every place has exactly one input transition and one output transition), and
> (iv) the net $N \backslash (S' \cup T')$ is strongly connected and contains some transition.

Figure 7.6 shows the only two CP-subnets of our usual example. Notice that a CP-subnet may contain only one transition t, provided the net $N \backslash \{t\}$ is strongly connected and contains some other transition.

By the definition of CP-subnets, the net generated by all nodes that do not belong to a CP-subnet is strongly connected. For well-formed free-choice nets we can show a much stronger result: this net is again well-formed. The next proposition shows how a live and bounded marking can be obtained.

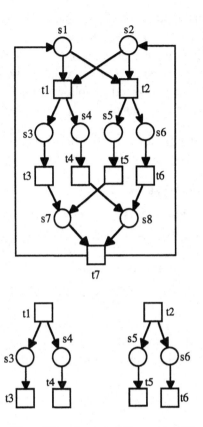

Fig. 7.6 Two CP-subnets of the net of Figure 5.1

Proposition 7.8   *Fundamental property of CP-subnets*

Let (N, M_0) be a live and bounded free-choice system. Let $\widehat{N}$ be a CP-subnet of N, and let $\widehat{S}$, $\widehat{T}$ and $\widehat{T}_{in}$ be the set of places, transitions and way-in transitions of $\widehat{N}$, respectively.

(1) There exists an occurrence sequence $M_0 \xrightarrow{\sigma} M$, such that $\mathcal{A}(\sigma) \subseteq \widehat{T} \setminus \widehat{T}_{in}$ and M enables no transition of $\widehat{T} \setminus \widehat{T}_{in}$.

(2) Let $\overline{N} = N \backslash (\widehat{S} \cup \widehat{T})$ and let $\overline{M}$ be the restriction of the marking M defined in (1) to the places of $\overline{N}$. Then $(\overline{N}, \overline{M})$ is a live and bounded free-choice system.

Proof:

(1)   Let t be an arbitrary transition of $\widehat{N}$. Since N is strongly connected and $\widehat{N}$ is transition-bordered, $\widehat{N}$ contains a path π leading from one of its way-in

transitions to t. Since $\widehat{N}$ is a T-net, every place in π has one single input transition, which is precisely its predecessor in the path. Therefore, by letting transitions of $\widehat{T}\backslash\widehat{T}_{in}$ occur, the number of tokens of this path does not increase, and it decreases when t occurs. So t can occur only a finite number of times in σ. Since t was arbitrarily selected, it follows that the length of the occurrence sequences using only transitions of $\widehat{T}\backslash\widehat{T}_{in}$ is bounded, which implies the result.

(2)   The proof is divided into three parts. In all of them we use that $\overline{N}$ is place-bordered, which holds because $\widehat{N}$ is transition-bordered.

(i) $(\overline{N}, \overline{M})$ is a free-choice system.

$\overline{N}$ contains a transition and is connected (even strongly connected) by the definition of a CP-subnet. Moreover, $\overline{N}$ contains a place because it is place-bordered. So $(\overline{N}, \overline{M})$ is a system. Finally, $(\overline{N}, \overline{M})$ is a free-choice system because N is free-choice and $\overline{N}$ is a subnet of N.

(ii) $(\overline{N}, \overline{M})$ is bounded.

Let $\overline{M} \xrightarrow{\sigma} \overline{L}$ be an occurrence sequence of $\overline{N}$. Since $\overline{N}$ is place-bordered, there exists an occurrence sequence $M \xrightarrow{\sigma} L$ of N such that $\overline{L}(s) = L(s)$ for every place s of $\overline{N}$. Then, since (N, M_0) is bounded, both (N, M) and $(\overline{N}, \overline{M})$ are bounded.

(iii) $(\overline{N}, \overline{M})$ is live.

Assume $(\overline{N}, \overline{M})$ is not live. Since $\overline{N}$ is strongly connected and $(\overline{N}, \overline{M})$ is bounded by (ii), we can apply Theorem 4.31 and conclude that $(\overline{N}, \overline{M})$ is not deadlock-free. So there exists an occurrence sequence $\overline{M} \xrightarrow{\sigma} \overline{L}$ of $\overline{N}$ such that no transition of $\overline{N}$ is enabled at $\overline{L}$. Since $\overline{N}$ is place-bordered, we have $M \xrightarrow{\sigma} L$ for some marking L such that

(a) $L(s) = M(s)$ for every place s of $\widehat{N}$ and

(b) $L(s) = \overline{L}(s)$ for every place s of $\overline{N}$.

We show that no transition of N is enabled at L, which contradicts the liveness of (N, M_0). By (a), and since no transition of $\widehat{T} \setminus \widehat{T}_{in}$ is enabled at M, no transition of $\widehat{T}\setminus\widehat{T}_{in}$ is enabled at L. By (b), and since $\overline{N}$ is place-bordered, no transition of $\overline{N}$ is enabled at L. It remains to prove that no transition of $\widehat{T}_{in}$ is enabled at L. Let t_{in} be a transition of $\widehat{T}_{in}$. By the definition of a way-in transition, some place s of ${}^\bullet t_{in}$ belongs to $\overline{N}$. Since $\overline{N}$ is strongly connected, some transition u of $s^\bullet$ belongs to $\overline{N}$. By (b), u is not enabled at L. Since t_{in} and u belong to the same cluster and N is free-choice, t_{in} is not enabled at L either.   □

Corollary 7.9

Let N be a well-formed free-choice net.

(1) If N has a CP-subnet $N' = (S', T', F')$ then the net $N \backslash (S' \cup T')$ is also well-formed.

(2) If N contains two or more transitions and, for some transition t, the net $N \backslash \{t\}$ is a strongly connected subnet, then this subnet is well-formed.

(3) If N contains two or more places and, for some place s, the net $N \backslash \{s\}$ is a strongly connected subnet, then this subnet is well-formed.

Proof:

(1) Follows immediately from Proposition 7.8.

(2) Under these conditions, $(\emptyset, \{t\}, \emptyset)$ is a CP-subnet. Then apply (1).

(3) Follows from (2) and the Duality Theorem.   □

The next result proves a structural property of CP-subnets.

Proposition 7.10

A CP-subnet of a well-formed free-choice net has exactly one way-in transition.

Proof:
Let $\widehat{N} = (\widehat{S}, \widehat{T}, \widehat{F})$ be a CP-subnet of a well-formed free-choice net N. The net N is strongly connected by the Strong Connectedness Theorem. Since the net $\overline{N} = N \backslash (\widehat{S} \cup \widehat{T})$ is nonempty, there exists an arc (x, y) of N such that x belongs to $\overline{N}$ and y belongs to $\widehat{N}$. Since $\widehat{N}$ is transition-bordered, y is a way-in transition. So $\widehat{N}$ has at least one way-in transition.

We use the Rank Theorem to prove that $\widehat{N}$ has at most one way-in transition. Let $\widehat{T}_{in}$ be the set of way-in transitions of $\widehat{N}$. The proof is divided into five parts:

(i) Every cluster of N containing at least one node of $\widehat{N}$ contains exactly one transition of $\widehat{N}$.

We claim that, for some T-component of N, all the nodes of $\widehat{N}$ are nodes of this T-component. Let s be a place of $\widehat{N}$. Since $\widehat{N}$ is transition-bordered and a T-net, s has exactly one input and one output transition in N. By the definition of a T-component, the input and the output transition of s belong exactly to the same T-components. This implies, by the connectedness of $\widehat{N}$, that *all* the nodes of $\widehat{N}$ belong to exactly the same T-components. Since N is covered by T-components by the T-coverability Theorem, all the nodes of $\widehat{N}$ are contained in some T-component, which proves the claim.

Let t and u be two different transitions of $\widehat{N}$. Since both t and u belong to some T-component, they have disjoint pre-sets. By the free-choice property, they belong to different clusters. So no cluster contains more than one transition of $\widehat{N}$.

It remains to show that every cluster that contains nodes of $\widehat{N}$ contains at least one transition of $\widehat{N}$. If a cluster contains a place of $\widehat{N}$ then it also contains its output transitions. There is at least one output transition since N is strongly connected, and every output transition belongs to $\widehat{N}$ since $\widehat{N}$ is transition-bordered.

(ii) If a cluster of N contains nodes of $\widehat{N}$ and $\overline{N}$, then it contains exactly one way-in transition of $\widehat{N}$.

Let c be a cluster of N containing nodes of $\widehat{N}$ and $\overline{N}$. By (i), it suffices to prove that c contains at least one way-in transition of $\widehat{N}$. Since $\widehat{N}$ is transition-bordered, c contains a place s of $\overline{N}$ and a transition t of $\widehat{N}$ such that (s,t) is an arc of N. Therefore t is a way-in transition of $\widehat{N}$.

(iii) $|C_N| = |C_{\overline{N}}| + |\widehat{T}| - |\widehat{T}_{in}|$ (recall that C_N and $C_{\overline{N}}$ are the sets of clusters of N and $\overline{N}$).

Divide the clusters of N into (1) those contained in $\overline{N}$, (2) those contained in $\widehat{N}$, and (3) those which contain nodes of both $\widehat{N}$ and $\overline{N}$. By (ii), the number of clusters of the first kind is $|C_{\overline{N}}| - |\widehat{T}_{in}|$. By (i), the number of clusters of the second kind is $|\widehat{T}| - |\widehat{T}_{in}|$ because every way-in transition is in a cluster containing a place of $\overline{N}$. Again by (ii), the number of clusters of the third kind is $|\widehat{T}_{in}|$.

(iv) $\text{Rank}(\mathbf{N}) \geq \text{Rank}(\overline{\mathbf{N}}) + |\widehat{T}| - 1$.

Since $\widehat{N}$ is a connected T-net, every T-invariant of $\widehat{N}$ is a multiple of the vector $(1 \ldots 1)$ (Proposition 3.16). Hence, we have $\text{Rank}(\widehat{\mathbf{N}}) = |\widehat{T}| - 1$.

Since $\widehat{N}$ is transition-bordered, no arcs connect places of $\widehat{N}$ with transitions of $\overline{N}$. If we assume without loss of generality that the first rows of the matrix $\mathbf{N}$ correspond to the places of $\overline{N}$ and its first columns to the transitions of $\overline{N}$, then $\mathbf{N}$ can be decomposed in the following way:

$$\mathbf{N} = \begin{pmatrix} \overline{\mathbf{N}} & A \\ 0 & \widehat{\mathbf{N}} \end{pmatrix}$$

for some matrix A. Thus we have

$$\text{Rank}(\mathbf{N}) \geq \text{Rank}(\overline{\mathbf{N}}) + \text{Rank}(\widehat{\mathbf{N}}) = \text{Rank}(\overline{\mathbf{N}}) + |\widehat{T}| - 1 \,.$$

(v) $\widehat{N}$ has at most one way-in transition.

N is a well-formed free-choice net by assumption, and $\overline{N}$ is a well-formed free-choice net by Proposition 7.8(2). By the Rank Theorem, we get

$$|C_N| = \mathrm{Rank}(\mathbf{N}) - 1 \quad \text{and} \quad |C_{\overline{N}}| = \mathrm{Rank}(\overline{\mathbf{N}}) - 1 \,.$$

Substituting in (iv) yields

$$|C_N| \geq |C_{\overline{N}}| + |\widehat{T}| - 1$$

Using (iii) we obtain $|\widehat{T}_{in}| \leq 1$. $\qquad\qquad\qquad\square$

Completeness of $\{\phi_A, \phi_S, \phi_T\}$

The completeness proof makes use of the fact that every well-formed free-choice net is either a T-net or has a CP-subnet.

Proposition 7.11

A well-formed free-choice net is either a T-net or has a CP-subnet.

Proof:

Let N be a well-formed free-choice net which is not a T-net. We show that N has a CP-subnet.

By the T-coverability Theorem, N is covered by T-components. Let C be a minimal T-cover of N, i.e., no proper subset of C is a cover. Since N is not a T-net, we have $|C| > 1$. We construct the (non-directed) graph $G = (V, E)$ as follows.

$$V = C$$
$$E = \{(N_i, N_j) \mid N_i \text{ and } N_j \text{ have at least one common node}\}$$

The graph G is connected because C is a cover of N and N is connected. Moreover, G has at least two vertices because $|C| > 1$.

We choose an arbitrary spanning tree[3] of G. Let N_1 be a leaf of the spanning tree. Then, N_1 has exactly one adjacent edge in the tree. When we remove N_1 from G, together with its adjacent edges, the remaining graph G' is still connected and nonempty. The vertices of G' are a cover of the subnet generated by all nodes of T-components in $C \setminus \{N_1\}$. It follows that this subnet is strongly connected, because it is covered by T-components and the graph G' is connected.

---

[3] A spanning tree is a cycle-free connected graph (V, E'); it can be obtained from G by successive deletion of edges that belong to a cycle.

Let X be a maximal set of nodes of N_1 satisfying the following properties:

(a) The net generated by X is connected, and

(b) No element of X belongs to a T-component of $\mathcal{C} \setminus \{N_1\}$.

Let N_X be the subnet of N generated by X. We prove that N_X is a CP-subnet. Let $N_X = (S_X, T_X, F_X)$.

(i) N_X is nonempty and connected.

   N_X is connected by definition. By the minimality of $\mathcal{C}$, there are nodes of N_1 that belong to no other T-component of $\mathcal{C}$ (otherwise, $\mathcal{C} \setminus \{N_1\}$ would be a cover of N). Since X is maximal, it contains at least one of these nodes, and is therefore nonempty.

(ii) N_X is transition-bordered.

   We have to prove ${}^\bullet s \cup s^\bullet \subseteq T_X$ for every place $s \in S_X$. Let s be a place of S_X and let t be a transition of ${}^\bullet s \cup s^\bullet$. By the definition of a T-component, every T-component containing t also contains s. By Condition (b) of the definition of X, the place s is contained in only one element of $\mathcal{C}$, namely N_1, and therefore the same holds for the transition t. This implies that the net generated by $X \cup \{t\}$ satisfies conditions (a) and (b) above. By the maximality of X we get $t \in X$.

(iii) N_X is a T-net.

   Let s be a place of N_X. The set ${}^\bullet s \cup s^\bullet$ is included in N_1 because N_X is a subnet of N_1 and N_X is transition-bordered. Since N_1 is a T-component, it is a T-net. So $|{}^\bullet s| = |s^\bullet| = 1$, and therefore N_X is a T-net.

(iv) The net $N \setminus X$ is strongly connected and contains some transition.

   $N \setminus X$ contains some transition because $|\mathcal{C}| > 1$, and therefore some transition of N does not belong to N_1.

   Let x and y be two arbitrary nodes of $N \setminus X$. Since N is strongly connected, it contains a path $\pi = u_1 \ldots u_k$ such that $x = u_1$ and $y = u_k$. If π is also a path of $N \setminus X$ then there is nothing to be shown. Otherwise we shall find another path of $N \setminus X$ which also leads from x to y.

   Let u_{i+1} and u_{j-1} be the first and last elements of π that belong to X (they may be the same node). By the maximality of X, u_i and u_j do not belong to N_X. Since the net generated by all nodes of T-components in $\mathcal{C} \setminus \{N_1\}$ is strongly connected, it contains a path $u_i\, v_1 \ldots v_l\, u_j$ Since this net is a subnet of $N \backslash X$, this path is also contained in $N \backslash X$. So the path

$$x \ldots u_i\, v_1 \ldots v_l\, u_j \ldots y$$

leads from x to y in $N \backslash X$. $\square$

Using this result, we shall now prove that, given an arbitrary non-atomic, well-formed free-choice net, a rule of the kit $\{\phi_A, \phi_S, \phi_T\}$ can be applied. This result implies the completeness of the kit, as follows. After the application of ϕ_A, ϕ_S or ϕ_T to a source well-formed net, the target net is also well-formed, and has moreover fewer nodes than the source net. Therefore, an exhaustive application of the rule to a well-formed free-choice net yields an atomic well-formed free-choice net.

We first show that if a net is well-formed, the conditions of application of the rules can be simplified. Recall for the next proofs that well-formed nets are strongly connected by the Strong Connectedness Theorem, and contain at least one place and one transition.

Proposition 7.12

Let N be a non-atomic well-formed free-choice net. Then

(1) ϕ_A can be applied iff N contains a place s and a transition t such that $s^\bullet = \{t\}$, $^\bullet t = \{s\}$ and $s \notin t^\bullet$.

(2) ϕ_S can be applied iff N contains a place s such that $N \backslash \{s\}$ is strongly connected.

(3) ϕ_T can be applied iff N contains a transition t such that $N \backslash \{t\}$ is strongly connected.

Proof:

(1) ($\Rightarrow$): Follows from the definition of ϕ_A.

($\Leftarrow$): We show that s and t satisfy the conditions of application of ϕ_A. Since N is well-formed, it is strongly connected, and so $^\bullet s \neq \emptyset$ and $t^\bullet \neq \emptyset$. By assumption, $s^\bullet = \{t\}$ and $^\bullet t = \{s\}$. So Conditions 1 and 2 hold.

Assume that Condition 3 does not hold. Then, there exist $u \in\, ^\bullet s$ and $r \in t^\bullet$ such that (u, r) is an arc of N. We prove $s \in t^\bullet$, which contradicts the hypothesis. By the T-coverability Theorem, N is covered by T-components. Let N_1 be a T-component of N which contains the transition u. It follows from the definition of a T-component that N_1 also contains s and r. Since t is the only output transition of s in N, N_1 also contains t. Therefore both t and u are input transitions of r. Since r has exactly one input transition in N_1, we have $t = u$, and therefore $s \in t^\bullet$.

(2) ($\Rightarrow$): Assume that ϕ_S can be applied. Then the target net is $N \setminus \{s\}$ for some place s. Since ϕ_S is strongly sound, $N \setminus \{s\}$ is well-formed, and therefore strongly connected.

($\Leftarrow$): We first prove that N contains at least two places. Assume that N only contains the place s. Since $N \setminus \{s\}$ is strongly connected, N contains exactly one transition. But a well-formed net containing exactly one place and one transition is atomic, which contradicts the hypothesis.

We now show that s is nonnegative linearly dependent. By Corollary 7.9(3), the net $N \setminus \{s\}$ is also well-formed. By the Rank Theorem, both N and $N \setminus \{s\}$ have a positive S-invariant, say I and $\overline{I}$. Assume without loss of generality $\overline{I}(r) > I(r)$ for every place r of $N \setminus \{s\}$ (multiply $\overline{I}$ by an adequate positive constant if necessary). Assume further that $\mathbf{s}$ is the last row of $\mathbf{N}$.

Define

$$I' = -\frac{1}{I(s)} I + (\overline{I}\, 0)$$

where $(\overline{I}\, 0)$ is obtained by appending a zero entry to $\overline{I}$.

Clearly, $(\overline{I}\, 0)$ is an S-invariant of N. Therefore, since S-invariants form a vector space, I' is also an S-invariant. By construction, we have, $I'(s) = -1$ and $I'(r) > 0$ for every place $r \neq s$.

Let Λ be the vector which coincides with I' except in the entry corresponding to the place s, for which $\Lambda(s) = 0$. Then Λ is nonnegative. Moreover, $\Lambda \cdot \mathbf{N} = \mathbf{s}$. So s is nonnegative linearly dependent.

(3) Similar to (2), exchanging places and transitions, and substituting T-invariants for S-invariants. $\square$

Theorem 7.13   *Completeness Theorem*

Let N be a non-atomic, well-formed free-choice net. Then a reduction rule of the kit $\{\phi_A, \phi_S, \phi_T\}$ is applicable to N.

Proof:

Consider three cases:

Case 1. N is both a T-net and an S-net.

Then N is a circuit. By Proposition 7.12(1), ϕ_A can be applied.

Case 2. N is not a T-net.

By Proposition 7.11, N contains a CP-subnet $\widehat{N} = (\widehat{S}, \widehat{T}, \widehat{F})$. Let t_{in} be the unique way-in transition of $\widehat{N}$.

We first claim that no input place of t_{in} belongs to $\widehat{S}$. By the definition of a way-in transition, some input place s of t_{in} does not belong to $\widehat{S}$. Since $N \setminus (\widehat{S} \cup \widehat{T})$ is strongly connected, s has some output transition $t \notin \widehat{T}$. Let r be an arbitrary input place of t_{in}. By the free-choice property, r is an input place of t. Since $\widehat{N}$ is transition-bordered and $t \notin \widehat{T}$ we get $r \notin \widehat{S}$.

Now, the proof is divided into three parts:

(a) If $|\widehat{S}| = 0$, then ϕ_T is applicable.

Since CP-subnets are connected, $|\widehat{S}| = 0$ implies that $\widehat{N} = (\emptyset, \{t_{in}\}, \emptyset)$. By the definition of a CP-subnet, $N \setminus \{t_{in}\}$ is strongly connected. Now apply Proposition 7.12(3).

(b) If $0 < |\widehat{S}| < 2(|\widehat{T}| - 1)$, then ϕ_A is applicable.

Every transition of $\widehat{N}$, with the exception of t_{in}, has at least one input place in $\widehat{S}$. By the claim above, t_{in} has no input places in $\widehat{S}$. Moreover, since $\widehat{N}$ is a T-net, the places of $\widehat{S}$ have exactly one output transition. Then, since less than $2(|\widehat{T}| - 1)$ input places have to be distributed among $|\widehat{T}| - 1$ transitions, some transition t of $\widehat{T}$ has exactly one input place s in $\widehat{S}$. Moreover, t is not a way-in transition, and therefore s is the only input place of t. Since $\widehat{N}$ is a T-net, t is the only output transition of s. Finally, we have $s \notin t^\bullet$, because otherwise t is the only input transition of s and then every path ending with s or t starts with s or t, which contradicts that N is strongly connected. Apply now Proposition 7.12(1).

(c) If $0 < |\widehat{S}| \geq 2(|\widehat{T}| - 1)$, then ϕ_S is applicable.

We shall prove that $\widehat{S}$ contains a place s such that the net $N \setminus \{s\}$ is strongly connected. The result follows by Proposition 7.12(2).

Since N is strongly connected, every node of $\widehat{T}$ belongs to some path leading from t_{in} to a way-out transition. We construct a subset R of $\widehat{S}$ which will have the following property:

Every node of $\widehat{T}$ belongs to some path leading from t_{in} to a way-out transition, *and containing only places of R.*

Divide the transitions of $\widehat{T}$ into the way-in transition t_{in}, the way-out transitions different from t_{in}, which we call T_{out}, and the rest, which we call T_{rest}. For every transition t of T_{rest}, select a path $\pi(t_{in}, t)$ from t_{in} to t and another path $\pi(t, T_{out})$ from t to a transition of T_{out}, both of minimal length. Put in R the predecessor of t in the path $\pi(t_{in}, t)$ and its successor in the path $\pi(t, T_{out})$. Moreover, for every transition t of T_{out}, select a path $\pi(t_{in}, t)$ from t_{in} to t, and put in R the predecessor of t in $\pi(t_{in}, t)$.

Let x be a node of $\widehat{N}$. We construct inductively a path leading from x to a way-out transition. Take x as the first element of the path, and then proceed as follows:

- if the last element of the path constructed so far is a place s, then add to the path its unique output transition;

- if the last element is a non-way-out transition t, then add to the path its successor in the path $\pi(t, T_{out})$;

This procedure terminates, because for every three consecutive nodes $t\,s\,t'$ of the path, where t and t' are transitions, the length of $\pi(t', T_{out})$ is smaller than the length of $\pi(t, T_{out})$ by the minimality of the paths.

By a similar procedure, we can construct a path leading from the way-in transition to x (we start this time with the last node, and construct the path backwards).

To prove that R is a proper subset of $\widehat{S}$, we first claim that the set T_{out} is nonempty. Since N is strongly connected and since $\widehat{S}$ is nonempty, there is a minimal path from some place s of $\widehat{N}$ to a way-out transition. Since t_{in} has no input places in $\widehat{S}$, this way-out transition is not t_{in} and therefore belongs to T_{out}. So T_{out} is nonempty which proves the claim.

Now we have

$$
\begin{aligned}
|R| &= 2\,|T_{rest}| + |T_{out}| && \text{(definition of } R) \\
&< 2\,(|T_{rest}| + |T_{out}|) && (T_{out} \text{ is nonempty}) \\
&= 2\,(|\widehat{T}| - 1) && (\widehat{T} = \{t_{in}\} \cup T_{rest} \cup T_{out}) \\
&\leq |\widehat{S}| && \text{(hypothesis)};
\end{aligned}
$$

Let s be a place of $\widehat{S} \setminus R$, which exists because R is a proper subset of S. We claim that the net $N\backslash\{s\}$ is strongly connected. Since N is strongly connected it suffices to show that $N\backslash\{s\}$ has a path π leading from the unique input transition u of s to the unique output transition v of s.

Take a path from u to a way-out transition of $\widehat{N}$ containing only places of R, extend it first with a path leading to the way-in transition t_{in} containing no nodes of $\widehat{N}$ and then extend it with a path leading from t_{in} to v containing only places of R. The first and the third path exist by the definition of R. The second path exists since the net $N\backslash(\widehat{S}\cup\widehat{T})$ is strongly connected.

Case 3. N is not an S-net.

Then N^d is not a T-net. By the Duality Theorem, N^d is well-formed and so, by Case 2, a rule is applicable to N^d. Recall that the places of N are the transitions of N^d and vice versa. An inspection of the rules shows that

$$(N^d, \tilde{N}^d) \in \phi_A \text{ iff } (N, \tilde{N}) \in \phi_A,$$

$$(N^d, \tilde{N}^d) \in \phi_S \text{ iff } (N, \tilde{N}) \in \phi_T, \text{ and}$$

$$(N^d, \tilde{N}^d) \in \phi_T \text{ iff } (N, \tilde{N}) \in \phi_S$$

Therefore, since a rule is applicable to N^d, the same holds for N. $\qquad\square$

7.5 Synthesis rules

The inverse of a reduction rule can be used as a *synthesis rule* to generate complex nets starting from atomic ones. A net is *synthesized* by a kit of synthesis rules if it is reduced by their inverses.

The formulation of the inverses of the reduction rules ϕ_S, ϕ_T and ϕ_A is straightforward. However, as pointed out in the introduction, it is possible to exploit the fact that atomic nets are well-formed. While a reduction rule can only be useful if it is strongly sound, a synthesis rule only needs to be sound, because the application of sound rules to well-formed free-choice nets yields well-formed free-choice nets.

By the definitions of strong soundness, the kit formed by the inverses of a strongly sound kit of reduction rules is also strongly sound. Since a sound kit suffices, we can try to weaken some rules, which may have the advantage that the conditions of application are easier to check. We show in this section that this is the case of the rule ϕ_T.

The conditions of application of ϕ_T require to find a nonnegative linearly dependent transition. This in turn needs to solve a system of linear inequalities in the nonnegative orthant. Although this is a polynomial problem, it is still time consuming. The following proposition allows us to do better.

Proposition 7.14

Let N be a net and let t be a linearly dependent transition of N. If the net $N\backslash\{t\}$ has a positive T-invariant, then t is nonnegative linearly dependent.

Proof:

Since t is linearly dependent, there exists a vector Λ such that $\Lambda(t) = 0$ and $\mathbf{N} \cdot \Lambda$ is equal to $\mathbf{t}$, the column of t in the incidence matrix $\mathbf{N}$. Let J be a positive T-invariant of $N\backslash\{t\}$, and let k be a number such that $(\Lambda + k\, J) \geq 0$. We have $C \cdot (\Lambda + k\, J) = \mathbf{t}$, which implies that t is a nonnegative linearly dependent transition. $\square$

We can now define the following synthesis rule.

Rule 4 *The rule ψ_T*

Let $N = (S, T, F)$ and $\tilde{N} = (\tilde{S}, \tilde{T}, \tilde{F})$ be two free-choice nets. $(N, \tilde{N}) \in \psi_T$ if:

1. $\tilde{S} = S$
2. $\tilde{T} = T \cup \{t\}$ *(where $t \notin T$)*
3. $\tilde{F} = F \cup F'$, where $F' \subseteq ((S \times \{t\}) \cup (\{t\} \times S))$
4. t *is a linearly dependent transition of $\tilde{N}$*
5. $^{\bullet}t \cup t^{\bullet} \neq \emptyset$ *in $\tilde{N}$*

In order to check if t is a (not necessarily nonnegative) linearly dependent transition, it suffices to solve an ordinary system of linear equations (using, for instance, Gauss elimination). Note that this is much easier than checking if t is nonnegative linearly dependent.

We finally show the that ψ_T is the inverse of ϕ_T within the class of well-formed free-choice nets.

Proposition 7.15

Let N and $\tilde{N}$ be free-choice nets. If N is well-formed then

$$(N, \tilde{N}) \in \psi_T \text{ iff } (\tilde{N}, N) \in \phi_T$$

Proof:

If N is well-formed then it has a positive T-invariant. It suffices to observe that then, by Proposition 7.14, a transition t of $\tilde{N}$ is linearly dependent iff it is nonnegative linearly dependent. $\square$

Using this proposition, it is immediate to show that the kit $\{\phi_A^{-1}, \phi_S^{-1}, \psi_T\}$ is sound. Moreover, it synthesizes all well-formed free-choice nets because the kit of its inverse is complete. The rule ϕ_S^{-1} can be replaced by a weaker rule in a similar way.

Exercises

Exercise 7.1
Show – by exhibiting suitable counterexamples – that if any of the conditions of application of ϕ_A is dropped the resulting rule is no longer strongly sound.

Exercise 7.2   *
Let (N, M_0), (N', M_0') be systems, where $N = (S, T, F)$ and $N' = (S', T', F')$, and let $f: T \to T'$ be an injective mapping. We say that (N', M_0') *simulates* (N, M_0) (with respect to f) iff there is a surjection $\beta: [M_0'\rangle \to [M_0\rangle$ such that the following holds:

(i) $M_0 = \beta(M_0')$.

(ii) Suppose $M_1 = \beta(M_1')$, $M_0' \xrightarrow{*} M_1'$ and $M_0 \xrightarrow{*} M_1$;

    (a) whenever $M_1 \xrightarrow{t} M_2$ then there exists $M_2' \in \beta^{-1}(M_2)$ and $w \in T'^*$ such that $M_1' \xrightarrow{w} M_2'$ and $f^{-1}(w) = t$;

    (b) whenever $M_1' \xrightarrow{w} M_2'$ with $w \in T'^*$, then $M_1 \xrightarrow{f^{-1}(w)} \beta(M_2')$.

(iii) For every $M \in [M_0\rangle$ the set $\beta^{-1}(M)$ is finite.

Prove:

1) If (N', M_0') simulates (N, M_0), then (N, M_0) is bounded iff (N', M_0') is bounded.

2) If (N', M_0') simulates (N, M_0), then (N, M_0) is live iff for every $t' \in f(T)$, t' is live in (N', M_0').

3) Let $(N, \tilde{N}) \in \phi_A$, where $N = (S, T, F)$ and $\tilde{N} = (\tilde{S}, \tilde{T}, \tilde{F})$ and let s and t be the place and the transition required by the definition of ϕ_A. Let $f: \tilde{T} \to T$ be the identity on $\tilde{T}$ (clearly, f is an injection). Let $\beta: [M_0\rangle \to [\tilde{M}_0\rangle$ be the surjection given by:

$$\tilde{M}(r) = \begin{cases} M(r) & \text{if } r \notin t^\bullet \\ M(r) + M(s) & \text{if } r \in t^\bullet \end{cases}$$

Let M_0 be a live and bounded marking of N. Show that (N, M_0) simulates $(\tilde{N}, \tilde{M}_0)$ with respect to f.

Conclude that ϕ_A is strongly sound, even if the source and target net are allowed to be arbitrary nets, not necessarily free-choice. Notice that if you did not use the three conditions of application of ϕ_A in your proof of (3) then your proof is not completely correct (because of Exercise 7.1).

Exercise 7.3

1) Prove that $\{\phi_A, \phi_T\}$ is strongly sound and complete for S-nets.

2) Prove that $\{\phi_A, \phi_S\}$ is strongly sound and complete for T-nets.

Exercise 7.4

Reduce the net underlying the vending machine of Chapter 1 to an atomic net.

Exercise 7.5

Find all the CP-subnets of the net of Figure 7.3 and of its dual net.

Exercise 7.6

Exhibit a well-formed, non-free-choice net N having a CP-subnet $\widehat{N} = (\widehat{S}, \widehat{T}, \widehat{F})$ such that the net $N \backslash (\widehat{S} \cup \widehat{T})$ is not well-formed.

Exercise 7.7

Let N be a well-formed free-choice net, let $\widehat{N}$ be a CP-subnet of N, and let $\overline{N}$ be the subnet of N generated by all the nodes that do not belong to $\widehat{N}$. Prove

$$\mathrm{Rank}(\mathbf{N}) = \mathrm{Rank}(\overline{\mathbf{N}}) + \mathrm{Rank}(\widehat{\mathbf{N}})$$

(a solution to this exercise can be found in Chapter 9, Lemma 9.3).

Exercise 7.8

Given a relation F, define $F(x \leftarrow y)$ as the result of substituting x by y in all the pairs of F. Define $F|_x$ as the relation obtained by removing from F all pairs containing the node x.

Consider the following rule ϕ'_A.

Rule 5 *The rule ϕ'_A (merging of transitions)*

> Let N and $\tilde{N}$ be free-choice nets, where $N = (S, T, F)$ and $\tilde{N} = (\tilde{S}, \tilde{T}, \tilde{F})$. $(N, \tilde{N}) \in \phi'_A$ if:

> **Conditions on N:**   *There exists $s \in S$ such that:*
> 1. $|{}^{\bullet}s| = |s^{\bullet}| = 1$, ${}^{\bullet}s \neq s^{\bullet}$
> 2. $(s^{\bullet})^{\bullet} \neq \emptyset$
> 3. ${}^{\bullet}(s^{\bullet}) = \{s\}$

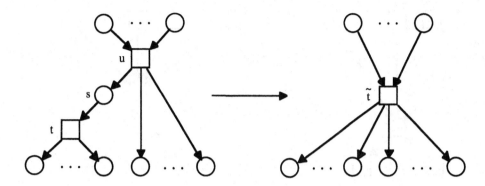

Fig. 7.7 The rule ϕ'_A

Construction of $\tilde{N}$:   *Let $\{t\} = s^\bullet$ and $\{u\} = {}^\bullet s$.*

4. $\tilde{S} = S \setminus \{s\}$
5. $\tilde{T} = (T \setminus \{t, u\}) \cup \{\tilde{t}\}$ *(where $\tilde{t} \notin T$)*
6. $\tilde{F} = F(t \leftarrow \tilde{t}, u \leftarrow \tilde{t}) \restriction s$

1) Show that ϕ'_A is strongly sound.

2) Show that if ϕ'_A is applicable to a net, then so is ϕ_A.

3) Show that the kit $\{\phi'_A, \phi_S, \phi_T\}$ is complete.

   ϕ'_A has the advantage of capturing more precisely than ϕ_A the idea of merging the occurrences of two transitions. However, it is not invariant under the dual transformation.

Exercise 7.9

   Consider the following rule ϕ''_A.

Rule 6 *The rule ϕ''_A (merging of places)*

   Let N and $\tilde{N}$ be free-choice nets, where $N = (S, T, F)$ and $\tilde{N} = (\tilde{S}, \tilde{T}, \tilde{F})$. $(N, \tilde{N}) \in \phi''_A$ if:

   Conditions on N: *There exists $t \in T$ such that:*

   1. $|{}^\bullet t| = |t^\bullet| = 1$, ${}^\bullet t \neq t^\bullet$
   2. ${}^\bullet({}^\bullet t) \neq \emptyset$
   3. $({}^\bullet t)^\bullet = \{t\}$

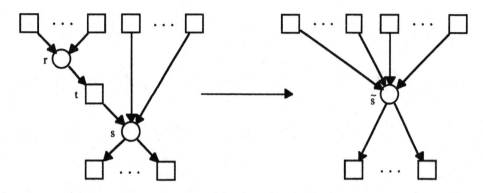

Fig. 7.8   The rule ϕ_A''

Construction of $\tilde{N}$:   *Let $\{s\} = t^\bullet$ and $\{r\} = {}^\bullet t$.*

   4. $\tilde{S} = (S \setminus \{s, r\}) \cup \{\tilde{s}\}$ *(where $\tilde{s} \notin S$)*

   5. $\tilde{T} = T \setminus \{t\}$

   6. $\tilde{F} = F(s \leftarrow \tilde{s}, r \leftarrow \tilde{s}) \,|\, t$

1) Show that ϕ_A'' is strongly sound.

2) Show that if ϕ_A'' is applicable to a net, then so is ϕ_A'.

3) Show that the kit $\{\phi_A'', \phi_S, \phi_T\}$ is complete.

   ϕ_A'' has the advantage of capturing more precisely than ϕ_A the idea of hiding the occurrence of a transition. However, it is again not invariant under the dual transformation (in fact, the rules ϕ_A' and ϕ_A'' are dual of each other).

Exercise 7.10

   Reduce the net of Figure 7.5 without transition t_{11} to an atomic net using the kit $\{\phi_A', \phi_S, \phi_T\}$. Same for the kit $\{\phi_A'', \phi_S, \phi_T\}$.

Bibliographic Notes

The results of this chapter are an improved version of some results of Esparza's Ph. D. Thesis [27] (see also [32] by Esparza and Silva and [30] by Esparza). In these references the rules are presented as rules on free-choice systems. Here we have chosen to present them as rules on free-choice nets for simplicity.

The net of Figure 7.5 is a slight modification of the main example in Hack's Master Thesis [42]. The notion of simulation used in Exercise 7.2 is due to Best [6].

Related work The use of (strongly sound) reduction rules as an analysis technique was first proposed and studied by Berthelot [3, 4, 5]. He provided a complete kit of rules for persistent systems, a behavioural generalization of T-systems.

Genrich and Thiagarajan obtained in [40] a complete kit of rules for Bipolar Synchronization Schemes. Bipolar Schemes can be seen as a subclass of free-choice systems. It has been conjectured that this is the subclass of free-choice systems without *frozen tokens*, but so far no proof exists. A free-choice system has frozen tokens if there exists a reachable marking M and a place s such that $M(s) > 0$ and $M \xrightarrow{\sigma}$ for some infinite sequence σ which does not contain any output transition of s. Loosely speaking, during the occurrence of σ the tokens on the place s are 'frozen', because they are never used.

Desel has studied the reduction problem for free-choice systems without frozen tokens in [20]. He provides four rules which reduce all and only the live and bounded free-choice systems without frozen tokens to either S-systems or T-systems. We describe here the "net part" of the rules, i.e., we omit how to obtain the marking of the target net as a function of the marking of the source net.

The first rule is ϕ_A. The second rule removes a nonnegative linearly dependent place, but only when the linear combination has a particularly simple form: $\mathbf{s} = \mathbf{r}$ for some other place r different from s. The third rule is the transition version of the second. The fourth rule is illustrated in Figure 7.9. It can be applied when there

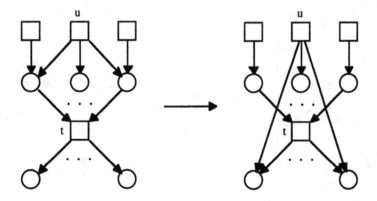

Fig. 7.9 One of Desel's rules

are two transitions t and u such that ${}^\bullet t \subseteq u^\bullet$, $|{}^\bullet t| > 1$, and every input place of t has some other input transition apart from u. The rule does not remove or add any node, it only changes the distribution of arcs: all the arcs leading from u to input places of t are removed, and new arcs leading from u to all the output places of t are added. However, this rule can only be applied a finite number of times if the net has a positive T-invariant.

It is not known if the fourth rule of [20] is necessary, i.e., if the kit containing only the other three rules can still reduce all the live and bounded free-choice systems without frozen tokens to S-systems or T-systems.

Kovalyov provides in [56] a complete kit of three rules for the class of free-choice systems satisfying that some transition is contained in every T-component. We describe here only the "net part" of the rules, and change the description of [56] slightly to allow for a better comparison with ϕ_A, ϕ_S and ϕ_T. The first rule can be applied to nets containing a place s such that $^\bullet s \neq \emptyset \neq (s^\bullet)^\bullet$, $^\bullet(s^\bullet) = \{s\}$, and $(^\bullet s \times (s^\bullet))^\bullet \cap F = \emptyset$, where F is the set of arcs of the net. These conditions of application generalize those of the rule ϕ_A: the conditions on the transition t are replaced by identical conditions on the set $s^\bullet$. The target net is constructed in two steps:

1. For every input transition t and every output transition u of s, add a new transition (t, u) satisfying $^\bullet(t, u) = {}^\bullet t$ and $(t, u)^\bullet = u^\bullet$. Loosely speaking, the occurrence of (t, u) produces the same effect as the occurrence of the sequence $t\, u$.

2. Remove the place s together with all its input and output transitions.

Figure 7.10 shows an example of application.

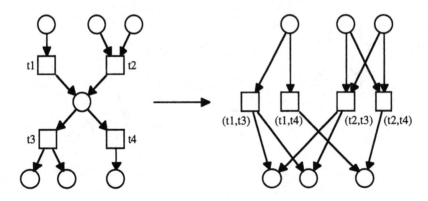

Fig. 7.10   One of Kovalyov's rules

The second rule removes a place s such that $\mathbf{s} = \mathbf{0}$ or $\mathbf{s} = \mathbf{r}$ for some place r different from s. The third rule is the transition version of the first.

The drawback of Kovalyov's kit of rules is that the number of reductions may be exponential in the size of the net. It is not known if the kit is complete for *all* free-choice systems.

Chapter 8 ——————————

Home markings

A home marking of a system is a marking which is reachable from every reachable marking; in other words, a marking to which the system may always return. The identification of home markings is an interesting issue in system analysis. A concurrent interactive system performs some initial behaviour and then settles in its ultimate cyclic (repetitive) mode of operation. A typical example of such a design is an operating system which, at boot time, carries out a set of initializations and then cyclically waits for, and produces, a variety of input/output operations. The states that belong to the ultimate cyclic behavioural component determine the central function of this type of system. The markings modelling such states are the home markings.

In Section 8.1 we show that live and bounded free-choice systems have home markings. In Section 8.2 we prove a stronger result: the home markings are the reachable markings which mark all the proper traps of the net.

8.1 Existence of home markings

Definition 8.1 *Home marking*

Let (N, M_0) be a system. A marking M of the net N is a home marking of (N, M_0) if it is reachable from every marking of $[M_0\rangle$.

We say that (N, M_0) has a home marking if some reachable marking is a home marking.

Using the results of Chapter 3, we can easily prove the following proposition.

Proposition 8.2 *Home markings of live S- and T-systems*

Every reachable marking of a live S-system or a live T-system is a home marking.

Proof:

Let M be a reachable marking of a live S-system or a live T-system (N, M_0). We prove that M is a home marking.

Let L be another reachable marking of (N, M_0). By the Second Reachability Theorem for S-systems (Theorem 3.8) and the Reachability Theorem for T-systems (Theorem 3.21), M_0 agrees with M and L on every S-invariant of the net N. So L and M also agree on all S-invariants. By the same two theorems, M is reachable from L.   □

This proposition does not hold for live free-choice systems, not even for live and bounded ones. For instance, the initial marking of the system shown in Figure 8.1 is not a home marking. In fact, it cannot be reached from any other (different) marking. However, the system does have home markings: one of them is the marking that puts one token in the places s_7 and s_8. This marking can be reached by the occurrence of the transitions t_3 and t_6.

We show in this section that all live and bounded free-choice systems have home markings. The proof uses two preliminary results. The first one is Lemma 8.3, which states that in the case of *bounded* systems the existence of home markings is equivalent to a confluence property. Confluence properties are those of the form

> *If two markings K and L of a net satisfy the property P, then K and $L* *have a common successor, i.e., $[K\rangle \cap [L\rangle \neq \emptyset$.*

The other result is the First Confluence Theorem[1] (Theorem 8.4), which states a confluence property of the *live* markings of free-choice nets.

Lemma 8.3

A bounded system has a home marking iff $[K\rangle \cap [L\rangle \neq \emptyset$ for every two reachable markings K and L.

Proof:

($\Rightarrow$): Every home marking belongs to $[K\rangle \cap [L\rangle$ by definition.

($\Leftarrow$): We prove that for every finite subset $\mathcal{M}$ of reachable markings, there exists a marking M which is reachable from every marking of $\mathcal{M}$. The result then follows by taking $\mathcal{M}$ as the set of reachable markings of the system, which is finite by boundedness.

The proof is by induction on the size of $\mathcal{M}$. If $\mathcal{M}$ is the empty set, we are done. Otherwise, $\mathcal{M}$ contains some marking M'. By the induction hypothesis, there exists a marking M'' reachable from every marking of $\mathcal{M} \setminus \{M'\}$. Since the set $[M'\rangle \cap [M''\rangle$ is nonempty by the assumption, it contains some marking M. Then M is reachable from every marking of $\mathcal{M}$.   □

---

[1]The Second Confluence Theorem can be found in the next chapter.

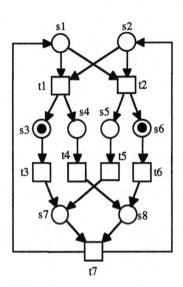

Fig. 8.1   A live and bounded free-choice system which is not cyclic

The First Confluence Theorem states that if two live markings K and L of a free-choice net satisfy the equation

$$L = K + \mathbf{N} \cdot X$$

for some nonnegative integer vector X, then $[K\rangle \cap [L\rangle \neq \emptyset$. For the proof, we construct two markings K' and L' such that $K \xrightarrow{*} K'$, $L \xrightarrow{*} L'$ and

$$L' = K' + \mathbf{N} \cdot X'$$

for some nonnegative vector X' *smaller* than X, i.e., $X' \leq X$ and $X' \neq X$. Iterating this construction as long as necessary, we obtain two markings K'' and L'', reachable from K and L such that

$$L'' = K'' + \mathbf{N} \cdot \mathbf{0} = K''$$

Since K'' and L'' coincide, they belong to $[K\rangle \cap [L\rangle$.

Theorem 8.4   *First Confluence Theorem*

Let N be a free-choice net. If K and L are two live markings of N such that $L = K + \mathbf{N} \cdot X$ for some nonnegative integer vector X, then $[K\rangle \cap [L\rangle \neq \emptyset$.

Proof:

By induction on the sum k of the components of X.

Base. $k = 0$. Then $X = \mathbf{0}$, and $K = L$.

Step. $k > 0$. Let $K \xrightarrow{\sigma\, t} K'$ be an occurrence sequence of minimal length satisfying $X(t) > 0$. Such a sequence exists by the liveness of K.

We claim that L enables σ. It suffices to prove $L(s) \geq K(s)$ for every place s in the pre-set of the transitions of σ.

Let t be an arbitrary transition that occurs in σ, and let $\sigma = \sigma_1 t\, \sigma_2$. Let s be an input place of t. Assume $L(s) < K(s)$. Since $L = K + \mathbf{N} \cdot X$, we have $X(u) > 0$ for some transition $u \in s^\bullet$. By the free-choice property, u and t are enabled at the same markings. Therefore, $\sigma_1 u$ is enabled at K. Moreover, it is shorter than $\sigma\, t$, which contradicts the minimality of $\sigma\, t$, and proves the claim.

By this claim, there exists a marking L' such that $L \xrightarrow{\sigma} L'$. We now have

$$
\begin{aligned}
L' &= L + \mathbf{N} \cdot \overrightarrow{\sigma} & \text{(Marking Equation)} \\
&= K + \mathbf{N} \cdot (\overrightarrow{\sigma} + X) & (L = K + \mathbf{N} \cdot X) \\
&= K + \mathbf{N} \cdot \overrightarrow{\sigma\, t} + \mathbf{N} \cdot (X - \overrightarrow{t}) \\
&= K' + \mathbf{N} \cdot (X - \overrightarrow{t}) & (K \xrightarrow{\sigma\, t} K', \text{ Marking Equation})
\end{aligned}
$$

The sum of the components of $X - \overrightarrow{t}$ is $k - 1$. The induction hypothesis implies $[K'\rangle \cap [L'\rangle \neq \emptyset$. Since K' and L' are reachable from K and L, $[K\rangle \cap [L\rangle \neq \emptyset$. □

Theorem 8.5   *Existence of home markings*

Live and bounded free-choice systems have home markings.

Proof:

Let (N, M_0) be a live and bounded free-choice system. By Lemma 8.3, it suffices to prove $[K\rangle \cap [L\rangle \neq \emptyset$ for every two reachable markings K and L.

Let K and L be two arbitrary reachable markings. Then, $M_0 \xrightarrow{\sigma_K} K$ and $M_0 \xrightarrow{\sigma_L} L$ for some sequences σ_1 and σ_2. By the Marking Equation

$$
K = M_0 + \mathbf{N} \cdot \overrightarrow{\sigma_K} \qquad L = M_0 + \mathbf{N} \cdot \overrightarrow{\sigma_L}
$$

So we have

$$
L = K + \mathbf{N} \cdot (\overrightarrow{\sigma_L} - \overrightarrow{\sigma_K})
$$

The First Confluence Theorem cannot be applied yet, because the vector $\overrightarrow{\sigma_L} - \overrightarrow{\sigma_K}$ may have negative components. To solve this problem, we take a positive T-invariant J of N, which exists because N is well-formed (Theorem 2.38), and a number k such that $\overrightarrow{\sigma_L} - \overrightarrow{\sigma_K} + k\, J \geq \mathbf{0}$. Then, we have

$$
L = K + \mathbf{N} \cdot (\overrightarrow{\sigma_L} - \overrightarrow{\sigma_K} + k\, J)
$$

and so $[K\rangle \cap [L\rangle \neq \emptyset$ by the First Confluence Theorem. □

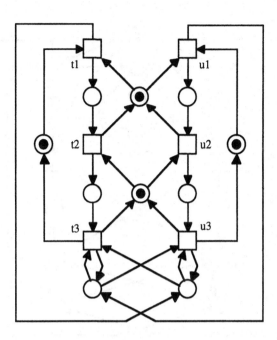

Fig. 8.2 A live and bounded system with exactly two infinite occurrence sequences

To finish the section we exhibit a live and bounded system without home markings. Let us first consider the system of Figure 8.2. This system has exactly two infinite occurrence sequences:

$$t_1\, t_2\, u_1\, t_3\, (u_2\, t_1\, u_3\, t_2\, u_1\, t_3)^\omega$$
$$u_1\, (u_2\, t_1\, u_3\, t_2\, u_1\, t_3)^\omega$$

Moreover, after t_1 or u_1 have occurred, the initial marking cannot be reached again, and therefore it is not a home marking. However, the system does have a home marking, namely the marking reached by the sequences $t_1\, t_2\, u_1\, t_3$ and u_1.

We now add some places and transitions and obtain the system of Figure 8.3, which is also live and bounded.

This new system has more than two infinite occurrence sequences, but all of them still start either with t_1 or with u_1. Again, once t_1 or u_1 have occurred, the initial marking cannot be reached again. Moreover, the intersection of the sets of markings reached by the sequences that start with t_1 and u_1 only contains the initial marking.[2] It follows that the system has no home markings.

---

[2] All these facts can be shown by direct construction of the reachability relation. The system has 21 reachable markings.

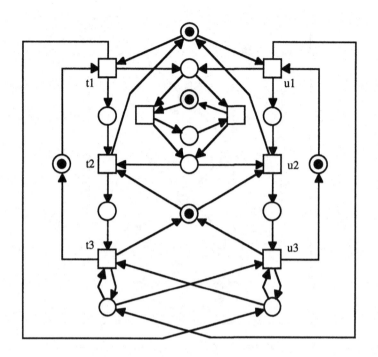

Fig. 8.3 A live and bounded system without home markings

8.2   A characterization of the home markings

We show that traps can be used to prove that a given marking is not a home marking. We will first consider an example. Let M_0 be the initial marking of the system shown in Figure 8.1. The set $\{s_1, s_2, s_4, s_5, s_7, s_8\}$ is a trap, and is moreover unmarked at M_0. The occurrence of t_3 leads to a marking M which puts a token in s_7, and therefore marks this trap. Since marked traps remain marked, M_0 cannot be reached from M, which implies that M_0 is not a home marking.

Proposition 8.6   *A property of home markings*

A home marking of a live system (N, M_0) marks every proper trap of N.

Proof:

Let M be a home marking of (N, M_0), and let R be a proper trap of N. Since liveness implies place-liveness, some reachable marking L marks R. Since M is a home marking, we have $L \xrightarrow{*} M$. Since marked traps remain marked, M marks the trap R.   □

The rest of the section is devoted to proving that this necessary condition is also sufficient for live and bounded free-choice systems, a result called in the sequel the Home Marking Theorem:

> *A reachable marking of a live and bounded free-choice system (N, M_0) is a home marking if and only if it marks every proper trap of N.*

We reduce the 'if' part of the Home Marking Theorem to a more convenient statement using the following lemma:

Lemma 8.7

Let (N, M_0) be a system having a home marking M_H and satisfying the following property: for every reachable marking K which marks all proper traps of N, if $K \xrightarrow{t} L$ for some transition t, then $L \xrightarrow{*} K$. Then every reachable marking which marks all proper traps is a home marking.

Proof:

Let M be a reachable marking that marks every proper trap of N. We show that M is a home marking.

Since M_H is a home marking, it suffices to prove $M_H \xrightarrow{*} M$.

Since M is a reachable marking of (N, M_0) and M_H a home marking, there exists an occurrence sequence

$$M = M_1 \xrightarrow{t_1} M_2 \xrightarrow{t_2} \cdots \xrightarrow{t_{n-1}} M_n \xrightarrow{t_n} M_H$$

Since M marks all proper traps of N and marked traps remain marked, all the intermediate markings $M_2, \ldots, M_n$ and M_H mark all proper traps of N too. By repeated application of the hypothesis, we get

$$M_H \xrightarrow{*} M_n \xrightarrow{*} \cdots \xrightarrow{*} M_2 \xrightarrow{*} M_1 = M$$

which proves $M_H \xrightarrow{*} M$.   □

Since live and bounded free-choice systems have home markings by Theorem 8.5, the 'if' part of the Home Marking Theorem reduces to:

> (A) *If a reachable marking K of a live and bounded free-choice system marks all proper traps of the net, and $K \xrightarrow{t} L$ for some transition t, then $L \xrightarrow{*} K$.*

We outline the proof of (A). To prove $L \xrightarrow{*} K$, we shall show that there exists an occurrence sequence

$$K = K_1 \xrightarrow{u_1} K_2 \xrightarrow{u_2} \cdots \xrightarrow{u_{m-1}} K_m \xrightarrow{t} K_{m+1}$$

called in the sequel the *auxiliary* sequence, satisfying the following two properties:

(1) for $i = 1, \ldots, m - 1$, the transitions t and u_i belong to different clusters, and

(2) for $i = 1, \ldots, m$, $K_{i+1} \xrightarrow{*} K_i$.

Since the net is a free-choice net, and by (1), the pre-sets of t and u_i are disjoint for $i = 1, \ldots, m - 1$. Therefore, since K enables t, the transitions t and u_i are concurrently enabled at the marking K_i. So we get the picture of Figure 8.4.

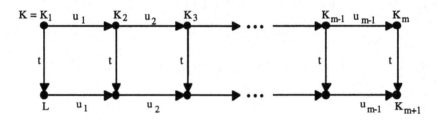

Fig. 8.4

By (2), this picture can be extended to the one of Figure 8.5, which contains a path leading from L to K_1. Therefore $L \xrightarrow{*} K$, because $K_1 = K$.

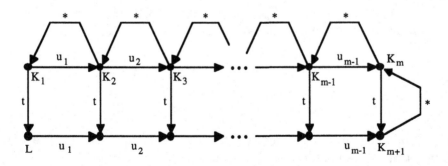

Fig. 8.5

Let us see how this works in an example. Let (N, K) be the free-choice system of Figure 8.6. The reader can easily check that this system is live and 1-bounded, and

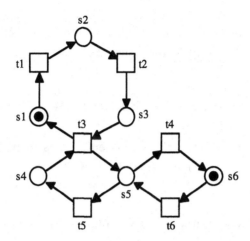

Fig. 8.6 A free-choice net and a home marking

that the marking K marks all proper traps of N. Let L be the marking obtained by the occurrence of t_1 (L marks s_2 and s_6). Making use of the 1-boundedness of (N, K), we represent a reachable marking by the set of places in which it puts one token; with this convention, $K = \{s_1, s_6\}$ and $L = \{s_2, s_6\}$.

We consider the auxiliary sequence

$$\{s_1, s_6\} \xrightarrow{t_6} \{s_1, s_5\} \xrightarrow{t_5} \{s_1, s_4\} \xrightarrow{t_1} \{s_2, s_4\}$$

which satisfies (1) and (2):

(1) t_1 does not belong to the clusters of t_6 and t_5, and

(2) $\{s_2, s_4\} \xrightarrow{t_2 t_3 t_5} \{s_1, s_4\} \xrightarrow{t_1 t_2 t_3} \{s_1, s_5\} \xrightarrow{t_4} \{s_1, s_6\}$.

We get $\{s_2, s_6\} \xrightarrow{\sigma} \{s_1, s_6\}$ for $\sigma = t_6\, t_5\, (t_2\, t_3\, t_5)\, (t_1\, t_2\, t_3)\, (t_4)$.

In Lemma 8.9, we give a criterion for the construction of the auxiliary sequence which guarantees that property (2) is satisfied. The sequence itself is constructed in Lemma 8.10.

Transition occurrences of activated T-components

It is easy to see that the statement (A) holds for live T-systems: by Theorem 8.2, $K \xrightarrow{t} L$ directly implies $L \xrightarrow{*} K$ for any reachable marking K. We show that the same property holds for activated T-components. Recall that a T-component N_1 of a net N is activated at a marking M of N, if the system $(N_1, M|_{S_1})$ is live, where S_1 is the set of places of N_1 (Definition 5.19).

Lemma 8.8

Let K be a marking of a net N which activates a T-component N_1 of N. If $K \xrightarrow{t} L$ for some transition t of N_1, then $L \xrightarrow{*} K$.

Proof:

Let K_1 and L_1 be the restriction of K and L to the set of places of N_1. Since N_1 is a T-component of N, we have $K_1 \xrightarrow{t} L_1$.

By the definition of an activated T-component, K_1 is a live marking of N_1. By Theorem 8.2, $L_1 \xrightarrow{\sigma} K_1$ in N_1 for some sequence σ. Since N_1 is a T-component, $L \xrightarrow{\sigma} K$ in N. $\square$

We shall use the following criterion for the inductive construction of the auxiliary sequence:

> Extend the sequence constructed so far by a transition which belongs to a T-component activated at the current marking.

By Lemma 8.8, a sequence constructed according to this criterion is guaranteed to satisfy the second property of the auxiliary sequence, namely that if $K_i \xrightarrow{t} K_{i+1}$ belongs to the sequence then $K_{i+1} \xrightarrow{*} K_i$. In the system of Figure 8.6, the initial marking K activates the T-component generated by $\{s_5, t_4, s_6, t_6\}$, and enables the transition t_6. This is the reason why we choose t_6 as the first transition of the auxiliary sequence.

We still need to prove that this criterion is always applicable. In fact, there are live and bounded free-choice systems in which no T-component is activated, and to which the criterion could not be applied (e.g. the system of Figure 8.1). However, we know that the first marking of the auxiliary sequence *marks all proper traps*, a property that the initial marking in Figure 8.1 does not enjoy. The first part of the following lemma shows that every marking which marks all traps activates some T-component, and therefore the criterion can be applied. The second part shows that we even have some freedom to choose this T-component, a fact that will be useful later.

Lemma 8.9

Let N be a well-formed free-choice net, let K be a marking of N which marks all proper traps, and let α be a total allocation of N. There is a T-component N_1 of N such that

(1) N_1 is activated at K, and

(2) every transition of N_1 enabled at K is α-allocated.

Proof:

Throughout the proof, we say that a place is marked (unmarked) if it is marked (not marked) at the marking K.

Let R be the set of unmarked places of N and let Q be the maximal trap of N contained in R. Since K marks all proper traps of N and Q is not marked, Q is the empty trap. Let C be the set of clusters containing places of R. By the Circuit-free Allocation Lemma (Lemma 4.26), there exists an allocation β with domain C which is circuit-free for R. So no circuit of N contains only unmarked places and β-allocated transitions.

The transitions of a cluster c of N are enabled at K iff none of the places of c is unmarked, i.e., iff $c \cap R = \emptyset$. We construct a total allocation γ as follows:

$$\gamma(c) = \begin{cases} \alpha(c) & \text{if } c \cap R = \emptyset \quad \text{(the transitions of } c \text{ are enabled at } K\text{)} \\ \beta(c) & \text{if } c \cap R \neq \emptyset \quad \text{(the transitions of } c \text{ are not enabled at } K\text{)} \end{cases}$$

Since γ is a total allocation, it is in particular cyclic. By the Cyclic Allocation Lemma (Lemma 5.16) there exists an occurrence sequence $K \xrightarrow{\tau\sigma}$ such that σ is infinite and its alphabet $\mathcal{A}(\sigma)$ contains only γ-allocated transitions.

By the Reproduction Lemma (Lemma 2.39), there is a semi-positive T-invariant J such that $\langle J \rangle \subseteq \mathcal{A}(\sigma)$. Let J' be a minimal T-invariant satisfying $\langle J' \rangle \subseteq \langle J \rangle$. Since minimal T-invariants induce T-components (Theorem 5.17), there is a T-component $N_1 = (S_1, T_1, F_1)$ of N such that $\langle J' \rangle = T_1$. Altogether we have

$$T_1 = \langle J' \rangle \subseteq \langle J \rangle \subseteq \mathcal{A}(\sigma)$$

Since $\mathcal{A}(\sigma)$ contains only γ-allocated transitions, all transitions of N_1 are γ-allocated. We now prove the two parts of the proposition.

(1) N_1 is activated at K.

By definition, K activates N_1 iff $K|_{S_1}$ (the restriction of K to S_1) is a live marking of N_1. By the Liveness Theorem of T-systems (Theorem 3.15), $K|_{S_1}$ is a live marking of N_1 iff every circuit of N_1 contains a place which is marked by $K|_{S_1}$. We prove indirectly that this is the case.

Assume that a circuit of N_1 contains only unmarked places. We prove that all its transitions are β-allocated, which contradicts the circuit-freeness of β for the set R of unmarked places. Let t be an arbitrary transition of the circuit. Since t is a transition of N_1, it is γ-allocated. Therefore, we have $t = \gamma([s])$ for the unique input place s of t that belongs to the circuit. Since $s \in R$, we have $\gamma([s]) = \beta([s])$, and therefore t is β-allocated.

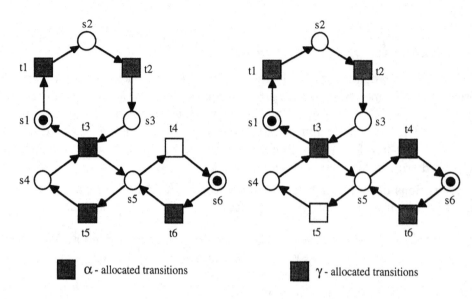

Fig. 8.7   The system of Figure 8.6 and two allocations

(2) Every transition of N_1 enabled by K is α-allocated.

Let t be a transition of N_1 enabled at K. Since N_1 contains only γ-allocated transitions, t is γ-allocated. Since K enables t, it marks every place of the cluster $[t]$, and so $[t] \cap R = \emptyset$. By the definition of γ we have $\gamma([t]) = \alpha([t])$, and therefore t is α-allocated. $\square$

Figure 8.7 illustrates this result. The figure on the left shows a total allocation α of the system (N, K) of Figure 8.6; α allocates every transition except t_4. The allocation β, not shown in the picture, allocates t_2, t_3 and t_4. It is circuit-free for the set $\{s_2, s_3, s_4, s_5\}$ of unmarked places.

The marking K activates the T-component generated by $\{s_5, t_4, s_6, t_6\}$. All its transitions are γ-allocated. The only one enabled at K is t_6, which is also α-allocated.

Construction of the auxiliary occurrence sequence

Recall that the auxiliary sequence must have K as first marking and t as last transition (the transition satisfying $K \xrightarrow{t} L$). We construct this sequence with the help of a total allocation α that points to the cluster $[t]$ (more precisely, to the set of clusters $\{[t]\}$) and moreover allocates t. Then, the Pointing Allocation Lemma (Lemma 6.5) can be used to show that every occurrence sequence of sufficient length that agrees with α contains t.

In the example of Figure 8.7, the allocation α points to the cluster $[t_1]$, and every infinite occurrence sequence that agrees with α contains occurrences of t_1.

Lemma 8.10

Let N be a well-formed free-choice net, let t be a transition of N, and let K be a live marking which marks every proper trap of N. There exists an occurrence sequence

$$K = K_1 \xrightarrow{u_1} K_2 \xrightarrow{u_2} \cdots \xrightarrow{u_{m-1}} K_m \xrightarrow{t} K_{m+1}$$

satisfying

(1) for $i = 1, \ldots, m-1$, the transitions u_i and t belong to different clusters, and

(2) for $i = 1, \ldots, m-1$, the marking K_i activates a T-component which contains u_i, and K_m activates a T-component which contains t.

Proof:

Since N is well-formed, it is strongly connected. By the first part of the Pointing Allocation Lemma 6.5, some allocation α, whose domain contains all the clusters of N except $[t]$, points to $\{[t]\}$. The total allocation β defined by

$$\beta(c) = \begin{cases} \alpha(c) & \text{if } c \neq [t] \\ t & \text{if } c = [t] \end{cases}$$

also points to $\{[t]\}$ and moreover allocates t.

By Lemma 8.9, there is a T-component $N_1 = (S_1, T_1, F_1)$, activated at K, such that every transition of N_1 enabled at K is β-allocated. Moreover, since $K|_{S_1}$ is a live marking of N_1, it enables at least one transition u_1 of N_1. Since N_1 is a T-component, the marking K also enables u_1 in N. Let K_2 be the marking of N defined by $K \xrightarrow{u_1} K_2$. Then K_2 is again a live marking of N, and it marks all traps because marked traps remain marked. So we can apply Lemma 8.9 to K_2. Repeating this construction infinitely often, we obtain an infinite occurrence sequence $K = K_1 \xrightarrow{u_1} K_2 \xrightarrow{u_2} K_3 \xrightarrow{u_3} \cdots$ such that

- for $i = 1, 2, 3, \ldots$, the marking K_i activates a T-component which contains u_i, and

- for $i = 1, 2, 3, \ldots$, the transition u_i is β-allocated.

Let $\sigma = u_1 \, u_2 \, u_3 \ldots$ Since N is well-formed and free-choice, the system (N, K) is bounded (Theorem 5.8(2)). By the second part of the Pointing Allocation Lemma, and since σ contains only β-allocated transitions, some transition of the cluster $[t]$ occurs in σ. Since $\beta([t]) = t$, this transition is t.

Let m be the smallest number satisfying $u_m = t$, and let $\sigma_m = u_1 \ldots u_m$. The sequence σ_m satisfies (2) because it inherits this property from σ. Since the infinite sequence σ contains only β-allocated transitions and t is the only β-allocated transition of $[t]$, no transition of σ_m except u_m belongs to $[t]$. So σ_m satisfies (1). $\square$

The Home Marking Theorem

Theorem 8.11   *Home Marking Theorem*

A reachable marking of a live and bounded free-choice system (N, M_0) is a home marking iff it marks every proper trap of N.

Proof:

($\Rightarrow$): Holds for arbitrary live systems by Proposition 8.6.

($\Leftarrow$): By Lemma 8.7, it suffices to prove: if a reachable marking K marks all proper traps of N, and $K \xrightarrow{t} L$ for some transition t, then $L \xrightarrow{*} K$. By Lemma 8.10, there exists an occurrence sequence

$$K = K_1 \xrightarrow{u_1} K_2 \xrightarrow{u_2} \cdots \xrightarrow{u_{m-1}} K_m \xrightarrow{t} K_{m+1}$$

such that

(1) for $i = 1 \ldots m - 1$, the transitions u_i and t belong to different clusters;

(2) for $i = 1 \ldots m$, the marking K_i activates a T-component which contains u_i, and K_m activates a T-component which contains t.

We prove separately $L \xrightarrow{*} K_{m+1}$ and $K_{m+1} \xrightarrow{*} K$:

- $L \xrightarrow{*} K_{m+1}$.

  K_1 enables t, because $K_1 = K$ and K enables t. By (1), the transitions u_i and t belong to different clusters for $i = 1 \ldots m - 1$. In particular, u_i removes no tokens from the places of $[t]$, which implies that K_i enables the sequences $t\, u_i$ and $u_i\, t$. Since these two sequences lead to the same marking, we have by repeated exchange of the transitions u_i and t

  $$K \xrightarrow{t} L \xrightarrow{u_1\, u_2\, \ldots\, u_{m-1}} K_{m+1}$$

- $K_{m+1} \xrightarrow{*} K$.

  By (2), we can apply Lemma 8.8 to the markings $K_1, \ldots, K_{m+1}$ and derive

  $$K_{m+1} \xrightarrow{*} K_m \xrightarrow{*} \cdots \xrightarrow{*} K_2 \xrightarrow{*} K_1$$

  So $K_{m+1} \xrightarrow{*} K_1 = K$. $\square$

8.3 Derived results

We show two consequences of the Home Marking Theorem.

Theorem 8.12   *Polynomiality of the home marking problem*

The following problem is solvable in polynomial time:

> Given a live and bounded free-choice system, to decide if a given reachable marking is a home marking.

Proof:

Let (N, M_0) be a live and bounded free-choice system, and let M be a reachable marking. We show that the condition of the Home Marking Theorem can be tested in polynomial time in the size of the net N. Let R be the set of places of N which are not marked by M. Every proper trap of N is marked by M iff the only trap contained in R is the empty trap. The algorithm given in Exercise 4.5 computes the maximal trap contained in a given set of places. Therefore, every proper trap of N is marked by M iff this algorithm, applied to R, yields the empty set as output. Since the algorithm runs in polynomial time in the size of N, the result follows.   □

This theorem implies in particular that it can be decided in polynomial time if the *initial* marking of a live and bounded free-choice system is a home marking. Systems satisfying this property are called *cyclic* and will be studied in the next chapter.

Theorem 8.13   *Occurrence sequences that reach a home marking*

Any occurrence sequence of a live and bounded free-choice system which contains each transition at least once yields a home marking.

Proof:

Since every place of a live and bounded system has an input transition, every proper trap becomes marked during the occurrence of the sequence. Since marked traps remain marked, every proper trap is marked when it ends. Apply then the Home Marking Theorem.   □

Exercises

Exercise 8.1

Prove that every bounded system (N, M_0) has a reachable marking M which is a home marking of (N, M).

Exercise 8.2

Exhibit a system (N, M_0) which has home markings, but also an infinite sequence $M_0\sigma$ such that none of the markings reached along the occurrence of σ is a home marking.

Exercise 8.3

1) Prove using a trap that the initial marking of the system shown in Figure 8.2 is not a home marking.

2) Prove that the system of Figure 8.3 has no home markings.

Exercise 8.4

Prove that if the null marking is a home marking of a live system, then the system contains no proper traps.

Exercise 8.5   *

Try to find a live and bounded system without home markings with fewer nodes than that of Figure 8.3 (if you succeed, please send it to the authors!).

Bibliographic Notes

Best and Voss proved in [11] that live and 1-bounded free-choice systems have home markings. Vogler observed in [76] that the result could be easily generalized to live and bounded free-choice systems. The proof of the text, based on the First Confluence Theorem, is due to Teruel and Silva [73]. The system of Figure 8.3 is taken from [11].

The Home Marking Theorem was proved by Best and the authors in [8]. Best, Cherkasova and Desel use it in [9] to give a compositional characterization of those markings M of a well-formed free-choice net N that are home markings of the system (N, M).

Chapter 9 ————————

Reachability and shortest sequences

We obtained in Chapter 3 a very satisfactory characterization of the reachable markings of live S-systems and live T-systems: a marking is reachable if and only if it agrees with the initial marking on all S-invariants. We also showed in Chapter 2 that, given an arbitrary system (N, M_0), a marking M of N agrees with M_0 on all S-invariants if and only if the equation

$$M = M_0 + \mathbf{N} \cdot X$$

has a (rational-valued) solution. Together, these two results reduce the reachability problem for live S- and T-systems to the problem of solving a system of linear equations.

The relation "agree on all S-invariants" no longer characterizes the reachable markings of live free-choice systems, not even of live and bounded ones. Consider the net of Figure 9.1 and the live and bounded markings K, which puts tokens on s_3 and s_6 (black tokens), and L, which puts tokens on s_4 and s_5 (white tokens). These two markings agree on all S-invariants, because the vector $(\,1\,1\,2\,0\,0\,2\,2\,)$ is a solution of the equation $L = K + \mathbf{N} \cdot X$. However, L is not reachable from K and K is not reachable from L.

Still, the relation "agree on all S-invariants" is useful to characterize the reachable markings of live, bounded and *cyclic* free choice systems. A system is cyclic if its initial marking is a home marking. In the first section of this chapter we obtain the following result, called the Reachability Theorem:

> *The reachable markings of a live, bounded and cyclic free-choice system are those which agree with the initial marking on all S-invariants and, moreover, mark all proper traps of the net.*

In the second section we prove the Shortest Sequence Theorem for free-choice systems, a companion of the Shortest Sequence Theorems for S- and T-systems presented in Chapter 3:

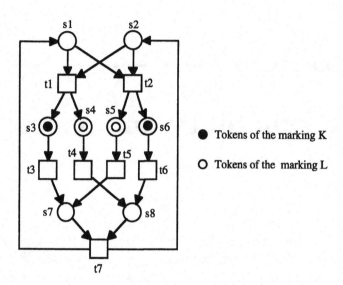

Fig. 9.1   A free-choice net and two live and bounded markings

Every reachable marking of a live and b-bounded free-choice system with n transitions can be reached from the initial marking by an occurrence sequence of length at most

$$b \cdot \frac{n \cdot (n+1) \cdot (n+2)}{6}$$

9.1   The Reachability Theorem

We shall prove the Reachability Theorem as a corollary of the Home Marking Theorem (see Chapter 8) and the following result:

If two live and bounded markings of a free-choice net agree on all S-invariants, then they have a common successor.

We call this result the Second Confluence Theorem, because it is similar to the First Confluence Theorem (Theorem 8.4). Both state that two markings K and L of a free-choice net N have a common successor, but under different conditions. In the First Confluence Theorem

(i) K and L must be live markings, and

(ii) the equation $L = K + \mathbf{N} \cdot X$ must have a *nonnegative, integer* solution X.

In the Second Confluence Theorem

(i') K and L must be live and bounded markings, and

(ii') they must agree on all S-invariants.

K and L agree on all S-invariants if and only if the equation $L = K + \mathbf{N} \cdot X$ has a *rational-valued* solution (Theorem 2.34). So the Second Confluence Theorem refines the First in the following sense: if K and L are not only live, but also bounded markings, then in order to ensure that they have a common successor it suffices to find a rational-valued solution of the equation $L = K + \mathbf{N} \cdot X$, instead of a nonnegative, integer one.

The proof of the Second Confluence Theorem can be outlined as follows. If the net is a T-net, then the Reachability Theorem for T-systems ensures that K and L are reachable from each other, and therefore any of them is a common successor of both. If the net is not a T-net, then it contains a CP-subnet (CP-subnets were defined and studied in Chapter 7). We let transitions of this CP-subnet occur from both K and L, in such a way that the projections of the two reached markings K' and L' on the places of the subnet are equal. After that we "freeze" the transitions of the CP-subnet, i.e., we forbid them to occur again. Since CP-subnets are transition-bordered, we preserve in this way these locally equal markings. If the rest of the net is a T-net, then we are done. Otherwise, it contains a CP-subnet, and we iterate the procedure until we get two markings which coincide everywhere, and are therefore the same. This marking is a common successor of K and L.

Let us see how this construction works in the example of Figure 9.1. We select the CP-subnet $\widehat{N}$ shown in Figure 9.2(a), and let the transitions t_3 and t_4 occur from the markings K and L, respectively, to yield the markings K' and L' shown in Figure 9.2(b). Notice that K' and L' coincide on the net $\widehat{N}$ (they are both the zero marking there).

Let $\overline{N}$ be the subnet generated by all nodes that do not belong to $\widehat{N}$. Let $\overline{K'}$ and $\overline{L'}$ be the markings K' and L' respectively, restricted to the places of $\overline{N}$ (Figure 9.2(c)). Both $(\overline{N}, \overline{K'})$ and $(\overline{N}, \overline{L'})$ are live and bounded T-systems. We have

$$\overline{K'} \xrightarrow{\ t_6\ t_7\ t_2\ t_6\ } \overline{L'}$$

Since no transitions of $\widehat{N}$ occur in the sequence $t_6\ t_7\ t_2\ t_6$, and $\widehat{N}$ is a transition-bordered subnet of N, we also have in N

$$K' \xrightarrow{\ t_6\ t_7\ t_2\ t_6\ } L'$$

Therefore, L' is a successor of both K and L.

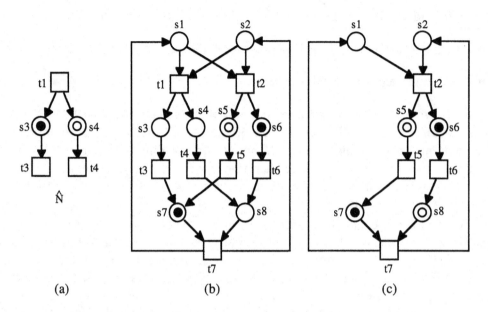

Fig. 9.2 The procedure applied to the markings of Figure 9.1

In this example it was easy to find occurrence sequences leading to markings K' and L' which coincide on $\widehat{N}$. To find such sequences in the general case we profit from the results on CP-subnets obtained in Chapter 7:

> *The markings K and L enable two occurrence sequences that contain only non-way-in transitions of $\widehat{N}$, and lead to two markings K' and L' at which none of these transitions is enabled*
> (was proved in Proposition 7.8(1))

> *K' and L' coincide in $\widehat{N}$, i.e., $\widehat{K'} = \widehat{L'}$*
> (will be proved in Lemma 9.2)

In order to use induction, we also have to show that the systems $(\overline{N}, \overline{K'})$ and $(\overline{N}, \overline{L'})$ enjoy the same properties as (N, K) and (N, L):

> *$(\overline{N}, \overline{K'})$ and $(\overline{N}, \overline{L'})$ are live and bounded free-choice systems*
> (was proved in Proposition 7.8(2))

> *$\overline{K'}$ and $\overline{L'}$ agree on all S-invariants of $\overline{N}$*
> (will be proved in Lemma 9.4)

We fix the following notations for the rest of the proof:

- N is a well-formed free-choice net, but not a T-net.

- $\widehat{N}$ is a CP-subnet of N (which exists by Proposition 7.11), $\widehat{\mathbf{N}}$ its incidence matrix, $\widehat{T}$ is its set of transitions, and t_{in} is its unique way-in transition (the uniqueness of t_{in} is guaranteed by Proposition 7.10).

- $\overline{N}$ is the subnet of N generated by the set of nodes that do not belong to $\widehat{N}$ ($\overline{N}$ is a well-formed free-choice net by Corollary 7.9(1)) and $\overline{\mathbf{N}}$ is its incidence matrix.

- The restriction of a marking M of N to the places of $\widehat{N}$ is denoted by $\widehat{M}$, and the restriction of M to the places of $\overline{N}$ by $\overline{M}$.

- K and L are live and bounded markings of N which agree on all S-invariants. σ_K and σ_L are occurrence sequences enabled at K and L, containing only transitions of $\widehat{T} \setminus \{t_{in}\}$, and leading to markings K' and L' at which no transition of $\widehat{T} \setminus \{t_{in}\}$ is enabled.

Our first goal is to prove $\widehat{K'} = \widehat{L'}$. We need the following lemma.

Lemma 9.1

For every transition t of $\widehat{N}$, there exists a path from t_{in} to t inside $\widehat{N}$ whose places are unmarked at K'.

Proof:

This path is constructed backwards by choosing for each place its unique input transition, and for each transition different from t_{in} one of its unmarked input places (which exist, because no transition of $\widehat{N}$ except possibly t_{in} is enabled at K').

This construction terminates, because otherwise (N, K') would contain an unmarked circuit in which all places have exactly one input transition. The places of such a circuit are a siphon of N. Since K is a live marking, the marking K' is also live and marks all proper siphons (Theorem 6.17(ii)), a contradiction.

Since $\widehat{N}$ is transition-bordered, the construction must end at the unique way-in transition of $\widehat{N}$, i.e., at t_{in}.   □

Lemma 9.1 also holds after substituting L' for K' because both markings enjoy the same properties.

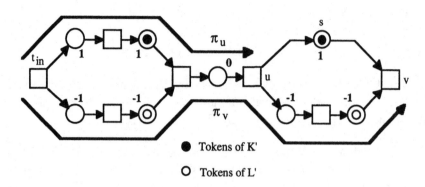

Fig. 9.3   Illustration of the proof of Lemma 9.2

Lemma 9.2

$\widehat{K'} = \widehat{L'}$.

Proof:

By assumption, K and L agree on all S-invariants. Since $K \xrightarrow{*} K'$ and $L \xrightarrow{*} L'$, the markings K' and L' also agree on all S-invariants.

We prove $K'(s) = L'(s)$ for every place s of $\widehat{N}$. We proceed indirectly and assume without loss of generality $K'(s) > L'(s)$ for some place s of $\widehat{N}$. Then, in particular, $K'(s) > 0$. We shall construct an S-invariant I such that $I \cdot K' \neq I \cdot L'$, which contradicts the assumption that K' and L' agree on all S-invariants.

Since $\widehat{N}$ is transition-bordered and a T-net, the place s has a unique input transition u and a unique output transition v. By Lemma 9.1, there exists a path π_u inside $\widehat{N}$, leading from t_{in} to u, whose places are unmarked at L', and there exists a path π_v, leading from t_{in} to v, whose places are unmarked at K'. In particular, since $K'(s) > 0$, the place s does not belong to π_v. We can further assume that no node appears in π_u or π_v more than once (see Figure 9.3).

Define the place-vectors I_u, I_s and I_v of N as follows

$$I_u(r) = \begin{cases} 1 & \text{if } r \text{ is in } \pi_u \\ 0 & \text{otherwise} \end{cases} \qquad I_s(r) = \begin{cases} 1 & \text{if } r = s \\ 0 & \text{otherwise} \end{cases} \qquad I_v(r) = \begin{cases} 1 & \text{if } r \text{ is in } \pi_v \\ 0 & \text{otherwise} \end{cases}$$

Define further $I = I_u + I_s - I_v$. For the T-net of Figure 9.3, the entries of I are shown in boldface.

We claim that I is an S-invariant. It follows from the definitions of I_u, I_s and I_v that $I \cdot M$ is equal to the number of tokens in the places of the path $\pi_u s v$ minus the number of tokens in the places of π_v. Observe that both paths start and end at the same nodes (t_{in} and v, respectively). Moreover, each place in these paths has exactly one input transition and exactly one output transition, because $\widehat{N}$ is transition-bordered and a T-net. Therefore, the occurrence of a transition t induces the same change in the number of tokens in π_u s v and π_v (either the two paths gain one token, or the two lose one token, or none of the two changes). So we have $I \cdot \mathbf{t} = 0$ for every transition t. This implies $I \cdot \mathbf{N} = \mathbf{0}$, which proves the claim.

Since the places of π_v are unmarked at K', and the places of π_u are unmarked at L', we have

$$I \cdot K' = (I_u + I_s) \cdot K' \geq I_s \cdot K' = K'(s)$$

$$I \cdot L' = (I_s - I_v) \cdot L' \leq I_s \cdot L' = L'(s)$$

Since $K'(s) > L'(s)$ by assumption, we obtain $I \cdot K' > I \cdot L'$, which finishes the proof. □

The next step is to prove that $\overline{K'}$ and $\overline{L'}$ agree on all S-invariants of $\overline{N}$. We need the following lemma:

Lemma 9.3

$\mathrm{Rank}(\mathbf{N}) = \mathrm{Rank}(\overline{\mathbf{N}}) + \mathrm{Rank}(\widehat{\mathbf{N}})$.

Proof:

Since $\widehat{N}$ has exactly one way-in transition t_{in}, every cluster of N is either a cluster of $\overline{N}$, or a cluster of $\widehat{N}$, or the cluster $[t_{in}]$, which contains elements of both $\widehat{N}$ and $\overline{N}$. So we have

$$|C_N| = (|C_{\overline{N}}| - 1) + (|C_{\widehat{N}}| - 1) + 1$$

where C_N, $C_{\overline{N}}$ and $C_{\widehat{N}}$ denote the set of clusters of N, $\overline{N}$ and $\widehat{N}$. Since N and $\overline{N}$ are well-formed free-choice nets, we obtain by the Rank Theorem

$$\mathrm{Rank}(\mathbf{N}) = |C_N| - 1 \quad \text{and} \quad \mathrm{Rank}(\overline{\mathbf{N}}) = |C_{\overline{N}}| - 1$$

Therefore

$$\mathrm{Rank}(\mathbf{N}) = \mathrm{Rank}(\overline{\mathbf{N}}) + (|C_{\widehat{N}}| - 1)$$

Every cluster of $\widehat{N}$ contains at least one transition, because $\widehat{N}$ is transition-bordered and N is strongly connected, and at most one transition, because $\widehat{N}$ is a T-net. So $|C_{\widehat{N}}| = |\widehat{T}|$, where $\widehat{T}$ is the set of transitions of $\widehat{N}$.

Since $\widehat{N}$ is a connected T-net, every T-invariant of $\widehat{N}$ is a multiple of the vector $(1 \ldots 1)$ (Proposition 3.16). Hence, we have $\mathrm{Rank}(\widehat{\mathbf{N}}) = |\widehat{T}| - 1 = |C_{\widehat{N}}| - 1$. □

Lemma 9.4

$\overline{K'}$ and $\overline{L'}$ agree on all S-invariants of $\overline{N}$.

Proof:

By Theorem 2.34, we have:

- Since K' and L' agree on all S-invariants of N, the equation $\mathbf{N} \cdot X = L' - K'$ has a rational-valued solution.

- To prove that $\overline{L'}$ and $\overline{K'}$ agree on all S-invariants of $\overline{N}$, it suffices to show that the equation $\overline{\mathbf{N}} \cdot X = \overline{L'} - \overline{K'}$ has a rational-valued solution.

It is a well-known result of linear algebra that an equation system $A \cdot X = B$, where A is a matrix and B a vector, has a solution if and only if the rank of A is equal to the rank of the matrix $[A\ B]$ obtained by adding B to A as rightmost column. Define $J = L' - K'$ and $\overline{J} = \overline{L'} - \overline{K'}$. Then we know

$$\mathrm{Rank}(\mathbf{N}) = \mathrm{Rank}(\,[\mathbf{N}\ J]\,)$$

and wish to show

$$\mathrm{Rank}(\overline{\mathbf{N}}) = \mathrm{Rank}(\,[\overline{\mathbf{N}}\ \overline{J}]\,)$$

Assume without loss of generality that the first rows of the matrix $\mathbf{N}$ correspond to the places of $\widehat{N}$ and its first columns to the transitions of $\widehat{N}$. Then, since $\widehat{N}$ is transition-bordered, $\mathbf{N}$ can be decomposed in the following way:

$$\mathbf{N} = \begin{pmatrix} \widehat{\mathbf{N}} & \mathbf{0} \\ A & \overline{\mathbf{N}} \end{pmatrix}$$

for some matrix A. Since K' and L' coincide on the places of $\widehat{N}$, the entries of J corresponding to places of $\widehat{N}$ are zero. So we get

$$[\mathbf{N}\ J] = \begin{pmatrix} \widehat{\mathbf{N}} & \mathbf{0} \\ A & \overline{\mathbf{N}} \end{pmatrix} \begin{pmatrix} \mathbf{0} \\ \overline{J} \end{pmatrix} = \begin{pmatrix} \widehat{\mathbf{N}} & \mathbf{0} \\ A & [\overline{\mathbf{N}}\ \overline{J}] \end{pmatrix}$$

From the form of this decomposition we can conclude

$$\mathrm{Rank}([\mathbf{N}\ J]) \geq \mathrm{Rank}(\widehat{\mathbf{N}}) + \mathrm{Rank}([\overline{\mathbf{N}}\ \overline{J}])$$

Therefore, we have

$$\begin{aligned} \mathrm{Rank}(\overline{\mathbf{N}}) &= \mathrm{Rank}(\mathbf{N}) - \mathrm{Rank}(\widehat{\mathbf{N}}) & \text{(Lemma 9.3)} \\ &= \mathrm{Rank}(\,[\mathbf{N}\ J]\,) - \mathrm{Rank}(\widehat{\mathbf{N}}) & (\mathrm{Rank}(\mathbf{N}) = \mathrm{Rank}(\,[\mathbf{N}\ J]\,)) \\ &\geq \mathrm{Rank}(\,[\overline{\mathbf{N}}\ \overline{J}]\,) & \text{(matrix decomposition of } [\mathbf{N}\ J]) \end{aligned}$$

So $\mathrm{Rank}(\overline{\mathbf{N}}) = \mathrm{Rank}([\overline{\mathbf{N}}\ \overline{J}])$, which finishes the proof. $\square$

We now collect all the results we have obtained and prove the Second Confluence Theorem according to our proof plan; the only point in which the plan has to be refined is the choice of the induction parameter.

Theorem 9.5   *Second Confluence Theorem*

If two live and bounded markings K and L of a free-choice net N agree on all S-invariants, then $[K\rangle \cap [L\rangle \neq \emptyset$.

Proof:

Let $N = (S, T, F)$. We prove the result by induction on

$$k = \sum_{s \in S}(|{}^\bullet s| + |s^\bullet| - 2)$$

Since N has live and bounded markings, it is well-formed, and therefore strongly connected. So every place has some input transition and some output transition. Therefore, k is nonnegative. Moreover, k is equal to 0 iff N is a T-net.

Base. $k = 0$. Then N is a T-net. By the Reachability Theorem for T-systems (Theorem 3.21), the markings K and L are reachable from each other, and therefore any of them is a common successor of both.

Step. $k > 0$. Then N is not a T-net. By Proposition 7.11, N has a CP-subnet $\widehat{N}$. Let $\widehat{T}$ be the set of transitions of $\widehat{N}$.

By Proposition 7.10, $\widehat{N}$ has exactly one way-in transition t_{in}. By Proposition 7.8, there exist two occurrence sequences σ_K, σ_L containing only transitions of $\widehat{T} \setminus \{t_{in}\}$, and leading to markings K', L' at which no transition of $\widehat{T} \setminus \{t_{in}\}$ is enabled. We show that the induction hypothesis can be applied to $\overline{N}$, $\overline{K'}$ and $\overline{L'}$, where $\overline{K'}$, $\overline{L'}$ are the projections of K', L' onto the places of $\overline{N}$. By Proposition 7.8, $(\overline{N}, \overline{K'})$ and $(\overline{N}, \overline{L'})$ are live and bounded free-choice systems. By Lemma 9.4, $\overline{K'}$ and $\overline{L'}$ agree on all the S-invariants of $\overline{N}$. It remains to prove $\overline{k} < k$, where $\overline{k}$ is the value of the induction parameter for $\overline{N}$. Since $\overline{N}$ is a subnet of N, we have $\overline{k} \leq k$. To prove $\overline{k} \neq k$, observe that $\overline{N}$ is a place-bordered subnet and so, e.g., the input places of t_{in} have less output transitions in $\overline{N}$ than in N.

By the induction hypothesis, there exist two occurrence sequences of $\overline{N}$

$$\overline{K'} \xrightarrow{\sigma_{K'}} \overline{M} \quad \text{and} \quad \overline{L'} \xrightarrow{\sigma_{L'}} \overline{M}$$

leading to the same marking $\overline{M}$. Since $\widehat{N}$ is transition-bordered, $\overline{N}$ is place-bordered. Therefore, $\sigma_{K'}$ and $\sigma_{L'}$ can also occur from K' and L' in the net N, without changing the markings on the places of $\widehat{N}$. So we have

$$K' \xrightarrow{\sigma_{K'}} K'' \quad \text{and} \quad L' \xrightarrow{\sigma_{L'}} L''$$

where

$$K''(s) = \begin{cases} \overline{M}(s) & \text{if } s \text{ belongs to } \overline{N} \\ K'(s) & \text{if } s \text{ belongs to } \widehat{N} \end{cases} \qquad L''(s) = \begin{cases} \overline{M}(s) & \text{if } s \text{ belongs to } \overline{N} \\ L'(s) & \text{if } s \text{ belongs to } \widehat{N} \end{cases}$$

By Lemma 9.2, $K'(s) = \widehat{K'}(s) = \widehat{L'}(s) = L'(s)$ for every place s of $\widehat{N}$, and so $K'' = L''$. Then we have $K \xrightarrow{\sigma_K \sigma_{K'}} K''$ and $L \xrightarrow{\sigma_L \sigma_{L'}} K''$, which proves the result.

$\square$

We now prove the Reachability Theorem as a corollary of the Home Marking Theorem and the Second Confluence Theorem.

Theorem 9.6   *Reachability Theorem*

Let (N, M_0) be a live and bounded free-choice system, which is moreover cyclic (i.e., M_0 is a home marking). A marking M is reachable from M_0 iff M and M_0 agree on all S-invariants and M marks every proper trap of N.

Proof:

($\Rightarrow$): Assume that M is reachable. Then it agrees with M_0 on all S-invariants by Theorem 2.33. Since (N, M_0) is cyclic, M_0 is a home marking. Since M is reachable from M_0, it is also a home marking. By the Home Marking Theorem, M marks every proper trap of N.

($\Leftarrow$): By the Second Confluence Theorem, the set $[M_0\rangle \cap [M\rangle$ contains some marking, say L. By the Home Marking Theorem (Theorem 8.11), M is a home marking of the system (N, M), and therefore $L \xrightarrow{*} M$. Since $M_0 \xrightarrow{*} L$, we get $M_0 \xrightarrow{*} M$. $\square$

An immediate consequence of this result is that the reachability problem of live, bounded and cyclic free-choice systems can be solved in polynomial time.

Theorem 9.7   *The reachability problem of live, bounded and cyclic systems*

The following problem is solvable in polynomial time:

> Given a live, bounded and cyclic free-choice system (N, M_0) and a marking M of N, to decide if M is reachable from M_0.

Proof:

Whether M and M_0 agree on all invariants can be decided in polynomial time by solving a system of linear equations (Theorem 2.34). Whether M marks all proper traps of N can also be decided in polynomial time (see Theorem 8.12). $\square$

It is an open question if this result also holds for non-cyclic, live and bounded systems.

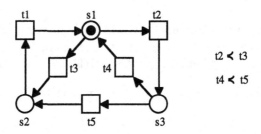

Fig. 9.4 A system and a conflict-order

9.2   The Shortest Sequence Theorem

The Shortest Sequence Theorem for T-systems (Theorem 3.27) states that, given a live and b-bounded T-system (N, M_0) with n transitions and a reachable marking M, there exists an occurrence sequence $M_0 \xrightarrow{\sigma} M$ such that the length of σ is at most

$$b \cdot \frac{(n-1) \cdot n}{2}$$

The Shortest Sequence Theorem for free-choice systems, which we prove in this section, states that for a live and b-bounded free-choice system with n transitions, the bound on the length of σ is

$$b \cdot \frac{n \cdot (n+1) \cdot (n+2)}{6}$$

The proof is based on the following two notions.

Definition 9.8   *Conflict order, ordered sequence*

Let N be a net and let T be the set of transitions of N. A conflict order $\preceq \subseteq T \times T$ is a partial order such that two transitions t and u are comparable (i.e., $t \preceq u$ or $u \preceq t$) iff ${}^\bullet t \cap {}^\bullet u \neq \emptyset$. If $u \preceq t$ and $u \neq t$, then we write $u \prec t$.

A sequence of transitions σ is ordered with respect to a conflict order $\preceq$, or just $\preceq$-ordered, if $u \prec t$ implies that u does not occur after t in σ. The sequence σ is ordered if it is ordered with respect to some conflict order.

Consider the system of Figure 9.4. It has three clusters, namely $c_1 = \{s_1, t_2, t_3\}$, $c_2 = \{s_2, t_1\}$, and $c_3 = \{s_3, t_4, t_5\}$. The sequence $t_2 \, t_5 \, t_1 \, t_3$ is ordered, because it is ordered with respect to the conflict order shown in the figure. On the contrary, the sequence $t_3 \, t_1 \, t_2 \, t_4 \, t_3$ is not ordered. To prove it, observe that t_2 occurs after t_3 and t_3 occurs after t_2. Since any conflict order satisfies either $t_2 \prec t_3$ or $t_3 \prec t_2$, this sequence cannot be ordered with respect to any conflict order.

With the help of these definitions and the following lemma, we can reduce the Shortest Sequence Theorem to a simpler assertion.

Lemma 9.9

Let (N, M_0) be a b-bounded system with n transitions, and let $M_0 \xrightarrow{\tau} M$ be an occurrence sequence such that τ is ordered. There exists another occurrence sequence $M_0 \xrightarrow{\sigma} M$ such that the length of σ is at most

$$b \cdot \frac{n \cdot (n + 1) \cdot (n + 2)}{6}$$

Proof:

Let k be the number of distinct transitions occurring in τ. We show that there exists an occurrence sequence $M_0 \xrightarrow{\sigma} M$ such that the length of σ is at most

$$b \cdot \frac{k \cdot (k + 1) \cdot (k + 2)}{6}$$

The result then follows because $k \leq n$.

We proceed by induction on k.

Base: $k = 0$. Then τ is the empty sequence, and there is nothing to be shown.

Step: $k > 0$. Let τ_1 and τ_2 be sequences such that $\tau = \tau_1 \tau_2$ and τ_1 is the maximal prefix of τ which is a biased sequence (Definition 3.22). Recall that in a biased sequence no two different transitions of the same cluster occur. Let $M_0 \xrightarrow{\tau_1} M_1 \xrightarrow{\tau_2} M$. By the Biased Sequence Lemma (Lemma 3.26), there is an occurrence sequence $M_0 \xrightarrow{\sigma_1} M_1$ such that the length of σ_1 is at most

$$b \cdot \frac{k \cdot (k + 1)}{2}$$

If $M_1 = M$, then we may take $\sigma = \sigma_1$, because

$$b \cdot \frac{k \cdot (k + 1)}{2} \leq b \cdot \frac{k \cdot (k + 1) \cdot (k + 2)}{6}$$

If $M_1 \neq M$, then τ_2 is nonempty. Let t be the first transition of τ_2. Since the sequence τ_1 is maximal, it contains a transition u of the cluster $[t]$ (otherwise, the sequence $\tau_1 u$ would also be biased). Since τ is ordered, u does not occur in τ_2. So the number of distinct transitions occurring in τ_2 is at most $k - 1$. By the induction hypothesis, there exists an occurrence sequence $M_1 \xrightarrow{\sigma_2} M$ such that the length of σ_2 is at most

$$b \cdot \frac{(k - 1) \cdot k \cdot (k + 1)}{6}$$

Define $\sigma = \sigma_1 \sigma_2$. Then $M_0 \xrightarrow{\sigma} M$ and the length of σ is at most

$$b \cdot \frac{k \cdot (k + 1)}{2} + b \cdot \frac{(k - 1) \cdot k \cdot (k + 1)}{6} = b \cdot \frac{k \cdot (k + 1) \cdot (k + 2)}{6}$$

$\square$

By this lemma, the Shortest Sequence Theorem can be reduced to the following assertion

> *Every reachable marking of a live and bounded free-choice system can be reached by an ordered occurrence sequence.*

Given a reachable marking M of a live and bounded free-choice system (N, M_0), we have to find a conflict order $\preceq$ and an occurrence sequence $M_0 \xrightarrow{\tau} M$ such that τ is $\preceq$-ordered. Since M is reachable, we know that there exists an occurrence sequence $M_0 \xrightarrow{\sigma} M$. We use the sequence σ as a guide to find both the conflict order $\preceq$ and the sequence τ. More precisely, the sequence τ will be a $\preceq$-ordered permutation of σ. Then, in order to show that $M_0 \xrightarrow{\tau} M$ is an occurrence sequence, it suffices to prove that τ is enabled at M_0. The fact that τ leads to M follows from $\overrightarrow{\sigma} = \overrightarrow{\tau}$ and the Marking Equation. The order $\preceq$ will be any of the conflict orders that *agree* with σ, which are defined next.

Definition 9.10   *Conflict orders that agree with a sequence*

Let σ be a sequence of transitions of a net. A conflict order $\preceq$ agrees with σ if for every cluster c either no transition of c occurs in σ, or the last transition of c that occurs in σ is maximal (i.e., the greatest transition of c with respect to $\preceq$).

Observe that a $\preceq$-ordered sequence agrees with $\preceq$, but not vice versa. For instance, the sequence $t_3\, t_1\, t_2\, t_4\, t_3$ agrees with the conflict order shown in Figure 9.4, but is not ordered with respect to it.

We shall prove the following:

> (A) *Let $M_0 \xrightarrow{\sigma} M$ be an occurrence sequence of a live and bounded free-choice system (N, M_0), and let $\preceq$ be a conflict order that agrees with σ. Some $\preceq$-ordered permutation of σ is enabled at M_0.*

Let us see that that (A) holds for a particular example. Let M be the marking of the system shown in Figure 9.4 which puts a token on the place s_2. We have $M_0 \xrightarrow{\sigma} M$ for the sequence

$$\sigma = t_3\, t_1\, t_2\, t_5\, t_1\, t_2\, t_4\, t_2\, t_5\, t_1\, t_3$$

The last transition of the clusters c_2 and c_3 occurring in σ are t_3 and t_5, respectively. Therefore, the only conflict order that agrees with σ is the one shown in the figure. If (A) holds, then there exists a $\preceq$-ordered permutation τ of σ such that $M_0 \xrightarrow{\tau} M$, i.e., a permutation of σ in which t_2 does not occur any more after the first occurrence of t_3, and t_4 does not occur any more after the first occurrence of t_5. In this example, the permutation happens to be unique:

$$\tau = t_2 \; t_4 \; t_2 \; t_5 \; t_1 \; t_2 \; t_5 \; t_1 \; t_3 \; t_1 \; t_3$$

The condition requiring the conflict order to agree with σ is essential. Every occurrence sequence leading to M must have t_3 as last transition, and therefore no permutation τ of σ in which t_2 occurs after the last occurrence of t_3 can lead to M.

We first prove (A) for S-systems, and then for live and bounded free-choice systems. In both cases, the proof constructs longer and longer prefixes of a $\preceq$-ordered permutation of σ, starting from the empty sequence and adding transitions one at a time. We call the prefixes of the permutations of a sequence *perms*[1]. The following lemma characterizes the $\preceq$-ordered perms of a sequence.

Lemma 9.11

Let σ be a sequence of transitions of a net, and let $\preceq$ be a conflict order. A sequence τ is a $\preceq$-ordered perm of σ iff it is $\preceq$-ordered and for every transition t it holds:

- $\overrightarrow{\tau}(t) \leq \overrightarrow{\sigma}(t)$, and

- if $\overrightarrow{\tau}(t) > 0$, then $\overrightarrow{\tau}(u) = \overrightarrow{\sigma}(u)$ for every transition u satisfying $u \prec t$.

$\square$

Proof:

($\Rightarrow$): If τ is a $\preceq$-ordered perm of σ then τ is $\preceq$-ordered by assumption and there exists a sequence ρ such that $\tau \rho$ is a $\preceq$-ordered permutation of σ. Therefore, for every transition t we have

$$\overrightarrow{\tau}(t) + \overrightarrow{\rho}(t) = \overrightarrow{\sigma}(t)$$

which implies $\overrightarrow{\tau}(t) \leq \overrightarrow{\sigma}(t)$. Moreover, if $\overrightarrow{\tau}(t) > 0$ and $u \prec t$ then $\overrightarrow{\rho}(u) = 0$ since $\tau \rho$ is $\preceq$-ordered.

($\Leftarrow$): Let ρ be a $\preceq$-ordered sequence satisfying

$$\overrightarrow{\rho}(t) = \overrightarrow{\sigma}(t) - \overrightarrow{\tau}(t)$$

for every transition t. Then $\tau \rho$ is a permutation of σ. This permutation is $\preceq$-ordered because both τ and ρ are $\preceq$-ordered, and because for every transition t that appears in τ, no transition u satisfying $u \prec t$ appears in ρ.

$\square$

---

[1]The reason of the name is twofold. First, 'perm' is a prefix of 'permutation'. Second, in British football pools one picks out a number of football teams from a list and sorts them in a particular order. The result is called a perm.

S-systems

We prove the statement (A) for S-systems. First, we need a lemma.

Lemma 9.12

Let $M_0 \xrightarrow{\sigma} M$ be an occurrence sequence of an S-system (N, M_0). Let $\preceq$ be a conflict order which agrees with σ, and let T_m be the set of maximal transitions (with respect to $\preceq$) occurring in σ. Then every circuit of N containing only transitions of T_m contains a place marked at M.

Proof:

Assume there exists a circuit of N which contains only transitions of T_m but does not contain any place marked at M. Let t, s, and u be three consecutive nodes of the circuit, where t and u are transitions and s is a place. Since t belongs to T_m, it occurs in σ. Let τ and ρ be sequences such that $\sigma = \tau\, t\, \rho$ and t does not occur in ρ. Since s is unmarked at M, but marked after the occurrence of t, an output transition of s occurs in ρ. In particular, since $\preceq$ agrees with σ, the maximal output transition of s occurs in ρ. By the definition of the set T_m, this transition is u.

So, for every pair of consecutive transitions t and u of the circuit, u occurs after t in σ. This contradicts the finiteness of σ. $\square$

Proposition 9.13   *Existence of a $\preceq$-ordered permutation for S-systems*

Let $M_0 \xrightarrow{\sigma} M$ be an occurrence sequence of an S-system (N, M_0), and let $\preceq$ be a conflict order that agrees with σ. Some $\preceq$-ordered permutation of σ is enabled at M_0.

Proof:

We prove that every $\preceq$-ordered perm τ enabled at M_0 can be extended to a $\preceq$-ordered permutation of σ, also enabled at M_0. Since the empty sequence is such a perm, this proves the result.

Throughout the proof we use the following conventions and notations. The terms 'perm' and 'permutation' always refer to the sequence σ. Similarly, 'maximal' and 'minimal' always refer to the conflict order $\preceq$. Finally, given a set of transitions U and a sequence ρ, we define

$$\overrightarrow{\rho}(U) = \sum_{t \in U} \overrightarrow{\rho}(t)$$

Let τ be a $\preceq$-ordered perm such that $M_0 \xrightarrow{\tau} M_1$. We prove that if τ is not a permutation, then there exists a transition t such that τt is also a $\preceq$-ordered perm, and M_1 enables t.

Since N is an S-net, a transition is enabled if and only if the unique place in its pre-set is marked. So it suffices to find a place s, marked at M_1, such that $\vec{\tau}(s^\bullet) < \vec{\sigma}(s^\bullet)$. Then, the minimal transition t of $s^\bullet$ satisfying $\vec{\tau}(t) < \vec{\sigma}(t)$ is a valid extension of τ, because the marking M_1 enables t and τt is again a $\preceq$-ordered perm.

We proceed indirectly and assume that no such place exists, i.e., we assume that every place s satisfies either $M_1(s) = 0$ or $\vec{\tau}(s^\bullet) = \vec{\sigma}(s^\bullet)$.

We make the following three claims.

(i) $M_1 = M$.

   Since M and M_1 are reachable from M_0 and N is an S-net, both M and M_1 put the same number of tokens in the places of N (Lemma 3.8). So it suffices to prove $M(s) \geq M_1(s)$ for every place s.

   Let s be a place. If $M_1(s) = 0$ then nothing has to be shown. If $M_1(s) > 0$, then, by the assumption, we have

$$
\begin{aligned}
M(s) &= M_0(s) + \vec{\sigma}(^\bullet s) - \vec{\sigma}(s^\bullet) & (M_0 \xrightarrow{\sigma} M) \\
&\geq M_0(s) + \vec{\tau}(^\bullet s) - \vec{\sigma}(s^\bullet) & (\tau \text{ is a } \preceq\text{-ordered perm}) \\
&= M_0(s) + \vec{\tau}(^\bullet s) - \vec{\tau}(s^\bullet) & (\text{the assumption}) \\
&= M_1(s) & (M_0 \xrightarrow{\tau} M_1)
\end{aligned}
$$

The other two claims concern the set U_m of maximal transitions t which satisfy $\vec{\tau}(t) < \vec{\sigma}(t)$. Notice that every such transition t satisfies in particular $\vec{\sigma}(t) > 0$, and therefore all the transitions of U_m occur in σ.

(ii) U_m is nonempty.

   Since τ is not a permutation of σ, some transition t that occurs in σ satisfies $\vec{\tau}(t) < \vec{\sigma}(t)$. Let t_m be the maximal transition of the cluster containing t. Since $\preceq$ agrees with σ and t occurs in σ, the transition t_m occurs in σ. Since τ is a $\preceq$-ordered perm and $t \preceq t_m$, we have $\vec{\tau}(t_m) < \vec{\sigma}(t_m)$. So t_m belongs to U_m.

(iii) $U_m^\bullet \subseteq {}^\bullet U_m$.

   Let s be a place of $U_m^\bullet$. We prove that s belongs to ${}^\bullet U_m$.

   Since s belongs to $U_m^\bullet$, we get $\vec{\tau}(^\bullet s) < \vec{\sigma}(^\bullet s)$. Moreover, since $M(s) = M_1(s)$ by (i), we also have

$$
\vec{\sigma}(^\bullet s) - \vec{\sigma}(s^\bullet) = \vec{\tau}(^\bullet s) - \vec{\tau}(s^\bullet)
$$

   It follows $\vec{\tau}(s^\bullet) < \vec{\sigma}(s^\bullet)$. Let t_m be the maximal transition of $s^\bullet$ that occurs in σ. Then $\vec{\tau}(t_m) < \vec{\sigma}(t_m)$, because τ is $\preceq$-ordered. So t_m belongs to U_m.

By (ii) and (iii), the net N contains a circuit γ whose transitions belong to U_m. Let T_m be the set of maximal transitions occurring in σ. We have $U_m \subseteq T_m$, because every transition of U_m occurs in σ. Therefore, every transition of the circuit γ belongs to T_m. We can now apply Lemma 9.12 to conclude that γ contains some place s marked at M. Since $M = M_1$, the place s is also marked at M_1. Moreover, since γ contains only transitions of U_m, some transition in the post-set of s belongs to U_m. This contradicts the assumption $\overrightarrow{\tau}(s^\bullet) = \overrightarrow{\sigma}(s^\bullet)$. $\square$

Free-choice systems

We now prove (A) for live and bounded free-choice systems. We shall show that if (A) does not hold for a live and bounded free-choice system (N, M_0), then it does not hold either for the system $(N_1, M|_{S_1})$, where N_1 is a certain S-component of N and $M|_{S_1}$ is the projection of M on the places of N_1. This contradicts Proposition 9.13.

The following lemma states that the projection of an occurrence sequence of an arbitrary system on one of its S-components yields a 'local' occurrence sequence of the component. The proof follows easily from the definition of an S-component, and is left for an exercise.

Lemma 9.14

Let $M_0 \overset{\sigma}{\longrightarrow} M$ be an occurrence sequence of a system (N, M_0). If N_1 is an S-component of N and $N_1 = (S_1, T_1, F_1)$, then $M_0|_{S_1} \overset{\sigma|_{T_1}}{\longrightarrow} M|_{S_1}$ is an occurrence sequence of $(N_1, M_0|_{S_1})$. $\square$

We will show that Proposition 9.13 also holds for live and bounded free-choice systems. First we need another technical lemma.

Lemma 9.15

Let N be a well-formed free-choice net and let α be an allocation with a nonempty domain C. Then there exists a T-component N_1 of N such that

(1) every transition of N_1 that belongs to C is α-allocated, and

(2) some transition of N_1 belongs to C.

Proof:
Let $\overline{C}$ be the set of clusters of N that do not belong to C. By the first part of the Pointing Allocation Lemma (Lemma 6.5) there exists an allocation β with domain $\overline{C}$ that points to C. Define the total allocation γ of N as follows:

$$\gamma(c) = \begin{cases} \alpha(c) & \text{if } c \in C \\ \beta(c) & \text{if } c \in \overline{C} \end{cases}$$

Let M_0 be a live and bounded marking of N (which exists since N is well-formed). By the Allocation Lemma (Lemma 4.24), there exists an infinite occurrence sequence $M_0 \xrightarrow{\sigma}$ such that σ agrees with γ. Since γ is a total allocation, σ only contains γ-allocated transitions. By the Reproduction Lemma (Lemma 2.39), there exists a semi-positive T-invariant J of N whose support $\langle J \rangle$ is included in the alphabet $\mathcal{A}(\sigma)$. Without loss of generality, we may assume that J is minimal. Then, by Theorem 5.17, J induces a T-component N_1 of N. We prove that N_1 satisfies (1) and (2).

To prove (1), let t be a transition of N_1 that belongs to C. Since t belongs to $\langle J \rangle$, and $\langle J \rangle$ contains only γ-allocated transitions, the transition t is γ-allocated. Since γ and α coincide on the set C, it is also α-allocated.

To prove (2), observe first that the allocation γ also points to C. So, for each place s of N_1 there is a path leading from s to a place of C which contains only γ-allocated transitions.

We claim that this path is contained in N_1. If a transition t of the path belongs to N_1, then, since N_1 is a T-component, every output place of t belongs to N_1, in particular the successor of t in the path. If a place r of the path belongs to N_1, then, since N_1 contains only γ-allocated transitions, the output transition of r which is γ-allocated also belongs to N_1. This transition is the successor of r in the path, which proves the claim.

Since the path ends with a place of C, a place of N_1 belongs to C, and so does its unique output-transition in N_1. $\square$

Proposition 9.16   *Existence of a $\preceq$-ordered permutation*

Let $M_0 \xrightarrow{\sigma} M$ be an occurrence sequence of a live and bounded free-choice system (N, M_0), and let $\preceq$ be a conflict order that agrees with σ. Some $\preceq$-ordered permutation of σ is enabled at M_0.

Proof:

Let τ be a $\preceq$-ordered perm of σ such that $M_0 \xrightarrow{\tau} M_1$. As in the proof of Proposition 9.13, we show that if τ is not a permutation of σ, then there exists a transition t such that τt is also a $\preceq$-ordered perm of σ, and M_1 enables t.

Let U be the set of transitions t satisfying $\overrightarrow{\tau}(t) < \overrightarrow{\sigma}(t)$. We will show that a transition of U is enabled at M_1. This implies the result as follows. Let t be a transition of U enabled at M_1, and let u be the minimal transition of the cluster $[t]$ that belongs to U. Then, u is enabled at M_1 because it belongs to $[t]$ and N is free-choice. We can then choose u to extend τ.

Assume that no transition of U is enabled at M_1. Let C be the set of clusters containing transitions of U. Then every cluster of C has a place unmarked at M_1.

Let $N = (S, T, F)$, and define a function $\alpha \colon C \to S$, which associates to each cluster c of C a place of c unmarked at M_1.

Let N^d be the dual net of N. Since the nets N and N^d have exactly the same clusters (Proposition 6.20(3)), the function α is an allocation of N^d. By the Duality Theorem (Theorem 6.21), N^d is a well-formed free-choice net. By Lemma 9.15, there exists a a T-component N_1^d of N^d such that

(1) every transition of N_1^d that belongs to C is α-allocated, and

(2) some transition s of N_1^d belongs to C (we call this transition s because it is a place of the net N).

Since N_1^d is a T-component of N^d, its dual net $N_1 = (S_1, T_1, F_1)$ is an S-component of N. By Lemma 9.14, we have $M_0|_{S_1} \xrightarrow{\ \tau|_{T_1}\ } M_1|_{S_1}$. We make the following three claims:

(i) $\tau|_{T_1}$ is a $\preceq$-ordered perm of $\sigma|_{T_1}$.

A subsequence of a $\preceq$-ordered sequence is itself $\preceq$-ordered. The other two conditions of the characterization of Lemma 9.11 follow immediately from the fact that they hold for τ and σ.

(ii) $\tau|_{T_1}$ is not a permutation of $\sigma|_{T_1}$.

By (2), some place s of N_1 belongs to C. Therefore, some transition t in the post-set of s belongs to U. This transition also belongs to T_1 because N_1 is an S-component of N. Therefore, $\tau|_{T_1}(t) < \sigma|_{T_1}(t)$.

(iii) The marking $M_1|_{S_1}$ enables no transition of U in the net N_1.

Let t be a transition of N_1 contained in the set U. By the definition of C, the transition t belongs to a cluster of C. By the definition of α, some input place s of t is unmarked at M_1 and satisfies $s = \alpha([t])$. By (1), s belongs to S_1. So $M_1|_{S_1}$ does not enable t.

By (iii), the sequence $\tau|_{T_1}$ cannot be extended to a $\preceq$-ordered permutation of $\sigma|_{T_1}$. Together with (i) and (ii), this contradicts Proposition 9.13. $\square$

This concludes the proof of the Shortest Sequence Theorem.

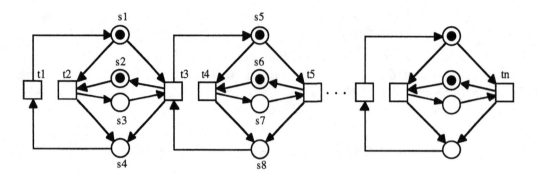

Fig. 9.5   A family of systems with exponential shortest sequences

Theorem 9.17   *Shortest Sequence Theorem*

Let (N, M_0) be a live and b-bounded free-choice system with n transitions, and let M be a reachable marking. There exists an occurrence sequence $M_0 \xrightarrow{\sigma} M$ such that the length of σ is at most

$$b \cdot \frac{n \cdot (n+1) \cdot (n+2)}{6}$$

Proof:

Since M is reachable, there exists an occurrence sequence $M_0 \xrightarrow{\tau} M$. By Proposition 9.16, there exists a $\preceq$-ordered permutation ρ of τ such that $M_0 \xrightarrow{\rho} M$. The result follows by Lemma 9.9. $\square$

It was shown in Chapter 3 that the bound given in the Shortest Sequence Theorem for T-systems is reachable. For every number n, there exists a b-bounded T-systems with n transitions and a reachable marking M such that the length of the shortest sequence that reaches M is *exactly*

$$b \cdot \frac{(n-1) \cdot n}{2}$$

For free-choice systems, the reachability of the bound is an open problem. In fact, we conjecture that a reachable bound should be quadratic in the number of transitions.

To finish the section, we exhibit a family of systems for which there exists no polynomial upper bound in the length of the shortest sequences. The family is shown in Figure 9.5. All the systems of the family are live and 1-bounded.

The shortest occurrence sequence that, from the initial marking shown in the figure, reaches the marking that puts a token in the places of the set $\{s_1, s_3, s_5, s_7, \ldots\}$ has exponential length in the number of transitions of the net. The proof of this fact is left for an exercise.

Exercises

Exercise 9.1

The *releasing* N^r of a net $N = (S, T, F)$ is the net constructed by exhaustive iteration of the following procedure. If N contains two places s and r and two transitions t and u such that $\{(s, t), (r, t), (s, u)\} \subseteq F$ but $(r, u) \notin F$, then

- remove the arc (s, t);
- add a new place s' and a new transition t';
- add new arcs (s, t'), (t', s'), (s', t).

Given a marking M of N, the marking M^r of N^r is defined as the marking which coincides with M on the places of N, and puts no tokens on the new places introduced by the procedure. Prove:

1) The releasing of a net is well-defined, i.e., the procedure described above always terminates, and yields a net.

2) The releasing of a net is a free-choice net.

3) If (N^r, M_0^r) is live, then (N, M_0) is live.

4) If M is a reachable marking of (N, M_0), then M^r is a reachable marking of (N^r, M_0^r).

5) If M is a reachable marking of (N^r, M_0^r), and $M = L^r$ for some marking L of N, then L is a reachable marking of (N^r, M_0^r).

6) Use (4) and (5) to prove that the reachability problem for free-choice systems is as hard as the reachability problem for *arbitrary* systems.

Exercise 9.2

Let N be a net, let $\widehat{N}$ be a CP-subnet of N, and let $\overline{N}$ be the subnet of N generated by all the nodes that do not belong to $\widehat{N}$. Prove:

1) For every T-component $\overline{N_1}$ of $\overline{N}$ (a) or (b) hold:

   (a) $\overline{N_1}$ is a T-component of N.

   (b) The subnet generated by the nodes of $\overline{N_1}$ and $\widehat{N}$ is a T-component of N.

2) For every S-component N_1 of N (a), (b), or (c) hold:

(a) N_1 is an S-component of $\overline{N}$.

(b) N_1 is an S-component of $\widehat{N}$.

(c) N_1 contains a path leading from a way-in transition of $\widehat{N}$ to a way-out transition of $\widehat{N}$.

Exercise 9.3

Prove the *Church-Rosser Property* of the reachability relation of live and bounded free-choice systems:

Let (N, M_0) be a live and bounded free-choice system, and let $L \xleftrightarrow{*} K$ be the smallest equivalence relation on the markings of N which includes $\xrightarrow{}$. Then $L \xleftrightarrow{*} K$ implies $L \xrightarrow{*} M$ and $K \xrightarrow{*} M$ for some marking M.

Exercise 9.4   *

Disprove the following conjecture by exhibiting a counterexample:

Let (N, M_0) be a live and bounded free-choice net and let M be a marking of N which agrees with M_0 on all S-invariants. Assume moreover that every trap marked at M_0 is also marked at M. Then M is reachable from M_0.

Exercise 9.5

Prove Lemma 9.14.

Exercise 9.6

Prove that the systems of the family shown in Figure 9.5 are live and 1-bounded. Prove that the occurrence sequences that lead to the marking indicated in the text have at least exponential length in the number of transitions of the net.

Bibliographic Notes

The Second Confluence Theorem was proved by the authors in [24]. The Shortest Sequence Theorem was proved in [25], also by the authors, but only for live and 1-bounded free-choice systems. The proof of Proposition 9.13 follows closely the proof of the BEST-Theorem of graph theory, which gives the number of Eulerian trails of a directed graph. For information on this result, see for instance the book of Fleischner [37].

Chapter 10 ————————————————

Generalizations

This chapter contains generalizations of three results on free-choice nets to larger net classes. In the first section, we show that one direction of Commoner's Theorem also holds for so-called *asymmetric-choice nets*. In the second and third section, we give necessary and sufficient conditions for an arbitrary net to be well-formed. When specialized to free-choice nets, these conditions coincide, and yield the Rank Theorem, but in the general case they are different.

Many other generalizations have been discussed in the literature. The bibliographic notes contain some examples.

10.1 Asymmetric-choice nets

We saw in Chapter 4 that free-choice nets are those in which for every two places s and r either $s^\bullet \cap r^\bullet = \emptyset$ or $s^\bullet = r^\bullet$ (Proposition 4.2(2)). Asymmetric-choice nets are defined by relaxing this condition:

Definition 10.1 *Asymmetric-choice nets*

A net is asymmetric-choice if for every two places s and r either $s^\bullet \cap r^\bullet = \emptyset$ or $s^\bullet \subseteq r^\bullet$ or $r^\bullet \subseteq s^\bullet$.

A system (N, M_0) is asymmetric-choice if N is asymmetric-choice.

Figure 10.1 shows an asymmetric-choice net. The addition of an arc from the place s_3 to the transition t_2 would spoil the asymmetric-choice property, because then the places s_1 and s_3 would have non-disjoint post-sets, but neither $s_1^\bullet \subseteq s_3^\bullet$ nor $s_3^\bullet \subseteq s_1^\bullet$ would hold.

We prove that the 'if' direction of Commoner's Theorem (if every proper siphon of a free-choice system includes an initially marked trap, then the system is live) also holds for asymmetric-choice systems. We shall reuse most of the proof of the free-choice case, presented in Chapter 4. This proof consists of two parts. First, it is shown that liveness and place-liveness coincide for free-choice systems (Proposition 4.19). Then, using this result, the 'if' direction of Commoner's Theorem

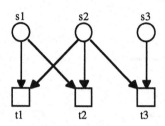

Fig. 10.1   An asymmetric-choice net

is proved without resorting to the free-choice property anymore (Theorem 4.21). Therefore, in order to extend Theorem 4.21 to asymmetric-choice systems, it suffices to extend Proposition 4.19. We can go even further: Proposition 4.19 is based on Lemma 4.18, and does not make direct use of the free-choice property either. So it suffices to generalize Lemma 4.18 to asymmetric-choice systems, which is done next.

Lemma 10.2   *Generalization of Lemma 4.18*

If a transition t of an asymmetric-choice system is dead at a marking M, then some input place of t is dead at some marking reachable from M.

Proof:

We prove the contraposition: if no input place of t is dead at any marking reachable from M, then t is not dead at M.

Let ${}^\bullet t = \{s_1, \ldots, s_n\}$. For every two places s and r in ${}^\bullet t$ we have $t \in s^\bullet \cap r^\bullet$ and therefore, by the asymmetric-choice property, either $s^\bullet \subseteq r^\bullet$ or $r^\bullet \subseteq s^\bullet$. So we can assume without loss of generality

$$s_1^\bullet \subseteq s_2^\bullet \subseteq \cdots \subseteq s_n^\bullet$$

Since no input place of t is dead at any marking reachable from M, there exists an occurrence sequence

$$M \xrightarrow{\sigma_1} M_1 \xrightarrow{\sigma_2} M_2 \longrightarrow \cdots \longrightarrow M_{n-1} \xrightarrow{\sigma_n} M_n$$

such that $M_i(s_i) > 0$ for $1 \leq i \leq n$. Assume without loss of generality that all the sequences σ_i are minimal, i.e., no intermediate marking marks s_i.

We show that M_n marks every place in ${}^\bullet t$, and therefore enables t. We proceed by induction on the index i and prove that, for $1 \leq i \leq n$ and $1 \leq j \leq i$, the marking M_i marks the place s_j.

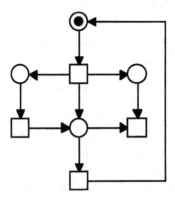

Fig. 10.2 A live asymmetric-choice system in which a proper siphon contains no marked trap

Base. $i = 1$. Then $M_i = M_1$, and M_1 marks s_1 by construction.

Step. $i > 1$. If $j = i$ then $s_i = s_j$ and M_i marks s_i by construction. Consider now the case $j < i$. By the induction hypothesis, M_{i-1} marks s_j. By the minimality of $M_{i-1} \xrightarrow{\sigma_i} M_i$, no transition of $s_i^{\bullet}$ occurs in σ_i. Since $j < i$, we have $s_j^{\bullet} \subseteq s_i^{\bullet}$. Hence no transition of $s_j^{\bullet}$ occurs in σ_i. So M_i marks s_j.

Since M_n enables t and M_n is reachable from M, t is not dead at M. $\square$

Replacing Lemma 4.18 by Lemma 10.2 in the proofs of Chapter 4, we get:

Proposition 10.3   *Generalization of Proposition 4.19*

An asymmetric-choice system is live iff it is place-live. $\square$

Theorem 10.4   *Commoner's Theorem for asymmetric-choice systems*

If every proper siphon of an asymmetric-choice system includes an initially marked trap, then the system is live. $\square$

The other direction of Commoner's Theorem cannot be generalized in a similar way. Figure 10.2 shows a live asymmetric-choice system in which the set of all places is a siphon. This siphon does not include an initially marked trap (in fact, the siphon contains no proper trap at all).

10.2   A necessary condition for well-formedness

Given a net N, not necessarily free-choice, define P_N as the set of pre-sets of the transitions of N. In other words,

$$P_N = \{\,{}^\bullet t \mid t \text{ is a transition of } N\,\}$$

We prove that if N is well-formed, then $\text{Rank}(\mathbf{N}) \leq |P_N| - 1$. If N is free-choice, then two transitions have the same pre-set if and only if they belong to the same cluster, and therefore $|P_N| = |C_N|$. So this result generalizes Proposition 6.13, one of the main propositions we used in Chapter 6 to prove the Rank Theorem, which states that a well-formed free-choice net satisfies $\text{Rank}(\mathbf{N}) \leq |C_N| - 1$.

Proposition 6.13 is proved by constructing $|T| - |C_N| + 1$ linearly independent T-invariants, where T is the set of transitions of N. This construction proves that the dimension of the set of T-invariants is at least $|T| - |C_N| + 1$. Since this dimension is equal to $|T| - \text{Rank}(\mathbf{N})$, we get $\text{Rank}(\mathbf{N}) \leq |C_N| - 1$.

For the non-free-choice case, we shall now construct $|T| - |P_N| + 1$ linearly independent T-invariants, along the lines we followed in Chapter 6. There we introduced the notion of regulation circuit, and now we need one more property.

Proposition 10.5   *Adding regulation circuits preserves well-formedness*

Let N be a well-formed net, and let U be a nonempty set of transitions with identical pre-sets, i.e., ${}^\bullet U = {}^\bullet u$ for every $u \in U$. Let N' be obtained from N by addition of a regulation circuit N_U of the set U. Then N' is also well-formed.

Proof:

Since N is well-formed, it has a live and bounded marking M. By boundedness, the system (N, M) has only finitely many reachable markings, say k. Define the marking M' of N' as the union of the markings M and $M_U = (k, \ldots, k)$; i.e., M' coincides with M on the places of N and puts k tokens on each place of the regulation circuit N_U. We prove that the system (N', M') is live and bounded.

(i) (N', M') is live.

Let $M' \xrightarrow{\sigma} L'$ be an arbitrary occurrence sequence, and let t be a transition. We construct an occurrence sequence $L' \xrightarrow{\tau} K'$ such that K' enables t. The sequence τ will be the concatenation of two sequences, τ_1 and τ_2.

Let L_U be the restriction of L' to the places of N_U, and let L be the restriction of L' to the places of N. Since both N and N_U are transition-bordered subnets of N', and moreover N and N' have the same set of transitions, we have

$$M_U \xrightarrow{\sigma|_U} L_U \quad \text{and} \quad M \xrightarrow{\sigma} L$$

Since N_U is an S-component of N', there exists a sequence $u_1 \ldots u_n$ of transitions of U such that $L_U \xrightarrow{u_1 \ldots u_n} M_U$ in the net N_U. We claim that the marking L enables some sequence τ_1 in the net N satisfying $\tau_1|_U = u_1 \ldots u_n$. For the proof, observe first that L is a live marking of N, because M is a live marking of N and $M \xrightarrow{\sigma} L$. Construct from L a minimal occurrence sequence leading to a marking that enables some transition of U. Such a sequence exists by liveness. Since all the transitions of U have the same pre-set, the marking reached by the sequence enables all the transitions of U, in particular u_1. Now extend the sequence with u_1. From the marking obtained after the occurrence of u_1, construct again a minimal occurrence sequence leading to a marking that enables some transition of U, and extend it with u_2. After n iterations of this procedure, we get a sequence whose projection on U is $u_1 \ldots u_n$.

Now we have:

- the restriction of τ_1 to the transitions of N (which is τ_1 itself) is enabled in N at the marking L,

- the restriction of τ_1 to the transitions in U (which is $u_1 \ldots u_n$) is enabled in N_U at the marking L_U, and leads to the marking $M_U = (k, \ldots, k)$.

Since both N and N_U are transition-bordered, and every input place of the transitions of τ_1 belongs to N or to N_U, we have that τ_1 is enabled in N' at the marking L'. Moreover, this sequence leads to a marking whose projection on the places of N_U is the marking M_U.

Since L is a live marking of N, there exists a sequence τ_2 such that $L \xrightarrow{\tau_1 \tau_2} K$ and K enables the transition t. Moreover, we can assume that no marking is reached more than once during the occurrence of τ_2. So the length of τ_2 is at most $k - 1$. Since every place of N_U contains k tokens after the occurrence of τ_1, we have $L' \xrightarrow{\tau_1 \tau_2} K'$ in the net N'. Moreover, every place of N_U contains at least one token at K'. So K' enables t in N'.

(ii) (N', M') is bounded.

If $M' \xrightarrow{\sigma} L'$ is an arbitrary occurrence sequence of N', then $M \xrightarrow{\sigma} L$ is an occurrence sequence of N and $M_U \xrightarrow{\sigma} L_U$ is an occurrence sequence of N_U. Moreover L and L_U are the restrictions of L' to the places of N and N_U. Therefore, it suffices to prove that (N, M) and (N_U, M_U) are bounded. (N, M) is bounded by hypothesis, and (N_U, M_U) is bounded because N_U is a circuit. $\qquad \square$

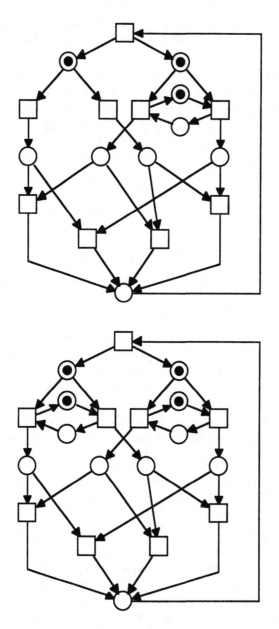

Fig. 10.3 The upper system is live and bounded, the lower system is not live

Notice that the result of combining a live marking of a net with a live marking of a regulation circuit is not necessarily a live marking of the composed system. Figure 10.3 shows a counterexample.

We construct a set of $|T| - |P_N| + 1$ linearly independent T-invariants of a well-formed free-choice net N. As in Chapter 6, the first element of this set, say J, satisfies $J(t) = J(u)$ for every two transitions t and u with the same pre-set. This can be equivalently stated as follows: for every element R of P_N and every two transitions t and u satisfying $R = {}^\bullet t = {}^\bullet u$, $J(t) = J(u)$. The other T-invariants satisfy this same property for all the elements of P_N *except one*, and the element that does not satisfy the condition is different for each T-invariant.

Lemma 10.6   *Generalization of Lemma 6.10*

Let N be a well-formed net. Then N has a positive T-invariant J such that $J(t) = J(u)$ for every two transitions t and u satisfying ${}^\bullet t = {}^\bullet u$.

Proof:

Let N' be the net obtained from N in the following way: for every element R of P_N, add to N a regulation circuit of the set of transitions having the pre-set R. By repeated application of Proposition 10.5, N' is well-formed. So N' has a positive T-invariant, say J (Theorem 2.38). J is also a T-invariant of N, because the pre- and post-set of a place of N coincides with its pre- and post-set in N'.

We prove that ${}^\bullet t = {}^\bullet u$ implies $J(t) = J(u)$. Let U be the set of transitions having the same pre-set as t and u. There exists a path $t\, s_1\, t_1 \ldots t_{k-1}\, s_k\, u$ inside the regulation circuit N_U, leading from t to u. Since J is a T-invariant of N', and the places $s_1, \ldots, s_k$ have exactly one input and one output transition, we have $J(t) = J(t_1) = \ldots = J(t_{k-1}) = J(u)$.   □

Lemma 10.7   *Generalization of Lemma 6.11*

Let N be a well-formed net and let t be an arbitrary transition of N. There exists a positive T-invariant J_t of N such that

- for every two transitions u and v, if ${}^\bullet u = {}^\bullet v$ and $u \neq t \neq v$, then $J_t(u) = J_t(v)$;

- for every transition u, if ${}^\bullet t = {}^\bullet u$ and $t \neq u$, then $J_t(t) > J_t(u)$.

Proof:

Completely analogous to the proof of Lemma 6.11, replacing "transitions that belong to the same cluster" by "transitions having the same pre-set".   □

The proof of the next result also follows closely that of the free-choice case, stated in Proposition 6.12.

Proposition 10.8   *Generalization of Proposition 6.12*

Let N be a well-formed net. Let T be the set of transitions of N, and let $\mathcal{J}$ be its space of T-invariants. Then $\dim(\mathcal{J}) \geq |T| - |P_N| + 1$.

Proof:

Choose a set of transitions U in the following way: for every element R of P_N, put in U all the transitions with pre-set R *except one*, arbitrarily selected. Clearly, we have $|U| = |T| - |P_N|$.

Let J be a positive T-invariant as in Lemma 10.6. For every transition $t \in U$ define a positive T-invariant J_t as in Proposition 10.7.

To show that the set $\{J\} \cup \{J_t\}_{t \in U}$ is linearly independent, proceed as in the proof of Proposition 6.12.   □

Finally, we obtain as an immediate consequence of this proposition:

Theorem 10.9   *A necessary condition for well-formedness*

If N is a well-formed net, then $\text{Rank}(\mathbf{N}) \leq |P_N| - 1$.   □

10.3   A sufficient condition for well-formedness

We show in this section that an *arbitrary* net N satisfying the four conditions of the Rank Theorem for free-choice nets is well-formed:

(a) it is weakly connected, and has at least one place and one transition,

(b) it has a positive S-invariant,

(c) it has a positive T-invariant, and

(d) $\text{Rank}(\mathbf{N}) = |C_N| - 1$, i.e., the rank of its incidence matrix is equal to the number of its clusters minus 1.

We also show that a marking of a net satisfying Conditions (a) to (d) is live and bounded if and only if it marks every proper siphon.

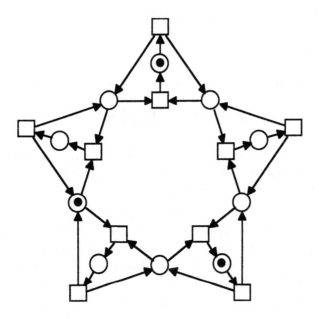

Fig. 10.4 An example (the dining philosophers)

Recall that a cluster of an arbitrary net is a minimal set of nodes satisfying the following two conditions:

- if the set contains a place s, then it contains the post-set of s, and,

- if the set contains a transition t, then it contains the pre-set of t.

Equivalently, a cluster generates a maximal connected subnet of the net obtained by removing all arcs from transitions to places.

Let us first consider an example. The system shown in Figure 10.4 models a version of the well-known *dining philosophers* in which a philosopher has to pick up both forks simultaneously. Its underlying net satisfies Conditions (a) to (c). It has six clusters (notice that all the nodes of the inner pentagon constitute one cluster). Since the rank of its incidence matrix is five, Condition (d) also holds for this net. Using the result we shall prove, it follows that this net is well-formed. Moreover, the initial marking marks every proper siphon, and so the system is live and bounded.

For the proof, we define a transformation rule ϕ, i.e., a binary relation on the class of all nets (see Chapter 7). The rule will be in fact a total mapping, i.e., each net will have exactly one image under the rule. Accordingly, $\phi(N)$ will denote the image of N under ϕ.

The mapping ϕ will satisfy the following three properties for every net N:

(1) $\phi(N)$ is free-choice.

(2) If N satisfies Conditions (a) to (d), then $\phi(N)$ also satisfies them.

(3) If $\phi(N)$ is well-formed, then N is well-formed.

Once this is proven, the result follows easily. If a net N satisfies Conditions (a) to (d), then the net $\phi(N)$ satisfies them too by (2). By (1) and the Rank Theorem, $\phi(N)$ is well-formed. By (3), N is well-formed.

The mapping ϕ will be the composition of a total mapping ϕ_1 and a partial mapping ϕ_2. The range of ϕ_1 and the domain of ϕ_2 will be the class of *feedback-free* nets, a structural concept defined below. The range of ϕ_2 will be the class of free-choice nets, as required in order to fulfill (1). We shall show that ϕ_1 and ϕ_2 satisfy (2) and (3), which implies that their composition, the mapping ϕ, also satisfies them.

We introduce the notion of a feedback and a feedback-free net.

Definition 10.10   *Feedbacks, feedback-freeness*

Let c be a cluster of a net. A feedback of c is an arc (t, s) from a transition t to a place s, both in c, such that there is no arc (s, t).

A net is feedback-free if none of its clusters has feedbacks.

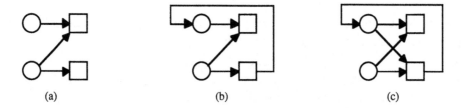

(a)   (b)   (c)

Fig. 10.5   Illustration of Definition 10.10

Figure 10.5 illustrates this definition using nets having only one cluster. The nets (a) and (c) have no feedbacks, the net (b) has a feedback.

Note that every free-choice net is feedback-free because in a cluster of a free-choice net every place is connected to every transition. The net shown in Figure 10.4 is another example of a feedback-free net.

Definition 10.11   *The mapping ϕ_1*

Let N be a net. The net $\phi_1(N)$ is defined as the result of performing the following operations for every cluster c of N and every feedback (t, s) of c:

- remove the arc (t, s);
- add a new place s' and a new transition t';
- add arcs (t, s'), (s', t') and (t', s).

It is easy to see that this construction always terminates, and does not depend on the order in which the feedbacks are treated. So the mapping ϕ_1 is well-defined. In Figure 10.6, the net shown in (a) is mapped by ϕ_1 to the net in (b).

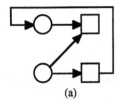
(a)
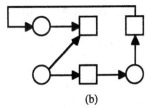
(b)

Fig. 10.6   Illustration of the mapping ϕ_1

Proposition 10.12   *Properties of the mapping ϕ_1*

Let N be a net.

(1) The net $\phi_1(N)$ is feedback-free.

(2) If N satisfies Conditions (a) to (d), then $\phi_1(N)$ also satisfies them [1].

(3) If $\phi_1(N)$ is well-formed, then N is well-formed.

Proof:

(1) The first step of Definition 10.11 removes a feedback from N, and the other two steps do not add any new one.

(2) It suffices to prove that the net N' obtained from N after performing the three steps of Definition 10.11 for one single feedback (t, s) satisfies Conditions (a) to (d), because once this is done the result follows by induction on the number of feedbacks of N.

---

[1] Actually, a net satisfying Conditions (a) to (d) is always feedback-free (see Exercise 10.5), and so ϕ_1 is the identity for such nets. However, to prove this fact we need this and the next results.

Let s' and t' be the new place and transition added to N. Assume without loss of generality that s' is the first row and that $\mathbf{s}$ is the second row of the incidence matrix $\mathbf{N}'$ of the net N', and that $\mathbf{t}'$ is its first column and $\mathbf{t}$ is its second column. Then $\mathbf{N}'$ looks as follows:

$$
\begin{array}{c|c|ccccc}
 & t' & t & & & & \\
\hline
s' & -1 & 1 & 0 & \cdots & 0 \\
\hline
s & 1 & 0 & & & & \\
 & 0 & & & & & \\
 & \vdots & & & \mathbf{N} & & \\
 & 0 & & & & &
\end{array}
$$

$(\mathbf{N}'(s,t) = 0$ and $\mathbf{N}'(x,y) = \mathbf{N}(x,y)$ for all other pairs (x,y) of nodes of N).

We prove that N' satisfies Conditions (a) to (d).

(a) N' is connected and has at least one place and one transition.

It inherits this property from N.

(b) N' has a positive S-invariant.

Let I be a positive S-invariant of N. Then $I' = (I(s)\ I)$ is an S-invariant of N'. It is positive because I is positive and $I'(s') = I(s) > 0$.

(c) N' has a positive T-invariant.

Let J be a positive T-invariant of N. Then $J' = (J(t)\ J)$ is a T-invariant of N'. It is positive because J is positive and $J'(t') = J(t) > 0$.

(d) $\text{Rank}(\mathbf{N}') = |C_{N'}| - 1$.

We claim that $\text{Rank}(\mathbf{N}') = \text{Rank}(\mathbf{N}) + 1$. To see this, add the first row of $\mathbf{N}'$ to the second row to get

$$
\begin{array}{c|c|ccccc}
 & t' & t & & & & \\
\hline
s' & -1 & 1 & 0 & \cdots & 0 \\
\hline
s + s' & 0 & & & & & \\
 & \vdots & & & \mathbf{N} & & \\
 & 0 & & & & &
\end{array}
$$

The net N' has one more cluster than N, namely $\{s', t'\}$. The result follows because $\text{Rank}(\mathbf{N}) = |C_N| - 1$ by assumption.

(3) As in (2), it suffices to prove the result for the net N' obtained from N after performing the three steps of Definition 10.11 for one single feedback (t, s).

Let $N = (S, T, F)$. Since N' is well-formed, it has a live and bounded marking M_0'. We can furthermore assume $M_0'(s') = 0$ (otherwise, let the transition t' occur until the place s' has been emptied). Define $M_0 = M_0'|_S$. We prove that (N, M_0) is live and bounded.

(i) The system (N, M_0) is live.

Let u be a transition of N, and let $M_0 \xrightarrow{\sigma} M$ be an occurrence sequence of N. We construct a sequence τ such that $M \xrightarrow{\tau} L$ and L enables u.

Let M' be the marking that coincides with M on the places of N and puts no tokens on the new place s'. Let σ' be the sequence obtained after replacing every occurrence of t in σ by the sequence $t\,t'$. By the construction of N', we have $M_0' \xrightarrow{\sigma'} M'$. Since (N', M_0') is live, there exists an occurrence sequence $M' \xrightarrow{\tau'} L'$ such that L' enables u. Define $\tau = \tau'|_T$ and $L = L'|_S$. Again by the construction of N' we have $M \xrightarrow{\tau} L$, and the marking L enables u.

(ii) The system (N, M_0) is bounded.

Let $M_0 \xrightarrow{\sigma} M$ be an arbitrary occurrence sequence of (N, M_0). Then, with the definitions of (i), we have $M_0' \xrightarrow{\sigma'} M'$. So for every reachable marking M of (N, M_0) there exists a reachable marking M' of (N', M_0') which coincides with M on S. Since (N', M_0') is bounded, so is (N, M_0). □

We now define the second mapping.

Definition 10.13   *The mapping ϕ_2*

Let N be a feedback-free net. The net $\phi_2(N)$ is obtained from N by adding arcs (s, t) and (t, s) for every place s and transition t satisfying

- $[s] = [t]$, and
- (s, t) is not an arc of N.

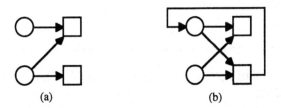

(a)   (b)

Fig. 10.7   Illustration of the mapping ϕ_2

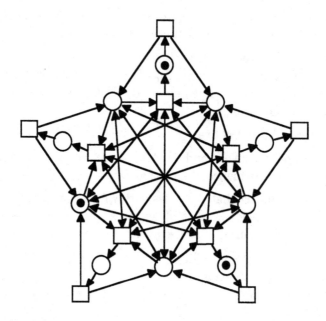

Fig. 10.8   The image of the net of Figure 10.4 under ϕ_2

The image under ϕ_2 of the net shown in Figure 10.7 is the net shown in (b). As another example, we consider again the net shown in Figure 10.4. This net has no feedbacks. It is mapped by ϕ_2 to the net of Figure 10.8[2]. The marking shown in Figure 10.8, which coincides with that of Figure 10.4, is live and bounded. Notice that the behaviours of the systems shown in the two figures are quite different: for example, the initial marking is a home marking of the system of Figure 10.4, which is not the case in the system of Figure 10.8.

Before proving the properties of ϕ_2, we need the following lemma:

Lemma 10.14

Let N be a feedback-free net.

(1) N and $\phi_2(N)$ have the same incidence matrix.

(2) If $M \xrightarrow{\sigma} M'$ is an occurrence sequence of $\phi_2(N)$ then it is also an occurrence sequence of N.

---

[2]In this example, we denote pairs of arcs (s, t), (t, s) by single arrows with two arrow heads.

Proof:

(1) The net $\phi_2(N)$ is constructed by adding new arcs to N. Since N has no feedbacks, $[s] = [t]$ and $(s,t) \notin F$ implies $(t,s) \notin F$ (where F is the flow relation of N). So whenever an arc (s,t) is added, the arc (t,s) is also added, and vice versa. Therefore, the incidence matrix does not change.

(2) We show the proposition for $\sigma = t$ where t is a single transition. The general case then follows by induction on the length of σ. By the definition of $\phi_2(N)$, the pre-set of t in N is a subset of the pre-set of t in $\phi_2(N)$. Hence, if M enables t in $\phi_2(N)$, M enables t in N. Since N and $\phi_2(N)$ have the same incidence matrix by (1), the vector $\mathbf{t}$ in N is equal to $\mathbf{t}$ in N'. Therefore, since $M' = M + \mathbf{t}$, the successor markings coincide. $\qquad\square$

Proposition 10.15 *Properties of the mapping ϕ_2*

Let N be a feedback-free net.

(1) The net $\phi_2(N)$ is free-choice.

(2) If N satisfies Conditions (a) to (d), then $\phi_2(N)$ also satisfies them.

(3) If $\phi_2(N)$ is well-formed, then N is well-formed.

Proof:

(1) Follows immediately from the definition of $\phi_2(N)$.

(2) For Condition (a), observe that the addition of new arcs cannot spoil connectedness. For Conditions (b) and (c), the result follows immediately from Lemma 10.14(1). For Condition (d), notice that, by the definition of $\phi_2(N)$, a new arc leading from a place s to a transition t is added to N only if s and t already belong to the same cluster. So the addition of these arcs does not change the clusters of the net, and therefore the nets N and $\phi_2(N)$ have the same set of clusters. Since the ranks of their incidence matrices coincide by Lemma 10.14(1), the result follows.

(3) Let M_0 be a live and bounded marking of $\phi_2(N)$. We claim that M_0 is also a live and bounded marking of N (recall that both nets have the same set of places).

(i) The system (N, M_0) is live.

Let M be a reachable marking of (N, M_0), and let t be a transition of N. We have to show that t is enabled at some marking L reachable from M.

We first claim that M is a live marking of $\phi_2(N)$. The proof makes use of Theorem 5.8(3), which states that a marking of a well-formed free-choice net is live iff every S-component has a marked place. Let $N_1 = (S_1, T_1, F_1)$ be an arbitrary S-component of $\phi_2(N)$. Since M_0 is a live marking of $\phi_2(N)$, it marks some place of S_1. By Proposition 5.7, the characteristic vector $\chi[S_1]$ is an S-invariant of $\phi_2(N)$. Since N and $\phi_2(N)$ have the same incidence matrices (Lemma 10.14(1)), $\chi[S_1]$ is also an S-invariant of N. Since the marking M is reachable from M_0 in N, the two markings agree on all S-invariants of N. Therefore, M marks a place of S_1. Since N_1 was arbitrarily chosen, every S-component of $\phi_2(N)$ is marked at M, and so M is a live marking of $\phi_2(N)$, which proves the claim.

It follows from the claim that $\phi_2(N)$ has an occurrence sequence $M \xrightarrow{\sigma} L$ such that L enables t. By Lemma 10.14(2), $M \xrightarrow{\sigma} L$ is an occurrence sequence of N as well, and L enables t in N.

(ii) The system (N, M_0) is bounded.

Since $\phi_2(N)$ is well-formed and free-choice, it has a positive S-invariant (Theorem 5.8(1)). Using Lemma 10.14(1), this vector is also a positive S-invariant of N. So every marking of N is bounded. $\square$

We are now ready to prove the main result of this section:

Theorem 10.16   *A sufficient condition for well-formedness*

Let N be a net satisfying the following conditions:

(a) it is weakly connected, and has at least one place and one transition,

(b) it has a positive S-invariant,

(c) it has a positive T-invariant, and

(d) $\mathrm{Rank}(\mathbf{N}) = |C_N| - 1$.

Then N is well-formed.

Proof:

Define $\phi(N) = \phi_2(\phi_1(N))$. By Propositions 10.12 and 10.15, $\phi(N)$ is a free-choice net satisfying Conditions (a) to (d). By the Rank Theorem, $\phi(N)$ is well-formed. By Propositions 10.12(3) and 10.15(3), N is well-formed. $\square$

It remains to show that a marking of a net satisfying the Conditions (a) to (d) of the Rank Theorem is live and bounded if and only if it marks all proper siphons.

Theorem 10.17   *A sufficient condition for liveness and boundedness*

Let N be a net satisfying Conditions (a) to (d) of Theorem 10.16. A marking of N is live and bounded iff it that marks all proper siphons.

Proof:

($\Rightarrow$): A live marking marks every proper siphon (Proposition 4.10).

($\Leftarrow$): Every marking of N is bounded because, by (a), N has a positive S-invariant. Let M be a marking of N that marks all proper siphons. We prove that M is live. Let M' be the marking of $\phi(N)$ which coincides with M on the places of N and puts no tokens on the new places. The proof is divided into six parts.

(i) M marks all S-components of N, i.e., every S-component of N has a place that is marked at M.

   The set of places of an S-component is a proper siphon, which is marked at M by the assumption.

(ii) M' marks all S-components of $\phi_1(N)$.

   Let S be the set of places of N. By the definition of the mapping ϕ_1, if S_1 is the set of places of an S-component of $\phi_1(N)$, then $S_1 \cap S$ is the set of places of an S-component of N. By the definition of M' and by (i), M' marks all S-components of $\phi_1(N)$.

(iii) M' marks all S-components of $\phi(N)$.

   Recall that $\phi(N) = \phi_2(\phi_1(N))$. By the definition of the mapping ϕ_2, if S_1 is the set of places of an S-component of $\phi_2(\phi_1(N))$, then S_1 is the set of places of an S-component of $\phi_1(N)$. By (ii), this set is marked at M'.

(iv) M' is a live marking of $\phi(N)$.

   Since $\phi(N)$ is a well-formed free-choice net by Theorem 10.16, we can apply Theorem 5.8(3), which states that every marking that marks all S-components is live. By (iii), M' enjoys this property.

(v) M' is a live marking of $\phi_1(N)$.

   As shown in the proof of Proposition 10.15, since M' is a live marking of $\phi(N) = \phi_2(\phi_1(N))$ by (iv), M' is a live marking of $\phi_1(N)$.

(vi) M is a live marking of N.

   As shown in the proof of Proposition 10.12, since M' is a live marking of $\phi_1(N)$ by (v), M is a live marking of N. $\square$

Exercises

Exercise 10.1

Exhibit an asymmetric-choice system which is not free-choice and which can be proved to be live using Theorem 10.4.

Exercise 10.2   *

A place s is called *self-controlling* if there is a transition $t \in s^{\bullet}$ such that:

- there is a path leading from t to another (different) transition $u \in s^{\bullet}$ which does not contain the place s, and

- there is a circuit containing s and t.

(notice that places having less than two output transitions are not self-controlling)

A system is not-self-controlling if no place of its underlying net is self-controlling.

Prove that a non-self-controlling system is live iff every proper siphon contains an initially marked trap.

Exercise 10.3

Exhibit a non-free-choice net that satisfies Conditions (a) to (c) of the Rank Theorem but does not satisfy $\text{Rank}(\mathbf{N}) \leq |P_N| - 1$ (By Theorem 10.9, this net is not well-formed).

Exercise 10.4

Let N be a well-formed net which is not a T-net such that the dual of N is asymmetric choice (i.e., if two transitions t and u share a common input place then either the enabledness of t implies the enabledness of u, or vice versa).

1) Prove that if N has exactly one cluster with at least two transitions then $\text{Rank}(\mathbf{N}) \leq |C_N| - 1$.

2) Disprove (by exhibiting a counterexample) that if N has more than one cluster with at least two transitions then $\text{Rank}(\mathbf{N}) \leq |C_N| - 1$.

Exercise 10.5

1) Prove that every net satisfying the Conditions (a) to (d) of Theorem 10.16 is covered by S- and T-components.

2) Use 1) to prove that every net satisfying the Conditions (a) to (d) of Theorem 10.16 is feedback-free.

Exercise 10.6

Let N be a net satisfying Conditions (a) to (d) of Theorem 10.16, and let M_0 be a live and bounded marking of N.

1) Show that (N, M_0) has a home marking.

2) Show that if (N, M_0) is cyclic then a marking M is reachable from M_0 iff it agrees with M_0 on all S-invariants.

Bibliographic Notes

Much effort has been devoted to investigating possible generalizations of the results on free-choice systems. Commoner's Theorem was extended to non-self-controlling systems by Griese [41] and to non-imposed-choice systems by Memmi [63]. The Coverability Theorems, the Rank Theorem, the First Confluence Theorem and other results have been extended to equal-conflict systems by Teruel and Silva [73, 74] (equal-conflict systems are the natural generalization of free-choice systems when weighted arcs are allowed, first defined by Starke [71]).

Weaker results (typically one direction of a strong theorem) have been generalized to larger classes, or even to arbitrary systems. This is the case of the three results shown in this chapter. The generalization of one direction of Commoner's Theorem to asymmetric-choice systems is due to Commoner, and can be found in Hack's Master Thesis [42] (where asymmetric-choice nets are called extended simple nets). The idea of the proof given in the text is taken from Best [6]. Theorem 10.9 (a necessary condition for well-formedness of arbitrary nets) is due to Colom, Campos and Silva [17], but the proof contains a mistake, which was subsequently corrected by Teruel and Silva [74]. Theorem 10.16 (a sufficient condition for well-formedness) is due to Desel [23].

Some results on free-choice systems not contained in this book have also been generalized. Hack shows in [44] that so-called state-machine allocatable nets are well-formed. This generalizes one direction of a result of [42], stating that a free-choice net is well-formed if and only if it is state-machine allocatable. Similarly, Esparza and Silva show in [31] (revised version) that the nets satisfying a certain condition expressed in terms of so-called "handles" are well-formed.

References

[1] AJMONE MARSAN, M. (ED.): *Application and Theory of Petri Nets 1993.* Lecture Notes in Computer Science, Vol. 691 – Springer-Verlag (1993)

[2] BARKAOUI, K.; LEMAIRE, B.: *An Effective Characterization of Minimal Deadlocks and Traps in Petri Nets Based on Graph Theory.* Proceedings of the 10th International Conference on Application and Theory of Petri Nets, 1989, Bonn, Germany, pp. 1–21 (1989)

[3] BERTHELOT, G.: *Verification de Réseaux de Petri.* Université Pierre et Marie Curie, Paris, Thése de 3eme Cycle (1978) (in French)

[4] BERTHELOT, G.: *Transformations et Analyse de Réseaux de Petri. Applications aux Protocoles.* Thése de Doctorat d'État, Université Paris VI (1983) Also: Laboratoire Informatique Théorique et Programmation, Internal Report 83-39, Université Paris VII (1983) (in French)

[5] BERTHELOT, G.: *Transformations and Decompositions of Nets.* In [12], pp. 359–376

[6] BEST, E.: *Structure Theory of Petri Nets: the Free Choice Hiatus.* In [12], pp. 168–205

[7] BEST, E.; DESEL, J.: *Partial Order Behaviour and Structure of Petri Nets.* Formal Aspects of Computing 2(2), pp. 123–138 (1990)

[8] BEST, E.; DESEL, J.; ESPARZA, J.: *Traps Characterise Home States in Free Choice Systems.* Theoretical Computer Science 101, pp. 161–176 (1992)

[9] BEST, E.; CHERKASOVA, L.; DESEL, J.: *Compositional Generation of Home States in Free Choice Systems.* Formal Aspects of Computing 4, pp. 572–581 (1992)

[10] BEST, E.; THIAGARAJAN, P.S.: *Some Classes of Live and Safe Petri Nets.* Concurrency and Nets / Voss, K.; Genrich, H.J., Rozenberg, G. (eds.), Advances in Petri Nets – Springer-Verlag, pp. 71–94 (1987)

[11] BEST, E.; VOSS, K.: *Free Choice Systems Have Home States.* Acta Informatica 21, pp. 89–100 (1984)

[12] BRAUER, W.; REISIG, W.; ROZENBERG, G. (EDS.): *Petri Nets: Central Models and Their Properties, Advances in Petri Nets 1986.* Lecture Notes in Computer Science Vol. 254 – Springer-Verlag (1987)

[13] CAMPOS, J.; CHIOLA, G.; SILVA, M.: *Properties and Performance Bounds for Closed Free Choice Synchronized Monoclass Queueing Networks.* IEEE Transactions on Automatic Control (Special Issue on Multi-Dimensional Queueing Systems) 36(12), pp. 1368–1381 (1991)

[14] CHENG, A.; ESPARZA, J; PALSBERG, J.: *Complexity Results for 1-safe Nets.* Lecture Notes in Computer Science, Vol. 761: Proceedings of the 13th Conference on the Foundations of Software Technology and Theoretical Computer Science / Shyamasundar, R.K. (ed.) – Springer Verlag, pp. 326–337 (1993). To appear in Theoretical Computer Science.

[15] CHVATAL, V.: *Linear Programming.* Freeman (1983)

[16] COHN, P.M.: *Algebra.* Wiley (1989)

[17] COLOM, J.M.; CAMPOS, J.; SILVA, M.: *On Liveness Analysis Through Linear Algebraic Techniques.* Proceedings of the Annual General Meeting of the ESPRIT Basic Research Action 3148 DEMON, Paris / Best, E. (ed.) (1990)

[18] COMMONER, F.: *Deadlocks in Petri Nets.* Applied Data Research, Inc., Wakefield, Massachusetts, Report CA-7206-2311 (1972)

[19] COMMONER, F.; HOLT, A.W.; EVEN, S.; PNUELI, A.: *Marked Directed Graphs.* Journal of Computer and System Sciences 5, pp. 511–523 (1971)

[20] DESEL, J.: *Reduction and Design of Well-Behaved Concurrent Systems.* Lecture Notes in Computer Science, Vol. 458: CONCUR '90 / Baeten, J.C.M.; Klop, J.W. (eds.) – Springer-Verlag, pp. 166–181 (1990)

[21] DESEL, J.: *Struktur und Analyse von free-choice Petrinetzen.* Doctor Thesis, Technische Universität München (1991) (in German)

[22] DESEL, J.: *A Proof of the Rank Theorem for Extended Free Choice Nets.* Lecture Notes in Computer Science, Vol. 616: Application and Theory of Petri Nets 1992 / Jensen, K. (ed.) – Springer-Verlag, pp. 134–153 (1992)

[23] DESEL, J.: *Regular Marked Petri Nets.* Lecture Notes in Computer Science, Vol. 790: WG '93, 19th International Workshop on Graph-Theoretic Concepts in Computer Science / Jan van Leeuwen (ed.) – Springer Verlag, pp. 264–275 (1993)

[24] DESEL, J.; ESPARZA, E.: *Reachability in Cyclic Extended free Choice Systems.* Theoretical Computer Science 114, pp. 93–118 (1993)

[25] DESEL, J.; ESPARZA, E.: *Shortest Paths in Reachability Graphs.* In [1], pp. 224–241. To appear in Journal of Computer and System Sciences.

[26] DÖPP, K.: *Zum Hackschen Wohlformungssatz für Free-Choice-Petrinetze.* Elektronische Informationsverarbeitung und Kybernetik EIK 19(1-2), pp. 3–15 (1983) (in German)

[27] ESPARZA, J.: *Structure Theory of Free Choice Petri Nets.* Ph. D. Thesis, Universidad de Zaragoza, Spain (1990)
Also: Research Report GISI-RR-90-03 of the Departamento de Ingeniería Eléctrica e Informática, Universidad de Zaragoza (1990)

[28] ESPARZA, J.: *Synthesis Rules for Petri Nets, and How They Lead to New Results.* Lecture Notes in Computer Science, Vol. 458: CONCUR '90 / Baeten, J.C.M.; Klop, J.W. (eds.) – Springer-Verlag, pp. 182–198 (1990)

[29] ESPARZA, J.: *A Solution to the Covering Problem for 1-Bounded Conflict-Free Petri Nets Using Linear Programming.* Information Processing Letters 41, pp. 313–319 (1992)

[30] ESPARZA, J.: *Reduction and Synthesis of Live and Bounded Free Choice Petri Nets.* Hildesheimer Informatik Fachbericht 91/11 (1991). To appear in Information and Computation (1994)

[31] ESPARZA, J.; SILVA, M.: *Circuits, handles, bridges, and nets.* Lecture Notes in Computer Science, Vol. 483: Advances in Petri Nets 1990 / Rozenberg, G. (ed.) – Springer-Verlag, pp. 210–242 (1990)
Also: Revised version: *Handles in Petri Nets.* Hildesheimer Informatik Fachbericht 91/3 (1991)

[32] ESPARZA, J.; SILVA, M.: *Top-Down Synthesis of Live and Bounded Free Choice Petri Nets.* Lecture Notes in Computer Science, Vol. 524: Advances in Petri Nets 1991 / Rozenberg, G. (ed.) – Springer-Verlag, pp. 118–139 (1991)

[33] ESPARZA, J.; SILVA, M.: *Compositional Synthesis of Live and Bounded Free Choice Petri Nets.* Lecture Notes in Computer Science, Vol. 527: CONCUR '91 / Baeten, J.C.M.; Groote, J.F. (eds.) – Springer-Verlag, pp. 172–187 (1991)

[34] ESPARZA, J; SILVA, M.: *A Polynomial-Time Algorithm to Prove Liveness of Bounded Free Choice Nets.* Theoretical Computer Science 102, pp. 185–205 (1992)

[35] ESPARZA, J.; SILVA, M.; BEST, E.: *Minimal Deadlocks in Free Choice Nets.* Hildesheimer Informatik Fachbericht 89/1 (1989)

[36] EZPELETA, J.; COUVREUR, J.M.; SILVA, M.: *A New Technique for Finding a Generating Family of Siphons, Traps and ST-Components. Application to Colored Petri Nets.* Lecture Notes in Computer Science, Vol. 674: Advances in Petri Nets 1993 / Rozenberg, G. (ed.) – Springer-Verlag, pp. 126–147 (1993)

[37] FLEISCHNER, H.: *Eulerian Graphs and Related Topics, Part 1, Vol. 1.* Annals of Discrete Mathematics, Vol. 45 – North Holland (1990)

[38] GENRICH, H.J.: *Das Zollstationproblem.* Internal Report of the Gesellschaft für Mathematik und Datenverarbeitung, Bonn, Germany, ISF/69-01-15 (1969) (in German)
Also: Revised version: ISF/71-10-13 (1971) (in German)

[39] GENRICH, H.J.; LAUTENBACH, K.: *Synchronisationsgraphen.* Acta Informatica 2, pp. 143–161 (1973) (in German)

[40] GENRICH, H.J.; THIAGARAJAN, P.S.: *A Theory of Bipolar Synchronization Schemes.* Theoretical Computer Science 30, pp. 241–318 (1984)

[41] GRIESE, W.: *Lebendigkeit in NSK-Petrinetzen.* Technische Universität München, Report TUM-INFO-7906 (1979) (in German)

[42] HACK, M.H.T.: *Analysis of Production Schemata by Petri Nets.* Cambridge, Mass.: MIT, Dept. Electrical Engineering, M.S. Thesis (1972)

[43] HACK, M.H.T.: *Corrections to 'Analysis of Production Schemata by Petri Nets'.* Cambridge, Mass.: MIT, Project MAC, Computation Structures Note 17 (1974)

[44] HACK, M.H.T.: *Extended State-Machine Allocatable Nets (ESMA), an Extension of Free Choice Petri Net Results.* Cambridge, Mass.: MIT, Project MAC, Computation Structures Group, Memo 78-1 (1974)

[45] HILLEN, D.: *Relationship between Deadlock-freeness and Liveness in Free Choice Nets.* Petri Net Newsletter 19, published by the Gesellschaft für Informatik, Bonn, Germany, pp. 28-32 (1985)

[46] HOLT, A.W.: *Final Report of the Project 'Development of the Theoretical Foundations for Description and Analysis of Discrete Information Systems'.* Applied Data Research, Inc., Wakefield, Massachusetts, Report CADD-7405-2011 (1974)

[47] HOWELL, R.R.; ROSIER, L.E.: *An $O(n^{1.5})$ Algorithm to Decide Boundedness for Conflict-free Vector Replacement Systems.* Information Processing Letters 25(1), pp. 27–33 (1987)

[48] HOWELL, R.R.; ROSIER, L.E.: *Completeness Results for Conflict-free Vector Replacement Systems.* Journal of Computer and System Sciences 37, pp. 349–366 (1988)

[49] HOWELL, R.R.; ROSIER, L.E.: *Problems Concerning Fairness and Temporal Logic for Conflict-free Petri Nets.* Theoretical Computer Science 64, pp. 305–329 (1989)

[50] JANTZEN, M.; VALK, R.: *Formal Properties of Place/Transition Nets.* Lecture Notes in Computer Science Vol. 84: Net Theory and Aplications / Brauer, W. (ed.) – Springer-Verlag, pp. 165–212 (1980)

[51] JONES, N.D.; LANDWEBER, L.H.; LIEN, Y.E.: *Complexity of Some Problems in Petri Nets.* Theoretical Computer Science 4, pp. 277–299 (1977)

[52] KARMARKAR, N.: *A New Polynomial-Time Algorithm for Linear Programming.* Combinatorica 4, pp. 373–395 (1984)

[53] KEMPER, P.: *Linear Time Algorithm to Find a Minimal Deadlock in a Strongly Connected Free-Choice Net.* In [1], pp. 319–338

[54] KEMPER, P.; BAUSE, F.: *An Efficient Polynomial-Time Algorithm to Decide Liveness and Boundedness of Free-Choice Nets.* Lecture Notes in Computer Science, Vol. 616: Application and Theory of Petri Nets 1992 / Jensen, K. (ed.) – Springer-Verlag, pp. 263–278 (1992)

[55] KHACHIYAN, L.G.: *A Polynomial Algorithm in Linear Programming.* Doklady Akademiia Nauk SSSR 244(S), pp. 1093–1096 (1979) (in Russian) Translated into English in: Soviet Mathematics Doklady 20(1), pp. 191–194 (1979)

[56] KOVALYOV, A.V.: *On Complete Reducibility of Some Classes of Petri Nets.* Proceedings of the 11th International Conference on Application and Theory of Petri Nets, Paris, pp. 352–366 (1990)

[57] KUMAGAI, S.; KODAMA, S.; KITAGAWA, M.: *Submarking Reachability of Marked Graphs.* IEEE Transactions on Circuits and Systems 31(2), pp. 159–164 (1984)

[58] LANDWEBER, L.H.; ROBERTSON, E.L.: *Properties of Conflict Free and Persistent Petri Nets.* Journal of the ACM 25(3), pp. 352–364 (1978)

[59] LAUTENBACH, K.: *Liveness in Petri Nets.* Internal Report of the Gesellschaft für Mathematik und Datenverarbeitung, Bonn, Germany, ISF/75-02-1 (1975)

[60] LAUTENBACH, K.: *Ein kombinatorischer Ansatz zur Beschreibung und Erreichung von Fairneß in scheduling-Problemen.* Applied Computer Science 8, pp. 228–250 (1977) (in German)

[61] LAUTENBACH, K.: *Linear Algebraic Techniques for Place/Transition Nets.* In [12], pp. 142–167 (1987)

[62] LAUTENBACH, K.: *Linear Algebraic Calculation of Deadlocks and Traps.* Concurrency and Nets / Voss, K.; Genrich, H.J.; Rozenberg, G. (eds.), Advances in Petri Nets – Springer-Verlag, pp. 315–336 (1987)

[63] MEMMI, G.: *Méthode D'Analyse de Réseaux de Petri, Réseaux a Files, et Application aux Systèmes Temps Réel.* Université Pierre et Marie Curie, Paris, Thése de Doctorat d'État (1985) (in French)

[64] MEMMI, G.; ROUCAIROL, G.: *Linear Algebra in Net Theory.* Lecture Notes in Computer Science, Vol. 84: Net Theory and Applications / Brauer, W. (ed.) – Springer-Verlag, pp. 213–223 (1980)

[65] MINOUX, M.; BARKAOUI, K.: *Deadlocks and Traps in Petri Nets as Horn-Satisfiability Solutions and some Related Polynomially Solvable Problems.* Discrete Applied Mathematics 29 (1990)

[66] MURATA, T.: *Circuit Theoretic Analysis and Synthesis of Marked Graphs.* IEEE Transactions on Circuits and Systems 24(7), pp. 400–405 (1977)

[67] MURATA, T.: *Petri Nets: Properties, Analysis and Applications.* Proceedings of the IEEE 77(4), pp. 541–580 (1989)

[68] PETERSON, J.L.: *Petri Net Theory and the Modeling of Systems.* Prentice Hall (1981)

[69] PLÜNNECKE, H.; REISIG, W.: *Bibliography of Petri Nets 1990.* Lecture Notes in Computer Science, Vol. 524: Advances in Petri Nets 1991 / Rozenberg, G. (ed.) – Springer-Verlag, pp. 317–572 (1991)

[70] REISIG, W.: *Petri Nets.* EATCS Monographs on Theoretical Computer Science, Vol. 4 – Springer-Verlag (1985)

[71] STARKE, P.: *Analyse von Petri-Netz-Modellen.* Teubner (1990) (in German)

[72] TERUEL, E.; CHRZASTOWSKI-WACHTEL, P.; COLOM, J.M.; SILVA, M.: *On Weighted T-Systems*. Lecture Notes in Computer Science, Vol. 616: Application and Theory of Petri Nets 1992 / Jensen, K. (ed.) – Springer-Verlag, pp. 348–367 (1992)

[73] TERUEL, E.; SILVA, M.: *Liveness and Home States in Equal Conflict Systems*. In [1], pp. 415–432

[74] TERUEL, E.; SILVA, M.: *Well Formedness of Equal Conflict Systems*. Lecture Notes in Computer Science, Vol. 815: Application and Theory of Petri Nets 1994 / Valette, R. (ed.) – Springer-Verlag, pp. 491–510 (1994)

[75] THIAGARAJAN, P.S.; VOSS, K.: *A Fresh Look at Free Choice Nets*. Information and Control 61(2), pp. 85–113 (1984)

[76] VOGLER, W.: *Live and Bounded Free Choice Nets have Home States*. Petri Net Newsletter 32, published by the Gesellschaft f'ur Informatik, Bonn, Germany, pp. 18–21 (1989)

[77] YEN, H.C.: *A Polynomial Time Algorithm to Decide Pairwise Concurrency of Transitions for 1-Bounded Conflict-Free Petri Nets*. Information Processing Letters 38, pp. 71–76 (1991)

[78] YEN, H.C.; WANG, B.Y.; YANG, M.S.: *A Unified Approach for Reasoning About Conflict-Free Petri Nets*. In [1], pp. 513–531

Index

List of symbols

General symbols

Sequences

Nets

Markings

$M(R)$	total number of tokens the marking M puts on the places of the set R	18
$[M\rangle$	set of markings reachable from M	19
$M \sim L$	M and L agree on all S-invariants	25
$M(\gamma)$	token count of the circuit γ at the marking M	47

Occurrence sequences

$M \xrightarrow{t} M'$	occurrence of a transition	18
$M \xrightarrow{\sigma} M'$	occurrence sequence	19
$M \xrightarrow{*} M'$	M' is reachable from M	19
$M \xrightarrow{\sigma}$	infinite occurrence sequence	19

Allocations

$\alpha(C)$	transitions of the set of clusters C allocated by α	73

Linear algebra

$\mathbf{N}$	incidence matrix of the net N	20
$\mathbf{s}$	row of the place s in the incidence matrix	20
$\mathbf{t}$	column of the transition t in the incidence matrix	20
$\langle I \rangle$	support of the (semi-positive) invariant I	31
$\mathrm{Rank}(\mathbf{N})$	rank of the matrix $\mathbf{N}$	112
$\dim(\mathcal{J})$	dimension of the vector space $\mathcal{J}$	123

Reduction and synthesis rules

ϕ_A	the abstraction rule	137
ϕ_S	the second reduction rule	142
ϕ_T	the third reduction rule	146
ψ_T	a synthesis rule	162
ϕ'_A	a variant of the abstraction rule	164
ϕ''_A	another variant	165

Net mappings

ϕ	composition of the mappings ϕ_1 and ϕ_2	215
ϕ_1	mapping to feedback-free nets	217
ϕ_2	mapping from feedback-free nets to free-choice nets	219

List of main results

Lemmata

Theorems